How to Invest

in

Gold Coins

DONALD J. HOPPE

How to Invest

in

Gold Coins

ARLINGTON HOUSE   NEW ROCHELLE, N.Y.

Library of Congress Catalog Card Number 70–115342

SBN 87000–076–4

MANUFACTURED IN THE UNITED STATES OF AMERICA

TO JOAN
and all else that is fine,
including gold

Contents

List of Illustrations

(between pages 160 and 161)

Figures

How to Invest

in

Gold Coins

Preface

IN ECONOMICS AND INVESTMENT THERE ARE ALWAYS LOST PIECES, missing numbers, and unexpected developments. Investment is an art, not a science, and in art one can only hope to understand the basic rules and principles; the events themselves will always partake of mystery. But if I have accurately perceived the basic rules and principles of gold-coin collecting and investing, and have presented them to the satisfaction of the reader (and this is my sincere intent), then the possibility that I may have overlooked, misinterpreted, or failed to anticipate some coming financial or economic event of consequence will not seriously impair the validity of this work. Equipped with sound rules and principles, and supplied with abundant technical and financial data, the gold-coin collector-investor possessing this book should be able to adjust to any unanticipated or extraordinary turn of events (at least I try to console myself with this thought).

Having presented my apology (or if the reader prefer, my alibi) for any shortcomings or omissions in this work, allow me to present a brief explanation of how and why it came to be done. First of all I cheerfully admit to being what has come to be known in financial and stock market circles as a "gold bug," that is, one who is convinced of, obsessed with, fascinated by, or otherwise hooked on the idea that gold still plays a significant if not an indispensable role in the affairs of men, and consequently that gold–oriented investments offer exciting opportunities for capital appreciation.

In my case the romance goes back quite a few years, probably beginning in Professor Arthur Vierthaler's art metals class at the University of Wisconsin, during the late forties. It was here that not a few of us recovered from the spiritual and physical injuries of war by going back to fundamentals. Fired by a dedicated teacher's intensity and enthusiasm, we studied the lore of precious metals and gems, and learned something of the historic techniques of gold and silver smithing, mostly by crafting objects of gold, silver, jade, and turquoise with our own hands. Many of his students went on to become noted artists, designers, and precious-metals craftsmen, while others became outstanding teachers themselves. But for the author there evolved a more erratic course.

For a while I continued, among other studies, my inquiries into the historic and esthetic nature of gold, eventually going on to graduate work in history and art history. But at the end of a year of graduate work I was no longer satisfied with the direction formal study was taking me. When the time came to make a decision, I accepted employment in Arizona, partly because it would allow sufficient free time and provide the geography for me to experiment with actual gold prospecting. It was a rather abrupt transition from the formal peace and tranquility of the Wisconsin Art History Library to the harsh reality of the Arizona desert, but I flattered myself that I had already seen too much of life to remain a cloistered scholar. Prospecting was more in my line.

Nature does not give up her secrets easily—for that matter, neither does man. Once I was shot at (several times) by some old "desert rat" who had no doubt been away from it all for too long; this kind could be downright inhospitable at times to anyone inadvertently trespassing on one of his lodes, real or imagined. More than once I stopped just short of falling into some long-abandoned mine shaft concealed almost entirely by brush and debris; another time I recovered just in time to avoid sliding over a cliff under an avalanche of loose rock. Furthermore, the number of times I was scared almost out of my wits by rattlesnakes is beyond recounting. To me, they were the worst of nature's booby traps and I never did get used to them, even though, unlike the man-made variety, they usually gave ample warning of their presence. Hazards and discomforts there were, and hard work as well. But looking back (from this safe and remote distance), I am now moved to conclude that I really had a grand time during my brief sojourn as a gold prospector.

My next significant encounter with gold was probably not until 1960. At that time I was, you might say, still prospecting, but definitely in another area: stock market and commodities trading. And in order to further my chances for success in the most difficult art of speculation, I began a program of intensive reading and study in the areas of financial history and monetary affairs.

One of the books that particularly attracted my attention was a slim paperback volume entitled *Twentieth Century Common Sense and the American Economic Crisis of the 1960's* (Great Barrington, Mass.: American Institute for Economic Research, 1960). This little book, written under the direction of Mr. E. C. Harwood by the editorial staff of the Institute,* clearly, logically, and un-equivocally demonstrated that if the United States did not desist from its postwar policy of reckless domestic monetary expansion, we would experience a drastic decline in our gold reserves and ultimately plunge the world into a most serious monetary crisis. Well, we did not desist, we did lose $8 billion more of gold, and the world has been plunged into a whole series of monetary crises.

Unfortunately the U.S. government and its money managers did not get the message, not in 1960, nor in the following nine years. In fact, it may well be doubted whether they have really got it yet. But the author had no trouble grasping it at the first reading; not being preconditioned by formal training in Keynesian economics (virtually the only kind taught in the last two decades), I was not hard to convince that debt was not wealth and paper was not gold. Therefore, I added the historic and contemporary role of gold in monetary affairs and the world's "gold problem" to my list of subjects deserving of intensive study and research.

About this time I also began attending coin shows and bourses

---

* An independent scientific and educational organization privately supported by several thousand sustaining members.

and saw for the first time gold coins offered for sale in real quantity and variety. Now when a gold bug gets bitten by the coin bug—you really have a case. At first I bought coins only for the enjoyment that comes with the discovery and acquisition of precious and historic objects; later I recognized the investment values of gold coins. And I began my study of them.

However, gold-mining stocks played an increasingly significant part in my trading operations as the world monetary cauldron continued to boil. By the break of 1966, nearly my entire trading account was in gold stocks. With some success I traded a more general list during the 1967 rally, but switched back to the golds in the late summer of that year. While all the perpetual bulls were still hypnotized by the wild gyrations of the ticker tape, I was keeping a closer watch on the international monetary scene. Despite all the fatuous optimism pouring forth from Washington and London, it was abundantly evident (to me at least) that things were deteriorating rapidly. The November 1967 devaluation of the British pound and the great gold crisis of March 1968 confirmed my judgment.

These events helped to provide the final determination and encouragement (and to net sufficient profit) for me to embark on a project that had long been on my mind, namely, to write a book or, more accurately, a series of books on the subjects of gold, financial history, current monetary problems, and the art of speculation. However, before beginning this rather ambitious program, I thought it would be helpful to condition myself by doing a preliminary work on a lighter subject, as I had not done any professional writing since concluding a period as a magazine writer some eight years earlier.

My choice for this preliminary exercise was to be a pamphlet or brief paperback on a subject that had become increasingly attractive to me: numismatic investment. How something that was so personally satisfying as numismatic collecting could also possess fantastic investment potential was a story that had to be told. But as I assembled notes and references for this effort, the idea gradually asserted itself that nothing less than a full-length, detailed study could even begin adequately to explore the subject. The idea of a brief pamphlet was abandoned shortly after I had begun to work on it, and I knew quite suddenly that numismatic investment had to be the theme of the first full-length book in my contemplated series.

I chose gold coins as the principal subject, not only because they were my personal interest, but because they represent the apex of numismatic collecting and investment. Furthermore, gold and gold coins are, as the reader will see, inextricably involved with the world's financial history, with our economic future, and even with our political destiny, whether we have gold-related investment positions or not. I began full-time work on the book in the early summer of 1968 and managed to complete it by Christmas of that year, with my enthusiasm for the subject undiminished, or if anything, even increased.

In the presentation of historical events and technical data, the author sought always to insure accuracy and objectivity, but I also set a high priority on getting this book to the reader in the shortest possible time in order for it to be of maximum benefit. In any case, there is not to my knowledge any possibility of a variance in fact or figure that can or will significantly alter any of the recommendations or conclusions expressed in this book.

Upon completing his book, any author must confess (if he is honest) that he owes unpayable debts to many of his predecessors, both living and dead. The traditional way of honoring them is with the footnote citation. This I have done, fairly I hope, but not to the point of pedantry. However, let me add here a few well-deserved extra notes for the living.

One of my principal references for the history of numismatics, which is surveyed very briefly in chapter one, was Mrs. Clain-Stefanelli's excellent Smithsonian research paper, *Numismatics: an Ancient Science*. Available from the Government Printing Office for only $1.00, it is an outstanding bargain, in my estimation. For monetary history in general, the most useful guide was Dr. Elgin Groseclose's *Money and Man*, a work destined, in my opinion, to remain a classic in its field. This book is also available as an inexpensive paperback and deserves to be included in any numismatic or financial library. And of course, how could any numismatist or numismatic writer carry on without those outstanding catalogues and guidebooks either authored by or produced under the editorship of the redoubtable Richard S. Yeoman, and published by the Whitman Division, Western Publishing Co. For recent numismatic events I relied upon the numismatic press, particularly the always entertaining and informative *Coin World*, ably edited by (Mrs.) Margo Russell.

Dr. Vladimir Clain-Stefanelli, Curator of the Division of Numismatics at the Smithsonian Institution, responded generously to my requests for illustrations.

Indeed, I owe much to many; nevertheless, I like to think that at least some of the comments, revelations, opinions and conclusions expressed herein are original. They were, however, not always above improvement, and my editor at Arlington House, Llewellyn Rockwell, deserves special thanks for his astute and cogent suggestions in this regard.

And finally, but certainly not the least in importance, was the valued assistance offered by my understanding wife Joan, who cheerfully laid aside other projects and considerations to aid in typing, proofreading and correcting the several versions of the manuscript. Her criticisms and suggestions were always welcomed and were never without significance; the book is better because of them. Her all-out effort in the last days was an indispensable help in getting the final version of the manuscript ready for delivery to the publisher on time.

Although the original manuscript was completed in December of 1968, world economic events continued to unfold with startling rapidity. It soon became clear that a thorough rewriting was needed to include the very important monetary and numismatic developments that had occurred during 1969.

Furthermore, some of my original predictions in the first draft of my manuscript had already come to pass, and consequently would be of little benefit to the reader. For example, I had predicted, in a moment of black pessimism, that the prime interest

rate in the U.S. would reach the unheard of figure of 8 to 9 percent
(it was then an unheard of 6½ percent). That unenviable goal
(8½ percent) was reached less than a year after I had written it.
(I have now raised my forecast to the 12–15 percent level.) Also,
I had stated that the French franc was probably next in line for
devaluation; it was duly devalued within the year.

I had thought it quite possible that further developments in the
international monetary drama might see a recourse to "floating"
currencies, that is, currencies no longer maintained at a fixed parity
in terms of gold, but allowed to find their own level in a free
foreign exchange market. As I write this preface, the *deutschmark*
has just been cut loose from its gold parity (temporarily, they say),
and serious discussions are getting under way within the IMF that
might well result in the introduction of a so-called crawling peg
system. Under this proposal all (paper) currencies *except the
dollar* would be allowed to float or "crawl" (mostly down) to their
true levels in the market place. It is my opinion that the next step
beyond the crawling peg or any other "flexible" international
monetary arrangement, and an inevitable one, will be to let the
dollar itself float (sink would be a more accurate word) to its real
value in terms of gold. This will be in essence the *de facto* worldwide devaluation, with a corresponding rise in the monetary price
of gold, which all our politico-economists say is never going to
happen.

The author also had advised (and still advises) that there would
be more inflation, more public unrest, further currency devaluations, great danger in the stock and bond markets, and continuing
gold and balance-of-payments problems for the United States.
It now appears that all these things have evolved and are continuing
to do so almost exactly as originally outlined.

Now I do not bring all this to the reader's attention in order to
boast of my prowess as an economic forecaster; actually I find it
rather depressing to think that an artist-historian turned economic
journalist can correctly anticipate, months in advance, the course
of economic and monetary events, a course which appears to take
our Treasury, banking and economic authorities completely by

surprise. But what I am trying to show is that ordinary common sense and an understanding of history are better guides to investment decisions and directions than allowing oneself to be tranquilized by the government handouts that too often pass for economic news in the popular press these days.

As anyone can see, the major result of this era of intensive monetary management has been a worldwide inflation. In the U.S. the money managers are, at this writing, desperately trying to halt a domestic inflation, which, by their own admission, is nearly out of control. Meanwhile, we are burdened with the highest interest rates and taxes in our history, adequate housing has risen in price far above the reach of those who need it most, the stock market has suffered severe setbacks, the bond market is a shambles, our balance-of-payments deficit is climbing towards disaster, and our once very substantial balance of trade has all but disappeared —so much for the miraculous benefits of neo-Keynesian economic and monetary management.

Inflation, deflation, and devaluation are subjects that should be of vital concern to investors, because investment success depends to a considerable degree on correctly anticipating and evaluating these trends and events. This is particularly true of numismatic investment, and most particularly so in the case of gold coins. Therefore, I have had to devote an appreciable part of this book to discussions of such matters, and I trust the reader will understand the necessity for such discussion.

In the purely numismatic area, the original manuscript had contained judgments that were, if I may say so, of some merit. I had written that the so-called common U.S. $5 and $10 gold pieces were far more scarce than their prices would seem to indicate, and therefore these coins could be recommended as an excellent buy; they forthwith rose in price from 50 to 100 percent. Nevertheless, there is still much potential, not only in the U.S. $5 and $10 pieces, but in virtually every recognized gold coin now extant.

I realize that I am asking the reader to accept all of the foregoing more or less as an act of faith, inasmuch as only my editors can verify it. However, you now have the evidence in your hand by which to judge me henceforth. From here on, the author is most definitely "on the record."

So the book was revised and all suggestions, recommendations, and predictions herein have been rewritten to make them as current as possible. As a consolation, I am inclined to think that we now have a better all-round book. Coin prices, however, continued to move (most inconsiderately) all the while I struggled to pin them down, and no doubt they will be further changed by the time this book gets to its readers. But this problem is really of minor consequence. Specific prices for specific coins are noted frequently in the course of the text, but these prices are primarily for the purposes of illustration. And what I have tried to illustrate, are basic principles. Prices will continue to change, but the basic rules, principles, and strategies of successful numismatic investment will remain constant.

Buying the *right coins* at the *right time* and following a consistent and well-planned long-term strategy of accumulation are far more important to investment success than attempting to anticipate or to be guided by short-term price movements. The momentary price of a rare coin (or of any other investment medium, for that matter) is in itself not really important. The only thing about price that is significant to the investor is whether or not it is about to go higher, or lower, by how much, and for how long. For questions like these, and many others that relate to gold coins, I have tried to provide adequate counsel. To what extent I have succeeded, only time will tell. But it has given me great pleasure to try. May you also find more than gold in numismatic investing—may you find contentment.

DONALD J. HOPPE
Crystal Lake, Illinois

PART 1

HISTORY,
GOLD COINS,
AND
THE INVESTOR

I

Coins of History

"The knowledge of the world is only to be acquired in the world and not in a closet."

—LORD CHESTERFIELD

COIN COLLECTING HAS A LONG HISTORY; WE PROBABLY CAN ASSUME that it originated with the development of coins themselves. The earliest coins are said to have been minted about 700 B.C. There is evidence that the ancient world quickly showed an interest in coins that went considerably beyond utilitarian concepts. And these "numismatic" interests seem to have expanded parallel to the universal acceptance and technical improvement of coinage that occurred during the classical ages.

The Greeks of antiquity, with their intensely esthetic minds, held coins in high esteem. The issuance of beautiful coin was a matter of national pride, and often an occasion for contest among the various Hellenic cities. By the end of the fifth century B.C., Greek coin engravers reached an artistic level that has probably never been surpassed. The coin—its origin and essence—was also a frequent and favored topic for discussion by the Greek philosophers. Aristotle had much to say on the subjects of coins and money. His definition of the coin as "an ingot of specific intrinsic content, with a legal value determined by the state" remains a model of brevity and lucidity.

Among the Romans, as in Greece, it was popular to present coins as gifts. Emperor Augustus was said to have distributed, not only his own coin, but "various unknown foreign coins and coins with portraits of ancient kings" to his favorites on festive occasions. The Roman aristocracy (even if not as discriminating as the Greeks) patronized the arts and consequently were enthusiastic collectors. Though not specifically mentioned, there are enough indications in various Roman texts to conclude that rare coins were frequently a part of the great Roman art collections.

There is little doubt but that the motives, habits, and rationalizations that prompt the collection of coins today were crystallized in the classical ages. Initially, the incentive to accumulate coins is a product of the same human refinements that compel our attraction to all objects of unusual interest. We find an irresistible mystery in such objects when they are curious or odd, have historical or geographical associations, are works of art or fine craftsmanship, or are even just sentimental souvenirs of dates, places, or events. With coins, however, the collecting urge becomes inextricably involved with our economic instincts and necessities, for coins, unlike other art works or antiquities, are a direct expression of wealth. Coins are also an actual living exhibit of history—a raw material for the archeologist, a guide to the history of art, a record of economic, social and political evolution—the resource of numismatics as a field of learned study, as a science.

It would be impossible, of course, to pinpoint exactly at what point in history the *investment* possibilities inherent in a collection of scarce, beautiful, or historic coins became an important consideration. It may be noted here, however, that a well-developed market for rare and historic coins appears to have existed in Imperial Rome. The Roman historian Pliny (the Elder) reported that scarce and unusual coins were in demand by wealthy collectors, who willingly paid high prices for them. Pliny also commented on the presence of numismatic forgeries—certainly another indication that the economic potential of coin collecting was thoroughly understood.

But the major activity of the ancient world, and particularly of the Roman Empire, was not any form of numismatics, popular though this type of collecting may have been. It was hoarding— simple, frantic, and at times desperate hoarding. The propensity of certain kings and emperors to devalue their coinage, by clipping, filing, reducing or debasing, made it so. The mighty emperors of Imperial Rome were particularly notorious for this dishonesty. It is a sad fact, but inflation is also probably as old as the history of money itself.[1]

The effects of inflation then were roughly the same as they are today: you spent your good coin, but received in return debased coin of less intrinsic value, which naturally would buy less than before. In time you spent the debased coin, only to receive in return coin still further diluted, which would buy still less—and so on and on. You soon learned; you kept the good coin of high intrinsic value for eventually it would buy as much as five or ten or even one hundred of the debased coin that was sure to follow.

The coin hoarder of old was obviously no mere monetary primitive. After all, the Greek philosophers had examined the subject of money and its effects with a clarity and sophistication that have yet to be surpassed. The coin hoarder, then as now, was only exhibiting the infrequent human characteristic of being completely rational. He was responding to an earlier version of Gresham's Law.[2]

The proponents of fiat currency schemes and various other cheap-money doctrines have always cited the coin and precious-metals hoarder as proof that sound, intrinsic value, commodity money is impractical and dangerous. What it really proves, to anyone who has the wit to see it, is that the weakness lies in the character of the money managers, not in the money. The evidence collected by the numismatist is inescapable. There in imperishable metals is the record of the frauds and official dishonesties that have occurred with discouraging regularity throughout the centuries.

Regardless of the sophistries of the economic experimenters, the fact remains that it is government, and government alone, that controls the issuance of money—both its quantity and quality (and in modern times regulates banking and credit also). Inflation or debasement can only occur with the acquiescence or active

support of the government. The hoarder of coin or bullion is inno-
cent of any hostile intent. He is not "selfish," unpatriotic, or an evil
"gnome" trying to sabotage the economic systems of the world.
The hoarder may plead not guilty to these charges—by reason of
self–defense.

The exoneration of the hoarder is no mere academic point for
the numismatic historian. The hoarding of precious metals, both
in bullion form and in the form of coins with high intrinsic value,
has again reached one of its recurrent peaks in economic history.
And the reason is the same as of old; another ballooning fiat money,
fiat credit scheme is trembling on the point of collapse. The "New
Economics" is in reality just another treatment of the old inflation.
The record of monetary instability and banking folly that has been
written in the twentieth century makes any further justification of
precious-metals hoarding unnecessary. The only question that remains is its wisdom, in the light of alternative methods of hedging.

Basically, the wisdom of the investor in precious metals (as the
hoarder is now called) would hardly seem open to challenge.
Franz Pick, considered by many to be the world's foremost authority on international currencies and monetary affairs, has in
recent years constantly advised that *"direct investment in precious
metals is the best inflation hedge."*[3] Dr. Pick also maintains that
the "smart" investor in this age of crisis will have 60 percent of
his investment portfolio in precious metals.[4]

Direct investment in precious metals—gold, silver and platinum
—is no problem for most of Dr. Pick's wealthy international clien-
tele.[5] If they are conservative, they simply buy their bullion for
cash and store it as a hedge against the inevitable depreciation
and devaluation of fiat paper currencies. If they are inclined towards speculation, they can buy options, or take positions in
"futures," or buy their bars on margin (that is, with a small down
payment and carry the balance on loan), thus obtaining greater
opportunity for profit. However, one also assumes the greater risks
of short-term errors in timing and judgment inherent in these
"leverage" methods. But for people with more modest means, the
only contact they are likely to have with precious metals will be
through the coin.

The unsophisticated accumulator of coins as sources of precious metals makes no error in principle, but unless he can get the coins out of the circulating media he will often pay too high a price for the intrinsic value received. Consequently, such "investments" frequently provide neither safety nor opportunity for profit. The problem is particularly acute in the area of gold. Gold coins are no longer part of the circulating media of any advanced nation. As a result all gold coins are presumed to have, in addition to their bullion content, a certain numismatic and esthetic value. And their price will reflect, in varying degrees, both types of value.

Therefore, the successful purchase of a gold coin for investment purposes requires a measure of numismatic sophistication, as well as a basic knowledge of the physical properties: weights, purities, conversion factors, exchange ratios, etc., inescapably a part of every gold transaction. (From the instances of "panic" buying that have accompanied the recurring gold crises since 1965, it is apparent that many would-be gold-coin investors are woefully deficient in both numismatic and fundamental technical and economic knowledge.)[6]

But regardless of the primary motive for buying gold coins, a combination of interests would seem to be unavoidable. In the case of the gold–coin investor, in order to be successful, he must develop a feeling for the intricacies of numismatics as well as a grasp of economic realities. And unless he is unusually wealthy, the numismatic or esthetic collector of gold cannot overlook the economic aspect of what is by its nature a substantial investment. Collecting gold coins as a form of gold investment may not be as direct or obvious as buying an ingot, but it is all to the good. The citizen who is barred by economics or law from owning bullion may have reason to feel offended on principle, but in reality he has cause to rejoice. There is far more (we hope to show) pleasure and profit in the possession of fine gold coins than there is in any artless bar of metal.

Some numismatic purists and scholars deplore the activities of investors and speculators in the coin field. Understandably, they would prefer to see numismatics confined to the requirements of historical and artistic study, and collections of the rarest and most valuable coins residing only in museums. Their motives are not without merit, but the verdicts of psychology and history make their position untenable.

We have noted previously that the collection of coins is often (psychologically) bound up with our feelings about money as a direct evidence of wealth. Nowhere is this dual nature of numismatics more pronounced than in the attitude of people toward coins of gold. The tradition of gold as the ultimate standard of value and measure of wealth has 3,000 years of history behind it. It is part of the basic foundation of civilization. It affects us all. "Good as gold" is the ultimate accolade. What legislation can dismiss it from our consciousness?

As to the psychology of collecting itself, one has only to peruse the popular numismatic press (*Coin World, Numismatic News,* for example) to see that the vast majority of coin collectors derive as much or more satisfaction from the pecuniary aspects of their avocation as they do from its creative and esthetic rewards. The merits of different coins as investments are a far more popular topic than their historic association or artistic significance. And why not? Have we in the West not developed the philosophy of dedication to our work and commerce for its creative and esthetic values as well as for its monetary ones? Then does it not follow that to combine business with pleasure and art with economics is a higher form of satisfaction than to relegate them to separate narrow compartments in our lives?

As for the historic evidence that the pecuniary aspects of numismatics are neither new nor undesirable, we must continue our brief history beyond classical times.[7]

In the period following the decline of Rome and the end of classical civilization, coin collecting suffered much the same regression that occurred in many areas of cultural and intellectual activity. During the dark centuries of barbarian domination, not only numismatics, but the very institution of money itself all but perished in the West.[8] However, there is evidence that, confused as this period was, some spark of interest in the science of coins remained. A collection of coins from ancient times—containing the portraits of forgotten kings and emperors, records of ancient victories, legends, and the procession of gods and heroes imperishably stamped upon them—was one of the few doors to knowledge about the past that remained open during the Dark Ages.

But the maturing of the medieval era eventually brought about the great compromise of Christian asceticism with classic humanism and set the stage for the glories of the coming Renaissance. This coming of age also established numismatics permanently as an important branch of learning, a pleasure of the cultivated, and a nice unobtrusive way of preserving and enhancing wealth. In any case, coin collections and studies were very much a part of the late Middle Ages.

By the end of the thirteenth century, new mints were active throughout Europe and money once again became the inseparable partner of commerce. The eminent Catholic theologian Thomas Aquinas saw fit to include in his *De regimine principus* a discussion of the function and evolution of money. And Nicholas Oresmius (1320–1382), in his *Tract on the Origin and Evolution of Money*,[9] can probably be credited with the first literary work devoted exclusively to numismatics and monetary history. The great Florentine humanist Petrarch not only wrote brilliantly on art, history, and numismatics, but was also intensely pleased by his own collection of ancient coins. He wrote with obvious excitement about the trips he made to Rome in search of new specimens.

The artistic and cultural explosion we call the Renaissance is too well known to elaborate upon here, except to say that numismatics, like all the arts, was pursued with dedication and enthusiasm that have not been equalled since. No member of the nobility, rich merchant, or well-to-do artisan, who could afford to decorate his dwelling with choice paintings and sculptures and ornament his wife with costly jewelry would risk the embarrassment of not possessing a cabinet of rare coins and fine medallions.

Antonius, the Cardinal of St. Marks, was known for his collection of ancient coins, which included 97 gold and over 1,000 silver coins. An inventory of the Medici collections taken in 1465 showed 100 gold and 503 silver coins. Alfonso V (1396–1458), king of Sicily and Naples, kept his coins in an ivory box that accompanied him on all his travels. Archduke Ferdinand (1529–1595) turned his ornate castle in the Tyrol into a veritable art museum, and installed there two elaborate cabinets to contain his extensive collection of Greek and Roman coins. The record is endless, and at the height of the Renaissance, truly fantastic. The roster of great coin collections reads like the *Almanac de Gotha*.[10]

Hubert Goltzius (1526–1583), a Dutch scholar and specialist in Roman coins, travelled widely about Europe in the sixteenth century to see the great collections and research them for his books. His list of these notable collections included 380 in Italy, over 200 in France, 200 more in Holland, and 175 in Germany; he observed that "there was no prince or lord who did not pride himself on owning coins, although there were still many among them who could not even read."[11]

Another Dutch scholar, Abraham van Goorle (1549–1609), also the author of a treatise on Roman coins, had a collection of 4,000 gold, 10,000 silver, and 15,000 bronze and copper coins. (This collection later passed into the hands of Charles I of England.) Flemish artist Peter Paul Reubens is known to have bought and later resold a collection of 18,000 coins. In 1598, in Leyden, the first known coin auction took place when a French collection was sold in this manner. (It should be consoling to numismatic purists that most of the magnificent collections privately built up by the great noble and royal houses of Europe eventually became the basis of the elaborate coin collections that now are part of the national museums of their respective countries.)[12]

From the Renaissance on, the evidence shows that investment and even speculation in paintings, sculptures, jewelry, and antiquities became commonplace. That the esthetic joys and satisfactions provided by the possession of a great work of art were more than a little enhanced by the realization of how much it cost, was obviously appreciated during these opulent centuries. Sheldon Cheney put it rather poignantly in writing about the artistic climax of the Renaissance as it swept over Holland in the seventeenth century: "There is witnessed the curious phenomena of thousands of Dutch citizens, in that prolific century, speculating in pictures, buying great numbers of prints and paintings, selling them or trading them at fairs, bargaining with the artists for lower prices—generally making a gambling commodity and an instrument of materialistic gain out of what should be a companion to man in his nobler haunts."[13] As coin collections were so often a part of the Renaissance passion for art, one could hardly expect that rare coins were exempt from similar attentions by speculators and investors.

The post–Renaissance and modern eras of coin collecting in Europe expanded in the established tradition of patronage and support by the wealthy, the noble and the cultured. Numismatics in the Renaissance had naturally been dominated by the Greek and Roman coins of antiquity, but the post–Renaissance trend in collecting included a growing interest in contemporary coinage. The coins of the modern centuries were not neglected by the Europeans, although from a scholarly point of view, a strong interest in the coins of the classic ages continued (and probably will continue) to be a feature of European collecting. Another development of note was the rise of the professional numismatist—scholars, professors and curators—and the building of the vast European museum collections.[14] The fall of many a royal house during the seventeenth, eighteenth, nineteenth and even twentieth centuries left magnificent coin collections to the public domain.

Numismatics in the United States followed, in a time-condensed version, a pattern similar to that of Europe. In the colonial era and in the early years of the Republic, coin collections were in the hands of very few—the gentlemen of wealth and leisure. And with the prevalence of classical thought and education, the emphasis was on Greece and Rome. The rapid growth of the Republic and the ascendancy of Jacksonian Democracy, however, soon had their effect, and interest in numismatics began to embrace the early coins of the United States and its colonial days as well as the contemporary coins and medals of Europe and even the Orient. We have the word of one of the founders of the first numismatic association in America, the Numismatic and Antiquarian Society of

Philadelphia, that when he and seven other citizens organized the group in 1858, "the mania for coin collecting was then raging fiercely, and desires had arisen with very many persons to become better acquainted with the science."[15]

The first regular coin publication, *The American Journal of Numismatics*, was begun in 1866 and its avowed purpose, in addition to providing information of historical value, was that it should "act as a check upon all nefarious and improper acts, either in the manufacture, collection or sale of coins and medals."[16] This comment would seem to indicate that interest in coin collecting was then at least popular enough to make "nefarious acts" profitable (and probably frequent). The statement was also prophetic, for calling attention to improper and dishonest acts and policing false or misleading advertising are still major endeavors and most valuable functions of the modern numismatic press.

By the close of the nineteenth century, the United States (and Canada) could claim collections to rival those of the great names of Europe. In 1889, there were over 400 American collections listed in a European catalogue of important world cabinets.[17] In the classical tradition, the Greek and Roman collections of Frank S. Benson, Clarence S. Bement, and J. Pierpont Morgan were equal to the best private collections on the Continent. Later, Enrico Caruso's golden tenor voice earned him a collection of gold coins that was one of the largest ever assembled, and Waldo E. Newcomer put together a collection of South American gold and silver coins that was among the best and most extensive of its kind in the world.

As for the twentieth century, we have an outstanding example of numismatics in the grand style: the world-famous Josiah K. Lilly collection, now considered the finest and most comprehensive private collection of gold coins ever formed. (Its appraised value has been set at $5,500,000.) This collection of 6,125 separate items is now the property of the citizens of the United States, having been donated by the estate of the late Mr. Lilly to the United States Museum of History and Technology (Smithsonian Institution).[18]

This book is by no means intended to be a thorough history of numismatics. (For those interested in pursuing this subject in greater detail, a few of the items listed in the bibliography will offer a starting point.) But a general background of such history is required as evidence that the collection of rare, beautiful and historic coins is a permanent part of the Western cultural tradition, and that the desire for such coins is so well established that the investment merits of recognized numismatic material would be, in general, beyond challenge. This fundamental pattern is of course subject to variations in enthusiasm and emphasis, which means that only the problems of *selectivity* and *timing* are of concern to the numismatic investor; he need not anticipate that his chosen investment medium will ever become obsolete.

There is also a point in Western history, indefinite though it may be, when the arts and other manifestations of culture cease to be predominantly the domain of the wealthy and the learned and become a mass phenomenon. And when this happens, the results are truly explosive. As for this phase of numismatics, it is the author's belief that it can be said to have begun in the United States in the Depression years of the 1930s.

The New Deal administration was at least partly instrumental in promoting a new awareness of the arts on the part of the public at this time through its broad concept of public works programs. The principal vehicle for this promotion was the WPA, which, in addition to its understandable concern with street paving, sewers, sidewalks and other strictly utilitarian areas, encouraged interest in such items as: art and design research, restorations of historic sites, paintings and murals for public buildings, writers projects, and community theater groups. These programs were of course primarily instituted to relieve unemployment, but their secondary effects of encouraging and sustaining the arts were not unconsidered.[19]

A particular interest in philately and numismatics was encouraged and greatly stimulated by the large number of commemorative stamps and coins issued during the Roosevelt years, particularly the famous "Farley issues" of stamps and the commemorative half-dollar series of coins. The direct sale of special

"proof sets" of United States coins to collectors was also begun
during these years by the U.S. mint. The subsequent sales record
of these proof sets provides a most interesting example of the
expansion of coin collecting since 1936, the first year of their issue.[20]

Fig. 1

U. S. MINT
PROOF-SET SALES 1936–1964

Year Minted	Sets Sold	Original Price	Current Value
1936	3,837	$1.89	$910.00
1937	5,542	1.89	370.00
1938	8,045	1.89	195.00
1939	8,795	1.89	160.00
1940	11,246	1.89	110.00
1941	15,287	1.89	100.00
1942	21,120	2.04	106.00
(sales discontinued during war years)			
1950	51,386	2.10	115.00
1951	57,500	2.10	75.00
1952	81,980	2.10	45.00
1953	128,800	2.10	35.00
1954	233,300	2.10	20.00
1955	378,200	2.10	28.00
1956	669,384	2.10	12.00
1957	1,247,952	2.10	7.00
1958	875,652	2.10	15.00
1959	1,149,291	2.10	8.00
1960	1,691,602	2.10	7.00
1960	(small date)	2.10	25.00
1961	3,028,244	2.10	5.00
1962	3,218,019	2.10	5.00
1963	3,075,645	2.10	5.00
1964	3,950,762	2.10	8.00

(sales discontinued due to coin shortage)
Last year of silver coinage (see footnote 21)

In addition to being a barometer of the rise of numismatic
interest over the past thirty years, the proof–set table tells a bit
about the investment possibilities of scarce coins. Note also the
beginning of what appears to be large-scale investment demand in

1961, the year in which worldwide monetary problems and economic mismanagement were becoming obvious. The production of proof sets was discontinued after 1964 because of the great "coin shortage" that resulted from the hoarding of silver coins for their intrinsic value, and from the consequent overtaxing of the U.S. mint capacity in trying to replace them with debased clad coinage.[21]

At present, the number of coin collectors (or at least of people who have some form of special interest in coins) in the United States has been estimated to exceed eight million.[22] The circulation of the weekly newspaper *Coin World*, probably as accurate as any other measure of active or significant participation in some phase of numismatics, exceeds 130,000 per issue. The number of collectors who have a particular interest in gold, regardless of their motives, is obviously substantial, but the actual total is of less importance than the amount of money that is potentially and actually available for the accumulation of gold collections. And it is safe to assume that those considering the purchase of gold will have more capital than the average coin collector.

In the past, proof sets and the commemorative half dollars have indeed proven to be satisfactory investments. And as a result of the world silver shortage and the great silver fiasco of the U.S. Treasury,[23] the silver dollars and silver crowns of the world have lately been much in demand. Precious-metals investors have been buying rolls and bags of the most common and consequently the cheapest of the large silver coins in huge quantities. Those with numismatic sophistication seek out the scarce types and dates in silver coins knowing, among other things, that many of their companion pieces will eventually disappear into the melting pot.

But what of the future? What is the best numismatic investment? Or for that matter, what is the best precious-metal hedge against inflation, currency debasement, and devaluation? Perhaps a clue to coming trends can be obtained from a bulletin recently mailed to a select group of collectors by a leading New York coin dealer, probably the most widely known dealer in the United States and one whose clients include the wealthiest and most prominent collectors in the country.[24] This bulletin indicates that coin dealers (and their clients) have a strong desire to acquire the following:

WE WOULD LIKE TO BUY:

Colonial Coins

U. S. Half Cents
—*Uncirculated and Proof*

U. S. Large Cents
—*Uncirculated and Proof*

U. S. Minor Coins:
2¢, 3¢ Nickel & Silver
—*Uncirculated and Proof*

U. S. Five Cents:
Shield, Liberty, Buffalo.
—*Uncirculated and Proof*

U. S. Half Dimes
—*Uncirculated and Proof*

U. S. Dimes:
1796–1828—All conditions.
Liberty Seated, Barber, Mercury
—*Uncirculated and Proof*

U. S. Twenty Cents
—*Uncirculated and Proof*

U. S. Quarters:
1796–1807—All conditions.
Liberty Seated, Barber, Liberty
Standing
—*Uncirculated and Proof*

U. S. Half Dollars:
1794–1807—All conditions.
Bust type, Liberty Seated,
Barber, Liberty Walking
—*Uncirculated and Proof*

U. S. Silver Dollars:
1794–1803—All conditions.
Gobrecht, Liberty Seated, Morgan
—*Uncirculated and Proof*

U. S. Gold Dollars

U. S. Quarter Eagles

U. S. Three Dollar Gold

U. S. Half Eagles

U. S. Eagles

U. S. Double Eagles

U. S. Pioneer & Territorial Gold

Foreign Gold
—*All countries and denominations*

Ancient Gold and Silver

Note that proof sets, mint sets, commemoratives, foreign crowns, freak die impressions, error coins and similar items, which are so frequently advertised in the numismatic press, are not mentioned on this list, which is really the "want list" of the most sophisticated coin collectors and investors in the United States if not the world. Note the overwhelming preference for the coins of the United States. Observe, too, that nearly all the U.S. coins listed, other than gold, are the very early and the very scarce issues. And finally, note that *all U.S. gold coins and all foreign gold coins regardless of date are urgently in demand.* The common denominator of all the items on this list can be summed up in one word: quality.

To be effective, the numismatic collector-investor must concentrate his efforts. The vast increase in the use of money and coin that has occurred since the Renaissance, or even from the early days of our Republic, makes the old leisurely "curio cabinet" approach to collecting obviously impractical. As long ago as 1885, British numismatist-scholar Stanley Lane-Poole observed that "to be a great general numismatist is beyond the powers of one man."[25] And today the endless variety of numismatic material available prevents anyone from becoming a recognizable general collector. In numismatics, as in all things, the modern era is the age of the specialist.[26]

There is undeniable investment merit in a great many types of numismatic material—one can hardly encompass them all in a single volume—but it is the author's belief that the collector or investor who specializes in gold coins enjoys certain obvious advantages:

1. The investment is in a precious metal that is historically acknowledged to be the ultimate standard of value.
2. There are far fewer varieties of gold coins than there are silver or bronze; it is easier to build an unusual and valuable collection with a relatively small number of coins.
3. Gold coins were originally minted in much smaller quantities than silver or bronze, and they were prone to be frequently remelted into bullion. Consequently they are relatively more scarce—and thus more valuable.
4. Each gold coin has a much higher intrinsic value than any comparable silver coin.
5. Gold coins were frequently hoarded and seldom widely circulated. Consequently many varieties are available to the collector in uncirculated or mint condition.
6. Gold coins usually have high artistic merit: the softness and ductility of gold make possible intricate die engraving and sharp, vivid striking. The value of gold justifies considerable artistic effort in the design of coins. The metal itself also has great esthetic attraction.
7. The intrinsic value of gold coins will be increased (in terms

of legal tender money) by any official currency devaluation. Their numismatic value will rise both through inflation and demand—more and more collectors, fewer coins for sale.

8. Gold coins are readily marketable. Since they are made of the most valued monetary metal and enjoy a numismatic tradition as the most desirable type of coin, gold coins can usually be sold without delay.

9. They are most easily stored and protected. Unlike most other art works or antiques, a substantial and valuable collection of gold coins can be kept in a small safe-deposit box.

10. Both the use of gold as a primary store of value and the tradition of numismatic collecting have twenty-five centuries of history behind them—neither is likely to go out of style.

11. Gold coins are immune to the effects of oxygen and age; they do not tarnish or corrode or deteriorate in any way, other than the wear of circulation.

12. Because they are so often viewed merely as a source of bullion, certain gold coins can occasionally be bought at *bargain* prices—when their numismatic value is underestimated or unrecognized.

It is once again apparent, in these "twelve points for the gold collector," that a collection of gold coins has a dual nature; it has a significant intrinsic value as well as a numismatic one. In the perilous economic and political climate of our day, it is indeed a point worth considering. To do so even briefly, one must examine the strength of those bonds that tie men to gold.

Notes

CHAPTER I

1. Elgin Groseclose, *Money and Man* (New York: Frederick Ungar, 1961). For the whole unhappy history of inflation.
2. For Gresham's Law see Glossary. As for hoarding, we are con-

sidering here its true meaning: accumulating coins solely for their intrinsic metal content in anticipation or fear of further coinage of the same face value being debased, i.e., becoming of less intrinsic value. The burying or hiding of large quantities of coin was universal in ancient times, and these caches are often referred to as "hoards," but in the absence of protective vaults, they were sometimes just a necessary instance of primitive banking.

3. *Wall Street Journal*, January 9, 1968.

4. *Ibid.*

5. They have to be wealthy; a subscription to Dr. Pick's *World Currency Report* costs $275 per year.

6. See chapter five.

7. The author's knowledge of numismatics has been enriched by Elvira Eliza Clain-Stefanelli, *Numismatics: an Ancient Science*, Paper 32, Museum of History and Technology (G.P.O., 1968).

8. Groseclose, *op. cit.* (The Byzantine, Arab and other Eastern empires, however, flourished at this time, and so did their use of coin.)

9. *Tractatus de origine, iure nec non et mutationibus monetarum.*

10. The genealogical register of European nobility and royalty.

11. Charles Ernest Babelon, *Traité des monnaies grecques et romaines*, vol. 1 (Paris, 1901).

12. However, many of these royal collections passed through several hands before finding their final resting places in museums. Some were broken up during wars and revolutions, only to be re-collected again. The huge van Goorle collection unfortunately did not survive intact.

13. Sheldon Cheney, *A World History of Art* (New York: Viking, 1947), p. 714.

14. The Vienna Cabinet, for example, contains over 400,000 coins and medals.

15. *Proceedings* (1867), p. 3.

16. *American Journal of Numismatics* (May 1866), p. 1.

17. *Guida numismatica universale*, 2nd ed. (1889).

18. The Lilly bequest was not entirely a gift; in return, the U.S. Treasury was obliged to grant the Lilly estate a tax write-off in the amount of $5,500,000. But according to the Smithsonian's numismatic curator, Dr. Vladimir Clain-Stefanelli, the bequest was well worth the price, and brings the National Museum's gold collection "almost to completion," and makes its foreign series in particular "the most complete in existence" (*Coin World*, June 12, 1968).

19. Dixon Wecter, *The Age of the Great Depression* (New York: Macmillan, 1948).

20. Compiled from dealers' retail prices for May and June 1969.

21. The Treasury has resumed production of proof sets, beginning

with the debased clad coinage of 1968. Demand for these sets remains surprisingly strong, but one wonders what the long-term outlook for such nonprecious metal coins will be. Would you treasure one of these "tin" proof sets as you would real coins of gold and silver?

22. The *Wall Street Journal* and *Coin World* favor this figure.

23. See William F. Rickenbacker, *Wooden Nickels* (New Rochelle, N.Y.: Arlington House, 1966).

24. Stack's, Inc., whose clients included among others, Josiah K. Lilly.

25. Stanley Lane-Poole, *Coins and Medals: Their Place in History and Art* (London, 1885), p. 2.

26. Since the post–Civil War era, American numismatists have overwhelmingly preferred the coins of their own country. As early as 1888, it was reported that three-fourths of the estimated 10,000 coin collectors in the U.S. at that time specialized in early U.S. and colonial coins (*New York World*, March 25, 1888).

II

The Color of Gold

"They who worship gold in a world so corrupt as this have at least one thing to plead in defense of their idolatry—the power of their idol. This idol can boast of two peculiarities; it is worshipped in all climates, without a single temple, and by all classes, without a single hypocrite."

—C. C. COLTON

FROM THE BEGINNING IT WOULD SEEM MANKIND HAS BEEN HELD in thrall by the color of gold. In the book of Genesis we read:

A river flowed out of Eden to water the garden and there it divided and became four rivers. The name of the first is Pishon; it is the one which flows around the whole land of Hav-i-lah, where there is gold; and the gold of that land is good.[1]

So it is that gold is the first metal mentioned in the Bible. Not only the first metal but the first element—before iron, copper, silver, stone or sand. It is the first inorganic material specifically referred to by name. It would appear that it was just a short trip down the river from paradise to the gold mines. But the implications of all this I will gladly leave to the contemplation of theologians and economists.

This, however, is certain: the use of gold as a primary store of value was highly developed long before the beginnings of the most rudimentary money systems. A great variety of gold ornaments and jewelry of beautiful design and elaborate workmanship is conspicuous among the treasures that have survived the ancient civilizations. The Minoans, Assyrians, Etruscans, and particularly the Egyptians are noted in this respect. The earliest known treasure, however, is some gold beads found in excavations of a Sumerian culture dating from before 4000 B.C.[2]

Gold, along with copper, appears to be one of the first metals discovered and exploited by man. Egyptian sculptured reliefs have been found that depict gold working and mining operations as early as 3000 B.C. In the great dynastic ages of Egypt, gold statuettes and ornaments of spectacular beauty, as well as gems and precious stones in elaborate gold settings, were prized possessions of the Pharaohs and other royalty. Huge quantities of these items were dutifully placed in their tombs when they departed this life. Tutenkhamon (d. 1360 B.C.), of archeological fame, but a rather minor Pharaoh, had a solid gold coffin weighing 2,400 pounds.[3]

The earliest use of gold as a monetary standard seems to have occurred among the Babylonians about 2000 B.C.; perhaps even earlier. The basic monetary unit of the Babylonian Empire was the shekel, not a coin at this time but an ingot of gold weighing about 8.34 grams and considered to have a value equivalent to a healthy ox. The reliability and the practicality of the shekel were most significant factors in the renowned commercial abilities of the Babylonians in the ancient world.

Nor were the early Greeks immune from the lure of gold—not even in their most heroic age. Stripped of its mythical disguise, the Homeric legend of the golden fleece is probably just an account of a Greek raid on Armenia about 1200 B.C., to steal the gold that was being produced there by an extensive river panning and washing operation. But for all their creative instincts, the Greeks, as well as the rest of the world, were at that time still five centuries away from the final evolution of gold into money. And when it came, it came not from the logical Greeks but from their neighbors, the Lydians.

The Lydians were an intelligent and industrious people of mixed aboriginal and Aryan stock who occupied what is now south-central Turkey. The minor Lydian Empire has been described as the industrial power of the ancient world. Its glory, however, was historically brief and its final destiny was to be overrun by the great Persian Empire of Cyrus. But somewhere along the way, in addition to their spectacular creation of coined money, they also found time to establish the first commercial inns and to invent the game of dice.

It was Gyges of Lydia who, around 700 B.C., established the first mint, in order to put the seal of his kingdom on uniform-sized lumps of natural gold—an alloy the Greeks called "electrum" (usually comprised of about 75 percent gold and 25 percent silver). Silver was coined on the island of Aegina soon afterwards. But it remained for another Lydian monarch, the legendary King Croesus (560–546 B.C.), to strike the first coins of pure gold.[4] These first gold "coins" were little more than bean-shaped lumps of metal with the heads of a lion and bull facing each other, and a double square marking the reverse. But they began an evolution in the economic affairs of men that has yet to be completed.

Gold coins have been minted by almost every government since that of the famed Croesus, whether permanent or provisional, secular or ecclesiastic, royalist or republican.[5] Consequently, immense quantities of gold coins have been struck in the 25 centuries since the invention of coinage. In the modern era, still more immense stocks of the yellow metal have been cast into ingots and retained as official monetary reserves, or as backing for paper money. Yet the desire for gold, the need to possess something of enduring value, has seldom been stronger than it is today. It is no mere historical accident that so many gold coins have survived from ancient times, or that the gold coins of modern history can be found so frequently in brilliant uncirculated condition. It is the nature of the metal itself, as well as the nature of man, that provides the answer.

The properties of gold that have made it the supreme metal for coinage and other monetary purposes do not require great elaboration. But considering that the government of the United States since 1933 has attempted to coerce its citizens into avoiding all

contact with what it lately has termed a "barbarous relic,"[6] it would
not be inappropriate to restate here the most obvious virtues of
the yellow metal:

Gold has some unique physical attributes. It is the most ductile
and malleable of all metals. A single ounce can be drawn into a
wire 35 miles long without breaking, or it can be hammered into
sheets as little as 1/250,000 of an inch.[7] It is unbelievably heavy;
a cubic foot of gold weighs more than half a ton, and at the rate
of $35 per ounce would be worth about $600,000. (At $70 per
ounce it would of course be equal to $1,200,000, and at $100 per
ounce, over $1,800,000.) Obviously, very small but valuable
amounts of gold can easily be stored, transported, hidden—or
smuggled.

Gold is a beautiful and noble metal. Its luster and deep yellow
color have, since the dawn of history, proved a powerful and at times
irresistible attraction for men—and women.[8] But what really ex-
cites man is that gold is not only beautiful, but virtually indestruc-
tible as well. Unlike most other metals, gold is totally immune to
the effects of oxygen.[9] It will not corrode, tarnish or rust. Coins of
gold that have been buried in the earth or have lain in the sea for
twenty centuries have been recovered and found to be as brilliant
as the day they were minted. Gold is the most stable and least
chemically active of all the metals; it is literally imperishable—the
most permanent of all man's material possessions.

Because of its desirable and imperishable nature, it has been
estimated that about 85 percent of all the gold produced throughout history is still available, the remaining 15 percent being
permanently lost. Of the total supply presently available to the
world, about 60 percent is held by governments as monetary reserves;[10] the rest is in the hands of corporations and individuals,
with individuals holding the lion's share.

Total world production of gold from the primitive workings of
the Egyptians in 3000 B.C. through 1966 is estimated not to exceed
2.5 billion troy ounces, which would equal about 80,000 tons.
This may seem like a lot of gold, but by comparison, the U.S. steel
industry when working at capacity can pour 80,000 tons of steel in

a single hour. How much is *all the gold in the world*? If it were gathered together—bars, coins, jewelry, ornaments, everything—and melted into ingots, the ingots could be stacked into a cube measuring 50 feet on a side.[11]

Gold and the Value of Money

From gold coinage's crude beginning in the lumps of Gyges and Croesus, money, man, and gold have been inseparable. It is true that nations not possessing enough gold, but having silver in quantity, have been successful in maintaining a workable monetary standard based on this other very desirable but less valuable metal. Copper, bronze, and even iron have also served adequately as minor coin. But on a worldwide and historical basis, gold has always remained the king of money.

Yet from the beginning man has had to struggle to understand, not only the endless complexities and technicalities that involuntarily grew out of the almost casual invention of coined money, but the moral problems and dilemmas it presented as well. The main issue is the nature of money itself, whether it is actual, i.e. a specified amount of gold or silver to be used more or less in direct barter, or whether it is conventional: a token signifying a quantity of capital or labor whose value is determined arbitrarily by the state. The issue was inevitable from the moment the Lydian state first set its seal upon a lump of gold, changing for all time the meaning of gold and the meaning of money.

It must be understood, however, that neither the clever Lydians nor any other state or government invented money. Ingots of metal, oxen, jars of wine, slaves, tools, and other common objects were variously recognized and widely used as money long before coins became common in the Mediterranean world. The early states merely intervened in the monetary structure as a regulating agency. But as soon as the tremendous economic power and other advantages of coined money were apparent, the issuance and control of such money were everywhere seized as a government monopoly.

Once the state had established undisputed control of the monetary mechanism, it was inevitable that those who viewed the state as the ultimate source of wisdom, order, and progress would evolve the philosophy that money was a convenience of the state, to be administered for the "general welfare" of the nation, or for the glory of the empire, or for something similar. Under this view, establishing the "value" of money was therefore a prerogative of government and not a normal result of the natural inclination of people to place a value on things in the order of their needs and desires. This belief found expression in the statements of neo–Keynesian economists and money managers after 1960, particularly those associated with the U.S. Treasury. These men argued that the dollar was "better than gold," reasoning that it was not gold that gave the dollar its value, but it was the dollar that gave value to gold because the U.S. Treasury was willing to pay 35 of its paper dollars for an ounce of gold. (The hypocrisy and emptiness of this argument were rudely exposed in 1968, when the international price of gold soared above $35 an ounce in spite of all the maneuvers, manipulations, threats, and intrigues employed by the U.S. government to prevent it.)

In the original conception of coinage, the state seal upon the metal was intended solely as a guarantee of weight and purity. The coin itself was still just a commodity—a commodity of convenience to be traded for commodities of necessity or desire. But it was not long before it occurred to the subtle mind of man that the seal of the state, with all the power and wealth and glory it signified, was adding a new intangible value to the recognized intrinsic value of the metal itself. For the state, whether representing the single will of an emperor or king or the collective will of an assembly or mass, possesses the power of fiat—the monopoly of the legal use of force. It can not only ask that the citizen respect the value it puts on its coins, but it can presume to have the authority and power to compel him to accept it. If this latter view is accepted as valid, the intrinsic value of money becomes secondary or even irrelevant.

For 25 centuries man has sought to master the economic and social revolution begun by this transmutation of gold into coin, and coin into the ultimate money, and money into a function of government. But his successes have been few. The philosophic division between the views of money as an actuality and money as a convention remains unresolved today. But what is significant is that historically the record of man's outstanding successes has been written when the monetary supremacy of gold was recognized and encouraged, and his most colossal failures have resulted from trying to manufacture the illusion of wealth from the promises and threats of the state. So far in history every attempt to eradicate the ties that have bound men to gold for 4,000 years has ended in disaster.

Gold, Fiat Money, and Gresham's Law

Ever since the Babylonian success, many other nations and groups of nations, at fortuitous periods in their history, have recognized that one of the primary advantages in the use of gold as money is its merit as a measuring device; it becomes a standard of value with which all other forms of wealth and all promises of wealth can be compared. Gold has all the attributes that would be required of a perfect value standard: it is highly prized for its own attractive nature, it is virtually imperishable, it is expensive in terms of the effort required to extract it from nature and refine it, and it is sufficiently scarce to be considered rare—but still available enough to be widely used. All that is necessary to maintain a "gold standard," with all the advantages of economic stability it offers, is that the *face value* and the *intrinsic gold value* of the monetary unit be kept identical. This is the essence of pure commodity money, and its ideal expression was found in gold coins of fixed value and unvarying purity.

But the Western mind is restive under restrictions of any sort and our history is replete with attempts to abandon the ancient "cross of gold." Since the glories of Imperial Rome, we have been enthralled by the apparent majesty and power of the state (particularly those who have had a part in the wielding of that power). It is regrettable but perhaps understandable that this apparently limitless power of the state, its right of fiat, should at times appear to be not merely the guarantor and regulator of money, but its actual creator. What a dream! If the state could actually create money by the mere exercise of its will, Brazil and Chile, presently buried under their mountains of fiat paper notes, would be among the richest countries in the world, while Switzerland with its 100 percent gold-backed currency of limited circulation would be one of the poorest.

Only a very few times in the history of the West have men been so bold as to dare to cut completely and openly the link between money and gold, and when they did the results have been catastrophic. Most of the rulers of the world's empires, whether absolute monarchs or populist politicians, have had the good sense to recognize that the fiat powers of the state depend eventually on a willingness to use brute force—and that naked force is, in the long run, the weakest basis for power. Confidence in its honesty and integrity, on the other hand, is the strongest type of power that a government can possess. (Switzerland has survived intact much longer by relying on honor than Germany has by believing in force.) Therefore, royal embezzlers, mountebank politicians, and academic theorists alike have been far more apt to introduce their fiat money schemes by subterfuge than by direct edict.

Typically the introduction of debased or fiat money begins slowly at first. The appearance of sound gold-based money is contrived, but the substance is gradually stolen and replaced with counterfeits: debased coin or fictitious receipts. However, the public is seldom deceived for long. Gresham's Law goes into effect: what good coin remains in circulation is quickly hoarded (it becomes a race between the government and its citizens to see who can hoard the most).[12] People become more and more reluctant to exchange their goods and services of recognizable value for money of doubtful or questionable value. Prices soar; inflation rages. With money no longer a trustworthy standard of value or measure of wealth, alternative means of preserving capital are sought. Works of art, precious metals, jewels, real estate, securities, and valuable objects of all kinds take on a new meaning (or perhaps regain an old one) as stores of value.[13] Speculation becomes a way of life. (Sound familiar?)

Once the momentum of debasement and inflation has begun, it is seldom if ever checked before the final destruction of the whole monetary system and the government responsible for it. The second phase of currency debasement is far more drastic than the first. Having been discovered in its deception, the government, if it wishes to pursue the delusion of fiat money further (and once started it invariably does), has only one option left—the uncertain powers of coercion. In this phase, wage and price controls are imposed, citizens are forced to accept the government's money under threat of severe punishment for refusing it, gold and silver are ordered to be surrendered, "hoarders" are threatened with arrest, citizens are forbidden to travel abroad, foreign investments are forbidden or curbed severely, tariffs and penalties are raised against foreign imports, exchange controls are instituted, and limits are put on interest rates.

The results of these measures are always the opposite of what is intended; trade stagnates, prices rise even faster, black markets develop, gold and silver disappear entirely, speculation becomes frantic, evasions and dishonesties are commonplace and all remaining confidence in the government evaporates. The government itself becomes the victim of its own inflationary debasement. Tax revenues decline due to the erosion of legitimate trade, the diversion of goods to the black market, and the pouring of money into nonproductive speculation. The costs of government rise rapidly and the burdens on it increase as a result of economic instability. In the end the government is obliged to create still more fiat money or debase the currency still further in order to finance its own operation—and the spiral gets another vicious twist. With each turn of the cycle the descent becomes more rapid. There is no way out except to return to the discipline of gold, and this requires that the debased purchasing media be officially devalued in terms of their gold equivalent or written off entirely as in a bankruptcy. In either case, the holders of the debased coin or fiat money are the losers.

Incredible as it sometimes seems, the United States and Great Britain have already gone far down the road leading to pure fiat money. Furthermore, the present United States government appears determined not only to maintain its "goldless" domestic money system, but to force its fiat money scheme on the rest of the world, through the International Monetary Fund or some similar agency. A new international paper currency is demanded as a substitute for gold in international payments. The fiat of an international authority is to be invoked to supplement the already oppressive economic powers of the individual nations.

The modern neo–Keynesian economists, academic theorists and political opportunists of all grades now dream on a far grander scale than the medieval alchemists. Those deluded souls toiled for centuries over bubbling cauldrons and blazing forges, muttering incantations, mixing vile concoctions, and invoking all the black arts in futile and bizarre attempts to find a magic formula that would turn iron or lead into gold. Alchemy was one of the more notable delusions of history and one of the most persistent. It gripped the mind of Europe for a thousand years, but produced not a single ounce of gold.[14]

But the modern alchemists, the believers in the fiat-money New Economics, claim to have worked the miracle. To them, realities are not as important as abstract ideas; real gold is not as significant as the *idea of gold*. Realities to this kind of thinker are finite, limited, irritating. But ideas and abstractions are infinite, limitless, and possessed of boundless possibilities. Real gold is expensive, hard to obtain; it has to be worked for, paid for in one way or another. But the idea of gold is merely an abstraction, and abstractions can be created from nothingness. Mere writings on a piece of paper, bookkeeping entries, promissory notes, or engraved certificates are sufficient evidence of this brilliant abstraction. There is only one difficulty: abstract ideas are like soap bubbles, absolute and perfect in their beauty and symmetry, a totally enclosed and unified system—but when you try to touch them they disappear.

The medieval alchemist failed because he foolishly tried to manufacture real gold from nothingness, but the modern money doctors think they have succeeded because they have gone beyond real gold to what they think is the far more impressive concept (mentally) of the *idea of gold*.

The common money of the United States, the Federal Reserve

note, and the proposed new international money or "drawing rights" controlled by the IMF are just such abstractions. They are defined in terms of gold but can never actually be redeemed in the metal.[15] They are intended forever to remain abstractions—evidences of debt that can never be repaid. Money is to be debt and debt is to be credit, and the debt is evidenced by interest-bearing notes or bonds. When due, the principal and the interest on the bonds are paid from the proceeds raised by the sale of more bonds. The more we get into debt the richer we are to become. The IOU's, called bonds, are deposited in the banks where they are called "assets," and therefore more "money" can be created from these assets to make new loans, and new loans mean more assets, and more assets mean more money—and so on into infinity. It is the perfect system, unified, self-contained, abstract—but if we try to touch it, it may one day disappear.

Lenin is said to have predicted that the free world would eventually destroy itself by debauching its own currency. Whatever else may be said of this Marxist Machiavelli, it is obvious that he was an astute observer of history. There is an old Swiss saying, "Good money is coined freedom." These hardy mountain people have also learned the lessons of history well. They know that their destiny depends, as did that of the ancient Byzantine Empire, on the world's respect for their money rather than for the military power they can display. It is no accident that the Swiss have become the indispensable bankers to the world; they have the world's most reliable money—backed 100 percent by gold. They sum up their future very simply: "No gold; no Swiss."

But if good money still circulates in parts of the West, despite the inflationary illness that has become chronic with us, the same can no longer be said of good intrinsic-value coin. Credit and monetary inflation can seldom be contained within the borders of those countries that originated it. The paper dollars of the U.S., when they can no longer be exchanged for intrinsic-value coin or bullion at home (our gold coins were taken from us long ago and nearly all our subsidiary silver has disappeared into the hoarder's vaults), reach out for the good coin of other countries.[16]

Despite laws to the contrary, the silver and gold coins of Canada,

Mexico and even Switzerland, for example, have been exported to the limit. And as a result, their mintage eventually had to be stopped and these coins replaced with base metal tokens, as in the United States. Gresham's Law respects no boundaries. Laws forbidding the movement of money, gold, and silver across international boundaries are and will be no more effective than were the laws forbidding the manufacture and importation of alcoholic beverages during the Prohibition era of the United States.

Good coin still exists in the Western world, but seldom anymore as legal tender. It is firmly in the hands of collectors, numismatists, investors, speculators, hoarders, and dealers. These diverse peoples possess diverse motives, but they have one thing in common: they recognize something of value when they see it.

The Private Citizen and Gold Today

Despite the patently obvious evidence of recent years that Gresham's Law is still irresistibly in operation, the student of monetary history and crowd psychology may yet have some reservations about gold investing. Before deciding on gold coins as a safe and profitable investment, with the obvious advantages already mentioned, one may properly question the extent to which man's historic faith in the reliability of gold as a standard of value has been or will be affected by the thirty-four-year campaign of the Keynesian economists to escape from the restrictions and disciplines of gold-based money. (The question is especially pertinent because of the defection of so many so-called conservative economists and bankers to the viewpoints of the New Economics.)

After all, we in what the French like to call the "Anglo–Saxon camp" have been told for a considerable time now, through our press and by the pronouncements of even some of our highest Treasury and banking officials, that gold, like the Deity in the eyes of some modern theologians, is dead; that the use of gold for monetary purposes or as a store of value is, in that already well worn cliché, a "barbarous relic." Furthermore, it is said that the sooner we are able to abandon it completely, the better it will be for us.

But perhaps the demise of gold as the center of the monetary universe has been reported, as was the death of Mark Twain, somewhat prematurely. Although the obituaries continue to be published, the world remains unconvinced. If gold is indeed dead, it has proven to be a rather lively ghost. The author's clipping files concerning monetary subjects indicate that more press copy on the subject of gold has been published during the last two years than at any time since the crisis years of 1933–34. Countless reports on the future of gold and the attendant opportunities for speculation it offers have also been prepared by private financial advisers and services (and sold at high prices) since the dying relic, the "echo of the past,"[17] has suddenly become a full-blown crisis. Some went so far as to declare that gold was America's number-one problem. But there is still little public agreement on whether the ancient idol will be finally and forever toppled from his throne or restored once more to past glory.

In the author's opinion, the decisive vote was given in 1967 and 1968, when repeated waves of gold speculation swept the gold markets of the world, shaking its very monetary foundations, breaking up the London gold pool and its fixed $35–per–ounce gold price and forcing the devaluation of the British pound sterling. The most revealing part of these episodes was that they imposed an ignominious retreat on the neo–Keynesian money managers of the West. In being forced into a tightfisted defense of their stock-piles of monetary gold, the position of the money managers would have been ludicrous but for the tragic effects of the inflation that had already eroded the wealth and vitality of countless peoples.

Ironically, it was these practitioners of the New Economics who had insisted all along that gold was only a superstition, a vestige of a barbarous past, and that we would have been better off to dump it all into the sea.[18] But now that it has apparently been found necessary, for the moment at least, for the United States and its partners in financial experiment to defend at all costs (that is, with whatever further sacrifices may be required of their citizens) what is left of their monetary gold stocks, it may be suggested (with tongue in cheek) that we dump our money managers into the sea instead.

However, it is obvious that the present show of defending gold by Britain and the United States, through various austerity programs, exchange controls, high taxes, etc., is a tactical expedient only. The ultimate goal remains the implementation of some new international paper-money scheme, an eventual total devaluation of the dollar, and the complete demonetization of gold. Therefore, stability in the price of gold and an end to the long-term inflation that has accompanied the ascendancy of the New Economics are nowhere in sight. Additional waves of gold speculation, gold-buying panics and recurrent gold crises are not only probable but inevitable.

What part the citizen of the United States and his British cousin have played in these events has been somewhat restricted, legally at least, by the actions of their respective governments. They have been prohibited by law and regulation from direct participation in the purchase, sale or ownership of gold in bullion or monetary form.

In most other civilized lands (and some that are not so civilized) the ownership of bar gold and gold in any other form is not only permitted but, as in the case of France and Switzerland, often tacitly encouraged. These enlightened countries believe that gold in the hands of private citizens is an aid to internal economic stability and complements rather than competes with the official reserves of their central banks. By allowing the free use of gold as a store of value, the other Western countries have eased somewhat the burden of inflation upon their citizens. Unfortunately, the insidious disease of inflation is, as a matter of record, chronic in every country that practices neo-Keynesian economics. But by permitting the private possession of gold in any form, France and Switzerland at least recognize that the least sophisticated and affluent of their citizens should have the right to defend themselves.[19]

The only other major nation, besides the U.S. and Britain, that prohibits free commerce in gold by its inhabitants is the Soviet Union. Private holdings or transactions in the yellow metal are considered there to be "economic crimes"—most serious offenses in a Marxist state. Those engaged in them are subject to the firing squad. (Yet it has been reliably reported that a flourishing black market in gold continues to exist in Russia and the other Marxist states.)[20] Curiously enough, the writer finds that the parallel presented by the United States and the Soviet Union, regarding the private holding of gold as an infringement on a state monopoly and therefore a crime, is neither unbelievable nor incongruous. Perhaps the "big brother" philosophy of economics is rather easily recognized whatever its stage of development.

Worldwide, the record of the neo–Keynesian money managers in the area of maintaining the purchasing power of their fiat currencies has been deplorable. But perhaps I am too harsh on the proponents of the New Economics; after all, monetary delinquency antedates Keynes by a considerable period; it is of course as old as money itself. The coin clippers and debasers caused as much ruin and suffering in ancient times as the paper-money inflationists have in the twentieth century.

But holding aside for a time further comments on the great questions concerning future trends of inflation and the coming rise in the price of gold, let us proceed directly to the problems and opportunities confronting people generally and citizens of the United States and Britain in particular who might wish to speculate on these possibilities, or who might want to invest in a gold-related activity as a hedge. Since possession of monetary gold (bullion) by citizens of the U.S. and Britain is unlawful, there remain only two (legal) avenues of gold investment open to them: the purchase of shares in gold-mining companies, and the collection of gold coins.

The gold coin was once a very vital part, at times the lifeblood, of the economic body. Today it is not so. The lifeblood of the New Economics is credit. The coin of gold, the ancient king of money, was forced to abdicate in disgrace during the depths of the Great Depression and it has been banished from the realm ever since. But the gold coin still has a meaning, and sometimes a very profitable one, for those who have the eyes to see it.

The provisions of the Gold Reserve Act of 1934 and the Executive Orders and banking laws of 1933, which originally demonetized and confiscated all outstanding gold coin in the United States, prohibited the individual possession of gold bullion (or any other recognizable use of gold as a store of value). However, they made no prohibitions regarding the ownership of gold-mining stocks,[21] and they also permitted the retention of gold coins of "recognizable numismatic value." Failure of the original legislation to define adequately what constituted recognizable numismatic value caused considerable confusion for some years, but in general, the parts of the gold regulations concerning numismatics were not rigidly enforced—at least not to the point of harassing collectors of gold coins.

It is now obvious that considerable quantities of U.S. gold coin were never surrendered at the time of the original order. Some coin was withheld because it was in the possession of foreign citizens, banks, or governments, and some because its owners chose to defy their government because of what they considered to be an arbitrary and unjust confiscation.[22] Considerable quantities of American gold coin also found residence in Canada.[23] At any rate, choice uncirculated U.S. and foreign gold coins were generally available through coin dealers in the United States after 1934 and they sold at prices that from today's vantage point were fantastically cheap.

Unusually strong demand for the more common gold coins, strictly as a speculation on a possible rise in the price of gold or as a hedge against inflation, occurred from time to time, notably in 1946, 1957 and 1961, but in general, the market for the so-called common type of gold coins remained unexciting—until 1967. In the truly numismatic area, however, astute and knowledgeable collectors gradually reaped a tremendous reward for their patience. During the postwar years, gold coins of unusual scarcity or rare numismatic value enjoyed a spectacular and continuous rise in price.

In the forties and fifties, the U.S. Treasury held most of the world's gold bullion, and consequently, the attitude of the government toward gold-coin collectors was one of indifference, even though the legality of possessing so-called common-date gold coins was somewhat questionable, at least until 1954. Prior to that year, the Treasury held the opinion that it alone had the right to determine whether or not any gold coin was of numismatic value. Determinations were to be made on the merits of each individual coin presented to the Treasury for ruling.

The pre–1954 criterion for judging a coin minted before 1933 was whether or not the coin in question had possessed a recognized numismatic value on or before April 5, 1933. Gold coins minted after 1933 were to be judged on the basis of the number issued, the purpose for which they were issued, their condition, mint mark, historical significance and other numismatic factors. However, there appeared to be no great rush of collectors to the Treasury Building to have their coins checked.

It must be admitted, however, that the Treasury Department of that era did not rigidly or aggressively enforce a narrow and legalistic interpretation of the "numismatic value" provision of the Gold Reserve Act. Had it done so, American numismatics would have suffered severe and irreparable damage; many fine gold coins which are now the prized possessions of American collectors would have been lost forever. "Numismatic value" is a term of varied and at times subtle meaning. Many regular-issue coins gradually become scarce or even rare, through natural attrition, while they are still technically part of the circulating medium, and these scarcity situations are invariably recognized at first only by the most astute and sophisticated collectors. By the time the numismatic value of such coins becomes common knowledge, it is usually well past the point where that value or the potential for numismatic value was actually acquired.

There is also the case of the unusually well struck or prooflike coin which was selected from a regular issue; certainly this type of coin has exceptional numismatic value even though the issue it was taken from was not particularly scarce. And how does one objectively judge the roll of uncirculated coins put away by the foresighted for the benefit of future generations of numismatists? And specimen coins retained because of their artistic merit or historical associations? Surely the final U.S. gold-coin series designed by Augustus St. Gaudens, one of America's most noted sculptors, would fall into this latter class. To have ruthlessly insisted on the surrender of *all* gold coins extant on or before April 5, 1933, that were still technically part of the circulating medium, and/or not obviously or generally recognized to be of unusual historic numismatic value, would have been catastrophic indeed, as far as numismatics is concerned.

But the Treasury officials of that day chose to be tolerant, if not amiable, and, except for preventing the importation of large numbers of post-1933 foreign gold coins, did little to disturb numismatic gold activity. Apparently, numismatists, collectors, and even hoarders were too few in number at that time to cause alarm on the Potomac. Whatever the reason, we can feel thankful that the Treasury authorities of the first quarter-century following the demise of gold coinage in the U.S. did not flail about with the typical bureaucratic myopia that has characterized their successors. In any case, the "common" U.S. gold coins (which, as we know now, are anything but common) and most pre-1933 foreign gold coins were allowed to be traded and collected more or less openly during the years prior to 1954.

In 1954, the Treasury Department recognized at last that the time had come to legitimize the numismatic gold market. Consequently, an amendment was made to the Gold Regulations, to the effect that *all gold coins minted prior to 1933* would subsequently be presumed to be rare and of recognized special value to collectors, without the necessity of further specific determinations by the Treasury. Coins minted after 1933 were still subject to specific Treasury Department rulings, which were to be based on the advice of the Curator of Numismatics of the United States National Museum. All U.S. gold coins and the vast majority of foreign gold coins were thus freed from the overhanging threat of confiscation, and a new era for American numismatics appeared to begin.

It might have been reasonable to expect after 1954 that further relaxations of the Treasury's Gold Regulations, particularly as they applied to numismatics, would be a natural development in time. But the subsequent course of American economic history ruled otherwise. By 1960, the underlying inflationary instability of the Western world had reached the point where the once seemingly unlimited gold reserves at Fort Knox had noticeably begun to shrink.

This unfortunate (and, in my opinion, wholly avoidable) turn of events precluded any possibility of further liberalization of the gold rules, numismatic or other. Instead, in 1961, the Kennedy Administration saw the necessity of establishing within the Treasury

Department the Office of Domestic Gold and Silver Operations (ODGSO), in order to institute a more rigorous control over the import and export of gold and silver, the licensing of jewelers, goldsmiths and industrial users of gold, and the import and sale of gold coins.

The most positive accomplishment of the new ODGSO was to reaffirm, as its own policy, the 1954 amendments to the Gold Regulations, which ruled that all gold coins minted prior to 1934 are rare and consequently of recognized numismatic value.[24] For gold coins minted after 1933, the office required a separate ruling in each case and the issuance of a special permit for the importation or possession of each post-1933 coin approved. (Once an initial ruling on a particular coin was made, however, no further permits or applications were necessary to purchase or hold other coins of the same identity within the United States, although a license to *import* any post-1933 gold coin is still required, whether it has been previously approved or not.)

By some obscure and tenuous logic, ODGSO also required (until 1969) a permit to *import* pre-1934 gold coins, even though the purchase or possession (or both) of such coins was unrestricted within the United States. I might add that the majority of applicants desiring to import pre-1933 as well as post-1933 gold coins were invariably refused.

The author once applied for a permit to import some pre-1933 Mexican gold coins offered by a Canadian dealer. The license was refused, even though the coins under consideration were the rarest of their series and selling for more than twice their intrinsic value, on the grounds that they were "not of exceptional numismatic value within the meaning of the Treasury Department Gold Regulations." In reply, I could only point out, politely (and in vain), that the Treasury Department Gold Regulations, which ODGSO was supposed to be administering, stated without qualification that *all* gold coins made prior to 1934 were to be considered of "recognized special value to collectors." The spectacle of federal regulatory agencies regulating themselves in a circle is at times wondrous to behold.

Fortunately, the 1954 amendments are now a well-established precedent, and they provided at least a basic protection for the numismatic gold collector. Furthermore, although it has required a change of administrations, ODGSO has finally come to recognize that some of its interpretations of the gold rules have been, in the words of its new director, "of dubious merit."[25]

On April 22, 1969, the Gold Regulations of the U.S. Treasury Department were amended to correct the obvious and unreasonable inconsistency introduced by Executive Order 11037, issued July 20, 1962, which required, among other things, a permit from ODGSO for the importation of pre-1934 gold coins. The new director of ODGSO, Mr. Thomas Wolfe, appointed by the Nixon Administration, admitted candidly that "it really didn't make a lot of sense" for ODGSO to prohibit or confiscate a pre-1934 gold coin coming from abroad, when the collector could walk across the street and buy the same coin in the U.S. without restriction.[26]

Therefore, the provisions requiring a license to import pre-1934 gold coins were eliminated. Collectors and dealers in the U.S. are now free to import such coins, provided they are genuine, subject only to the usual customs regulations and import duties.* Counterfeits or restrikes, however, are subject to confiscation, regardless of a pre-1934 date. The Gold Regulations were further amended to require import licenses only for gold coins struck from 1934 through 1959. The granting of such licenses is to be subject to the usual criterion of judgment. No gold coins struck after 1959 will be admitted, except for those issues already granted exemption by ODGSO prior to April 30, 1969. (A list of the exempt post-1959 gold coins will be found on page 286.)

The 1969 modifications of the Gold Regulations bring a wel-

---

* It appears, however, that there still may be formidable difficulties to contend with. Some of the early reports from collectors who ordered coins by mail from abroad, subsequent to the April 1969 modifications of the Gold Regulations, are hardly reassuring. They tell of lengthy delays while coins are held in customs houses pending "inspection," and worst of all there have been reported incidents where rare coins were mutilated by having their "authenticity" tested by means of a metal punch wielded by some thickheaded or vindictive customs or postal inspector. I do not know whether these indefensible practices are yet widespread, are destined to become so, or merely represent isolated cases. In any event, I feel that collectors should be alerted to these possible dangers.

come breath of fresh air into the bureaucratic smog that has shrouded the rulings and statements of the Treasury and ODGSO since 1961. However, one can only regret the arbitrary cut-off date of 1959, which automatically excludes such highly desirable numismatic treasures as the Canadian $20 centennial gold coin of 1967, and most of the post–1960 commemorative gold coins of Israel.

Fortunately, past history has demonstrated that common sense eventually triumphs, even in the Treasury; we can therefore continue to hope that the absolute 1960 cut-off ruling will also be reconsidered one day.

By contrast, however, British gold collectors were apparently dealt a severe blow when in 1966 the Bank of England issued regulations requiring the registration of *all* coin collectors and limiting collectors to no more than four gold coins minted after 1837. But fortunately, as was the case with the original numismatic provisions of our own Gold Reserve Act of 1934, these rules were softened considerably in their administration. Although not specifically stated in the regulations, it has been made known that "collectors may possess two gold coins or sets of any one type or series, that is, two 1887 five-pound pieces, two 1902 two-pound pieces, two 1937 proof sets, etc.—only holders of large quantities of common-date sovereigns will be required to surrender them."[27]

The citizen of the United States, if interested in acquiring a speculative or investment position in gold, is then limited to gold-mining stocks or gold coins. The citizen of Great Britain has the same options except that he is much more limited in the area of coins. The natives of Canada, France, Switzerland, Germany, South Africa, and innumerable other areas of the world, presumably not as far along on the path of enlightenment as we, are free to do as they please regarding gold.

There has been some talk that once gold was successfully demonetized by the U.S., the free holding of gold by its citizens would be permitted. If this is ever tried, it will be as a last desperate bluff to prove that the dollar is better than gold. But like our former policies of trying to hold down the international price of gold by selling it freely through the London "gold pool" and trying to hold down the price of silver through massive Treasury sales, it will be just another phenomenal failure. By its demented economic and fiscal policies of the last three decades, the U.S. government has forfeited all confidence in its ability to maintain the value of its currency. If U.S. citizens were now granted the right to cash in some of their paper dollars for gold, what is left of our national gold reserve would disappear in a month.

In Russia and the Marxist countries of Eastern Europe, there are of course no gold-mining stocks. If it were not for the Communist ideology, however, no doubt there would be; the Soviet Union is thought to be the third largest producer of gold in the world (after South Africa and Canada), although the actual production figures are a closely guarded state secret. It is also reported that the Russians pay production costs equivalent to $100 an ounce for their gold. Despite Lenin's boast that gold would one day pave the public rest rooms in the worker's paradise, the Russians seem to have found other uses for it—like buying vitally needed equipment and raw materials in Europe, Africa and Asia.

But as we have said, private trafficking in gold bullion in the Soviet Union is considered (as in the United States) a most serious crime. Surprisingly, coin collecting, including gold coins, is permitted. The state mints occasionally issue gold commemorative coins and medals, and sometimes restrikes of older gold coins. We can assume they are sold on a strict one-to-a-customer basis at home, although some of these restrikes have been widely exported to the West (and smuggled into the United States) for profitable sale. However, whether a *tovarich* can acquire a collection of gold coins without arousing the suspicion that he is surreptitiously planning an "economic crime" I do not know, but I imagine the mental hazards are discouraging.

The general worldwide availability and popularity of gold coins as an investment and speculative medium, and the rather intense activity of recent months call for diligent, thorough and hopefully objective investigations into the merits, hazards, techniques and problems involved in the purchase and collection of gold coins.

That is the main purpose of this volume. It is hoped that it will also serve an auxiliary purpose by revealing something of the extent of monetary deterioration in the West and by showing the absolute necessity, as well as the advantages, of finding alternative stores of value to rapidly depreciating paper currency.

An analysis of the virtues, risks and comparative values of various gold-mining stocks is not within the scope of this work except as it serves to compare the character of gold-mining issues as a group with coins and other forms of investment.

Notes

CHAPTER II

1. Revised Standard Version: GENESIS 2: 10–12.
2. Cheney, *op. cit.*, p. 38.
3. Said to be the largest single object of gold in existence.
4. According to the ancient Greek historians, Xenophanes and Herodotus. Numismatic specimens of these first coins have been recovered.
5. Robert Friedberg, *Gold Coins of the World*, 2nd ed. (New York, 1965).
6. A peculiar notion that seems to gain prominence in direct but inverse proportion to the decline in our monetary gold stocks. In 1946, when the U.S. Treasury contained most of the world's gold, our government was equally insistent on proclaiming that gold was the only real money and that gold must be the foundation of all international monetary arrangements. One is reminded of the old proverb: "Those who fail in an enterprise do not thereafter speak highly of it."
7. William L. Graham, Jr., *The Coming Gold Crisis* (Glenview, Ill.: Hickory Press, 1966), p. iv.
8. Freud has suggested that part of this attraction is derived from the subconscious association of gold with the erotic fantasies of childhood—a notion I find too abstruse to comment on.
9. Gold is not entirely unique in this respect. There are six rare metals of the "platinum type"—platinum, palladium, ruthenium, osmium, rhodium, and iridium—that are also immune to normal atmospheric

conditions. But they are all considerably more scarce and expensive than gold. Of the six only platinum has been used for coinage in the past. Between 1828 and 1845, Russia minted three denominations of platinum coins. (Recently the island kingdom of Tonga announced plans to mint commemorative coins of palladium.)

10. Most monetary reserves are kept in the form of ingots or bars (the 30-kilogram size is preferred—about 66 lbs.), but considerable quantities of gold coins are also held by many countries, including France and Mexico, as part of their central bank reserves.

11. Statistics on gold production are derived principally from *U.S. Bureau of Mines Bulletin*, no. 630 (G.P.O., 1965), with embellishments by author.

12. In 1966–67 all U.S. silver coins disappeared in just such a manner, with the public probably outreaching the Treasury for most of them.

13. Cynical Frenchmen used to say they could judge the future of the franc by the trend of the antique markets. When the antique business was booming they knew the franc was headed for devaluation again. (The antique business in the United States is now better than ever.)

14. Charles Mackay, *Extraordinary Popular Delusions and the Madness of Crowds*, 2nd ed. (London, 1852; reprint ed., with Foreword by Bernard M. Baruch, New York, 1932), p. 100.

15. The U.S. *dollar* is "defined" by law of Congress to be an amount of gold equal to 1/35 of a troy ounce (13.71 grains) of fine gold. The Continental nations have let it be known that any future IMF currency or "drawing rights" must also be defined as a specific amount of gold to get their approval.

16. Those dollars that "buy" foreign coins eventually return as a claim on the American gold stock and the cycle will continue until: a) all good foreign coins are gone, or b) all our gold is gone.

17. Headline of a feature article in *Chicago Daily News*, February 26, 1968, read: "Gold backing an echo of past."

18. See John Maynard Keynes, *General Theory of Employment, Interest and Money* (New York, 1936), for these and similar ideas.

19. The wealthy and sophisticated can more easily obtain and better judge the value of such things as stocks, real estate, works of art, antiques, etc. Precious metals have traditionally been the "poor man's" inflation hedge. Witness the popularity of gold ornaments among the masses of India.

20. Occasional accounts in the Soviet press concerning trials and sentences for gold dealing, hoarding and similar "economic crimes" tend to verify this.

21. Prior to and following the banking acts of 1933–34, which included devaluing the dollar by 41 percent, the stocks of gold-mining companies underwent an enormous increase in price. The

shares of Homestake Mining Co., for example, rose 1,600 percent, reaching their peak in 1936.

22. The Supreme Court in a narrow (5–4) decision ruled otherwise.
23. Until the recent series of gold crises of 1966–69, American gold coins could readily be obtained at the Bank of Nova Scotia and several Canadian banks at a price only slightly over their bullion value.
24. The bureau's ruling was based on an assumption that nearly all American gold coins were surrendered and melted in 1933–34, and therefore those that remained outstanding were rare. (That was the essence of its original statement, at any rate.)
25. Thomas G. Wolfe, Speech to Professional Numismatists Guild, *Coin World*, May 21, 1969.
26. *Ibid.*
27. Information from Spinks, Ltd., Coin Dealers, *Numismatic Circular* (London, August 1966).

III

From Caesar to Napoleon

"The history of money is the history of civilization."

—ALEXANDER DEL MAR

ANYONE WHO BECOMES INTERESTED IN GOLD COINS, WHETHER AS a numismatist-collector or as an investor, will find that a fair amount of study and reading is involved. As was pointed out in the first chapter, successful investment in gold coins requires at least a general knowledge of numismatics and, as with any other serious investment program, a working knowledge of economics and finance. Bernard Baruch, the great speculator-financier and adviser to presidents, recommended the reading of economic history, and particularly the study of the great financial delusions of the past, to all who would succeed at any sort of investment or speculation. It is common enough advice, that anyone who proposes to employ any significant amount of money in the stock market had better be prepared to spend at least one hour a day in study and research— and I assure the reader that a great deal more time than that is involved if one is really serious about making the stock market a consistently profitable venture.

How much time the gold-coin collector-investor should spend in study and research will depend probably on the extent of his collection and the amount of money involved. It will not be arbitrarily fixed by this writer; the ancient lure of gold and the fascination of rare coins will draw whoever possesses them willingly enough into the study of their nature and meaning. As for understanding contemporary economic trends, which admittedly shift and evolve with bewildering complexity, reading the financial press is helpful. The *Wall Street Journal* of course is *the* daily paper devoted exclusively to finance and always well worth reading.

However, if one hasn't the time or the inclination to read the *Journal* every day, a conscientious review of a good financial weekly is recommended. *Barrons* is one of the best-known weekly newspapers devoted to investment and finance and its news coverage of national and international developments affecting gold and silver is excellent. Receiving economic and financial news on a weekly basis has, perhaps, even a certain advantage in that it tends to encourage a more reflective outlook concerning current events. One must avoid succumbing to the emotional contagions that are inescapably a part of daily news reporting. The gold-coin investor should take a much longer view of things than the typical stock market or commodity speculator.

For the really serious and sophisticated student of investment and finance, the weekly *Commercial and Financial Chronicle* contains highly technical articles by the world's leading economists and bankers, covering current developments in domestic and international finance. But it is expensive; better read it at your library or broker's office if you can. In general, it would probably not be worthwhile to subscribe unless you have other sizable gold or silver investments, such as stocks or futures.

But no one, no gold-coin collector-investor, can be excused from a thorough reading of the weekly numismatic press. *Coin World*, published every Wednesday at Sidney, Ohio, has been in print since 1935, has a large circulation, and is generally available at the larger newsstands or through coin dealers. *Numismatic News* is another excellent journal. Both are available by mail at a modest subscription rate if they can't be obtained locally.

The numismatic press not only gives complete coverage of general numismatic interests, but also reviews all important political and economic developments that might affect the price of gold and silver, or the price trends of various coins. There are also several good monthly magazines devoted to numismatics, with *Numismatic Scrapbook* being an outstanding example. I would also suggest that from your newspaper reading you begin and maintain a clipping file or scrapbook of the more important and informative articles on gold and gold coins. It will become a valuable and always-current reference, and will be a great help in sharpening your numismatic and investment skills. It may provide an interesting diversion as well.

The numismatic investor will find that building a modest private library on the subject will prove not only personally rewarding, but eventually financially profitable. Out-of-print books on numismatics, investment, economics and monetary history have grown quite valuable in recent years. Old coin catalogues, for example, that sold for a dollar or so in the late forties were worth $15 to $30 twenty years later, and have become collector's items in themselves. Books on gold and gold mining also form a special category of interest for rare book collectors. Old books about speculation and investment, economic crises, the history of money, financial delusions of the past, and virtually every other economic or monetary subject are always wanted by professional speculators and investors.

Professional stock market speculators and traders number among them some of the most literate and cultured people in the world of business—or any other field, for that matter. Some of the better literature, some of the more profound philosophical appreciations of life, and some of the shrewder observations about the nature of man and his problems often can be found in the writing devoted to speculation and investment.[1]

Therefore, if you are investing in gold coins or considering such investment (or any other form of investment or speculation), and are not already doing so, I strongly recommend that you:

1. Read the numismatic press.
2. Read the financial press.
3. Become familiar with the basic outlines of economic and monetary history.

4. Read and collect books on numismatics, coin catalogues, magazines, etc.
5. Build your own personal reference library.

Reading and study are one of the requirements and one of the rewards of successful gold-coin investing. As for starting a personal reference library, the brief bibliography in this book will offer some suggestions, but few if any firm recommendations. After all, a personal library should be personal; it should grow primarily from the natural inclinations of the individual investor.

The Coin Debasers

We have already touched upon the propensity of peoples in the classic and medieval worlds to hoard good coin in the fear or anticipation of subsequent issues of the same face value being reduced in intrinsic value. Why they were so often compelled to this view can be readily realized from even an abbreviated review of the history of coin and money after Gyges.

From the primitive mints of Gyges and Croesus, the institution of coinage spread with great rapidity throughout the Mediterranean world. As it was the Greeks who emerged to dominate that world, it was the Greeks who first experienced the complications and trials of a money economy. The widespread use of coined money brought a great boom to the area. The convenience and abundance of coin released men from the tedious and awkward economy of barter and brought new and seemingly unlimited opportunities for the expansion of trade and commerce. The money economy also provided new and unlimited opportunities for going into debt.

Cities began to flourish as never before and, just as in our own time, there was a vast exodus from the rural areas into the trading and shipping centers, which held the promise of affluence and excitement. Banks were established and the money changer, previously unknown, became a powerful factor in the economic life of the world. A distinct creditor and debtor class appeared—with the debtors naturally becoming far more numerous. In ancient times it was possible, and not uncommon, for a borrower not only to pledge land and livestock as security for a loan, but to offer his wife, his children or himself as collateral. If the loan was defaulted, these human "chattels" were subject to being sold into slavery to satisfy the debt.

At the end of the first century following the general use of coined money, the Greek civilization was not only no longer prosperous, but bordering everywhere on complete collapse. All over Attica, stone pillars inscribed with the amount of a loan, the rate of interest, the date of maturity, and the name of the lender dotted the landscape; it was a rare farm that did not exhibit one of these monuments. As for the nonpropertied population, the greater part of the working class, rural and urban, was already in danger of being sold into slavery. Everywhere there were suffering and discontent; armed insurrection seemed imminent.

The immediate cause of the problem was a general and severe depression, which had settled over the land after decades of unprecedented prosperity and expansion. The opening of a vast new trade in grains, wine and manufactured goods with the more primitive Italian states led to a drastic undercutting of domestic prices and drove thousands of small farmers and artisans into bankruptcy. The trouble was compounded by the previous decades of "easy money" credit inflation. The friendly neighborhood moneylender was always ready to make a loan—after all, what better security could there be than the very life of the borrower? (How much like today, when men are induced to forfeit so much of their freedom and pledge most of their working lives to the yoke of 30- and 35-year mortgages.)

The Athenian economic crisis, like that of our own Great Depression, was so severe that it could only be met by the most direct and drastic action. Fortunately the Athenians were able to select the right man for the job: the learned and aristocratic Solon, who took the office of *Archon* in 594 B.C. Assuming extra-legal powers, Solon issued a decree called *Seisachtheia* ("shaking off the burdens"). This decree cancelled at once all outstanding agricultural and personal debts. The hated mortgage pillars were pulled down and all persons in bondage from previous debt defaults were ordered released.

The legality and morality of the *Seisachtheia* were widely questioned but never seriously challenged, although the landlords, bankers, and other creditors were deprived of property and assets without due process and without opportunity for redress. Many of them, also having obligations to meet, were forced into bankruptcy themselves. Partially to relieve their condition and to restimulate the economy and to renew the movement of money, Solon also devalued the *drachma* by 27 percent, from 73 to 100 to the *mina* or ancient Greek pound.

Perhaps the most remarkable thing about the Solonian reform was that it was never necessary to repeat it. The clear-thinking Greeks of the classic age, perhaps the most intellectual people in all history, learned well the lessons taught by the crisis and resolved never to let similar conditions occur again. Speculative enthusiasm and excesses were discouraged if not cured, and the Greek mind saw that the limitations of a cash economy were far more acceptable than the evils of excessive credit. The remainder of Solon's program forbade the pledging of persons as chattels for loans, expanded the opportunities for citizenship, dissolved the oppressive oligarchy (which included in its body some of the more rapacious moneylenders), and negotiated new commercial treaties guaranteeing more equitable prices.

Throughout the remainder of classical Athenian history, currency depreciation was never resorted to again. In fact, in the subsequent Athenian democracy, the *diakists* or leading judges and legislators were required to take an annual oath to maintain the purity of the coinage. It was upon this new soundness of their currency that the Athenian state built a new and greater commercial system, which eventually ruled the whole Mediterranean basin.

The new basic coin of Athens was the silver *drachma* (66 grains of 99 percent pure silver), originally adopted from the silver coin of Aegina. Although gold coins were frequently struck, silver was available in much greater quantity and remained the monetary standard of the Hellenic world until the Macedonian conquest. Then

Philip II and Alexander the Great introduced their small gold "staters" and these coins remained the prized money of the Near East long after the armies that brought them were gone.

The long and honored tradition of sound intrinsic-value money established in the Hellenic world after the reform of Solon, and spread, to the Near and Far East by the armies of Philip and Alexander is in sharp contrast to the Western experience with money. To this day we still do not recognize the enormous depth of feeling for gold and silver that exists in the Levantine world, in the Middle East, and in Asia—for ours is the heritage of Rome.

Sincere admirers of Roman civilization, who rightfully appreciate the West's lasting inheritance of Roman law and justice, political administration, engineering, literature, and innumerable minor arts, are invariably surprised and confounded by the almost total inability of the Roman administrators to cope with the institution of money.

The earliest money of the practical Romans was neither gold nor silver but an ingot of copper—the *as*—weighing one pound. At first the *as* was passed by weight, but later it was stamped with the seal of the state, broken into smaller pieces and passed by sight. By the fourth century B.C., the *as* had evolved into a heavy round stamped copper slug, the *as grave*. With so large a coin passing by sight, the temptation surreptitiously to debase it by reducing its weight proved irresistible to the authorities. By the middle of the third century B.C., the weight of the *as* had dropped to four ounces. By the end of the First Punic War, around 240 B.C., it had shrunk to a mere two ounces, and by 70 B.C. it weighed no more than half an ounce.[2]

The Roman *denarius* fared somewhat better at first. Originally introduced in 277 B.C. to compete with the trusted Athenian *drachma*, the *denarius* was minted at the same weight and fineness (66 grains of 99 percent pure silver). At the time of the ascension of Julius Caesar, the *denarius* had declined in weight only slightly, to 60 grains—a tribute in a way to the general virtue and integrity of the Roman Republic.

But in the Empire things were indeed different. Caesar and his successor Augustus began what could have been the foundation for an efficient and reliable monetary system. The value of all coins was determined by weight and based on the ancient Roman measure, the *libra* or pound. The principal coin was to be a new gold *aureus*, 126 grains of fine gold, minted at the rate of 40 to the *libra*. The silver *denarius* was continued at 84 to the *libra* and valued at 25 to the *aureus*. All went well when the emperors were, in the words of Shakespeare's Brutus, "honorable men"—but unfortunately they were not honorable men for long, at least not long enough.

However, Caesar's gold *aureus* did remain undisturbed for 75 years (not a bad record at that, considering that the U.S. gold dollar lasted just short of 100 years before encountering its first official devaluation). Fittingly, it was the infamous Nero who took the first fatal step by reducing the weight of the *aureus* from 40 to 45 to the *libra*, and the *denarius* from 84 to 96 to the *libra*. Under successive administrations the degeneration became much more marked. During the reign of Trajan, the purity as well as the weight of the coin was reduced. Under Severus (A.D. 193–211) the depreciation reached a point where the fine silver content of the *denarius* was only 26 grains, with the coin being more than 50 percent base metal.

Caracalla (A.D. 215) officially reduced the *aureus* again, from 45 to 50 to the *libra*, although this was purely an academic exercise —the imperial mints had long since been surreptitiously issuing the gold *aureus* with a base metal content as high as 40 to 50 percent. As for the *denarius*, it had already sunk so low in weight and silver content that it was little more than a copper penny. Consequently, Caracalla introduced a new silver coin, the *antoninius*, weighing about 84 grains. But this new coin soon began the same sickening downward spiral that had destroyed the *denarius*. By the end of the reign of Gallienus (A.D. 268) the *antoninius* was no more than a base metal token with a thin plating of silver (the first clad coinage!).

About the period after Gallienus, the great classical historian Theodor Mommsen was moved to write: "In the last half of the third century there existed no longer in the Roman Empire any money having an intrinsic value corresponding to its nominal value, not even a piece of brass or billon."[3] For a while the imperial treasury demanded taxes be paid with sound gold or silver, while it made its own payments with debased coin or copper, but this soon proved impossible to enforce. What gold and silver were left rapidly fled beyond the borders of the Empire. Price controls and legal tender laws were passed in profusion, to no avail. The decline of Rome and the decline of its money went hand in hand. Rioting and lawlessness, dishonesty and corruption were aggravated by the spectacle of emperors and governments that were little more than liars and embezzlers themselves.

At last, with its treasury empty, its farms rotting in neglect, industry stagnant and mired in financial disorder, trade reduced to almost a barter level and a frantic speculation devouring the last vestige of organized commercial activity, the mightiest empire the world has ever seen drifted helplessly into barbarism. It never recovered from the monetary madness of the third century. Long before the Huns and Vandals set foot within its boundaries, the Roman Empire committed suicide by monetary debasement and inflation.

During the long dominance of Rome, the Greek tradition of sound coinage was subdued but never really extinguished. Following the agonizing decline and final collapse of the Western Roman world, there arose from its ashes a new empire in the East, Greek by language and custom, Roman by tradition and heritage. The coin of this strange hybrid, the so-called Byzantine Empire, was the gold solidus or *bezant*, perhaps the most significant coin of all time. Its history deserves more than a brief statement.

The gold solidus was first minted by the founder of the capital of the Eastern Empire, Constantine. His immediate successors maintained the coin without significant alteration, except to improve its uniformity and purity until its weight became fixed at 65 grains of fine gold.[4] It was minted at this standard for *eight hundred years* —undoubtedly the most outstanding achievement in the history of money.

The *bezant* became the unquestioned standard of value from the raw camps of the Huns along the Danube to the opulent courts of the Moguls of Western India. Through most of the Middle Ages, the princes and feudal lords seldom if ever bothered to mint gold for their own uses, but kept their accounts and made payments in *bezants*.

The Byzantine Empire survived as a political entity for over twelve hundred years. Its rulers were regarded with awe from the Baltic to Ceylon, and its commerce extended from the lonely coast of Northern Europe to the warm seas south of China. It raised and equipped vast armies and launched great fleets, built stately churches and magnificent palaces. Its emissaries were received with honor in the farthest reaches of the medieval world. During the Dark Ages in Europe, Byzantine culture and wealth flourished. Assault after assault upon its frontiers was repulsed; for nine hundred of those twelve hundred years its capital was never seriously threatened by an enemy force.[5] All these things were impressive, but what really excited the wonder and respect of the medieval world was the *bezant*.

An Egyptian merchant of the sixth century, one Cosmas Indicopleustes, who travelled widely and recorded his observations in a book called *Christian Topography*,[6] gave this testimony regarding the power of the *bezant*: "With their gold piece all nations do trade; it is received everywhere from one end of the earth to the other; it is admired by all men and every kingdom, for no other kingdom hath its like."

The sound coinage of Byzantium was of course only one of several factors that contributed to the commercial success and social progress of the Empire, but that its importance was early recognized can be judged from the following regulations concerning Byzantine banking: all bankers and money changers were required to take oath never to file, clip, or in any way debase the coinage, never to issue false coin and never to allow any of their servants to take charge of the business during an absence. The penalty for any violation of these canons was drastic: the offender's hand was cut off.

The decline of Byzantine power and influence coincides with

the decline of the *bezant*. In the reign of Alexius Comnenus (1081–1118), the eight centuries of trust were irrevocably destroyed when this unpopular monarch reduced the gold content of his coin, in order to pay debts incurred by his corruption and extravagance. Alexius employed the old Roman strategy of paying the public debts with his own debased coinage, while demanding that taxes be paid in the pure coinage of his predecessors.[7]

Although the Byzantine state managed a precarious survival for two hundred fifty years after Alexius Comnenus, it never recovered its former glory. Further debasements and official dishonesties followed with increasing frequency, and with them came political and social unrest, military and court intrigues, cheating and corruption in all walks of life. When the final act came and Byzantium fell before the onslaught of Islam, the name which had once been renowned as the standard of honesty and integrity was in total disgrace; "byzantine" had become synonymous with corruption and debauchery.

One of the most interesting lessons that can be learned from the Byzantine monetary experience is that despite the constant and free export of *bezants* to all parts of the medieval world, there was never any "shortage" of gold. During the 800 years of sound coinage, bullion from the mines and hoards of Asia and the Near East freely flowed into Byzantium to be sold and exchanged for the prized *bezants*. As for those *bezants* that travelled so far from the Empire, most eventually returned to be spent again with Byzantine merchants. Quite a contrast with the latter days of Rome, when neither the edicts of Caesar nor the swords of the legions could bring forth a single ounce of precious metal, and the base Roman coins were so universally despised and rejected that the once extensive foreign commerce of the Roman Empire all but perished.

The final eclipse of what was left of the old Hellenic world by the Islamic conquest left the West without any stabilizing influence, and the general reintroduction of money into Europe during the late Middle Ages was unfortunately redirected almost exclusively to the Latin example. In these times, and even into the sixteenth and seventeenth centuries, the princes and kings did a smashing business in coin debasement. The right to degrade, debase, and devalue their currencies was looked upon by the kings and rulers of the premodern era as one of their sovereign prerogatives. The seigniorage or profit derived from coining money with an intrinsic value less than the face value (and then surreptitiously or even openly degrading it further from time to time) was considered an important if not vital source of revenue for the crown. These potentates seemed not to understand the economic burden that flagrant monetary abuse imposed upon their long-suffering subjects, or the extent to which commerce was being stifled and discouraged by financial confusion and uncertainty. If they did, they cared not, for the chief monetary characteristic of Western Europe from Caesar to Napoleon was a constant currency depreciation.

What happened to the Hellenic ideal of sound intrinsic-value money under the resurgence of Roman tradition can be seen in the fate of the Arabian *dinar* when it fell into Christian hands. The gold *dinar* of the Arab world was the unit of account for Moslem Spain under its Moorish dynasties. For over 400 years the gold *dinar* had circulated from Bagdad to Barcelona at its original weight of 65 grains .975 fine without significant alteration.[8] Only in the last 50 years of Moorish control (1094–1144) had the *dinar* of Spain been reduced slightly and issued at 60–62 grains. But no sooner had it been transferred to Christian administration than it was subject to a flagrant and catastrophic depreciation.

The Christian conquerors of Spain adopted the Moslem *dinar*, but changed its name to the *maravedi* and immediately reduced its weight to 56 grains. Spain hardly had time to make the acquaintance of the new *maravedi* before its debasement began in earnest. By the beginning of the reign of James I of Aragon in the thirteenth century, the *maravedi* had sunk to a mere 14 grains. Under the rule of Alfonso the Wise it contained only 10 grains of gold and soon after that it became too small to continue in circulation.

Consequently, the *maravedi* was changed to a silver coin of 26 grains, but the fate of the silver *maravedi* was no better than its gold predecessor. Eventually the silver *maravedi* was so debased that it could be used only as a theoretical unit of account; its silver content

at the time of Ferdinand and Isabella was less than 1.5 grains—
not enough to bother to put in a coin. Other examples of the ruinous
practice of coin debasement that plagued Europe for so many
centuries are too numerous to mention here. It must be candidly
asserted, however, that all the clipping, filing, and cheating on the
weights of coin were but a prelude to what was to come with the
introduction of paper money.

The Paper-Money Magicians

The discovery of the Americas brought a river of gold to the
shores of Europe for the following 250 years, and with the gold
came a great new commercial expansion and wave of prosperity.
But no matter how much wealth was extracted from the mines of
Mexico or Peru, it never seemed enough to satisfy the avarice of
some kings and princes.

The reign of the Sun King, Louis XIV, of France is a case in
point. Louis's constant military adventuring, his lavish expenditures
on grand palaces, gardens and chateaux, and his general corruption
and monetary profusion were enthusiastically imitated by sub-
ordinates of every rank. Upon his death in 1715, the country found
itself on the verge of ruin. The national debt amounted to 3,000
million *livres* and the net revenue of the government after expenses
was only three million. The new regent, the Duke of Orleans, tried
the time-hallowed method of devaluing the coinage, but this
stratagem served only to throw the country into greater commercial
disorder. Poverty, depression, and lawlessness soon lay over the
land and talk of revolution was everywhere.

Into this seemingly hopeless economic quagmire came a handsome 45-year-old Scotsman, a gambler and adventurer named John
Law, who had gained the confidence of the Regent during their
joint visits to the gaming halls of Paris. Law had been trained in
his father's Edinburgh bank as a young man, but had lived by his
wits most of his adult years. He was forced to flee his native land
at the age of 26 after killing a man in a duel over the affections of a
young lady, and had travelled widely on the Continent thereafter,

supporting himself mainly by his remarkable abilities with cards and dice.

A dabbler in economic theory, Law had written a few pamphlets concerning a scheme of his for establishing a bank that could issue notes based on the value of land or other wealth, rather than on specific reserves of gold or silver. Law was readily received by the Regent in 1716 and given permission to open a bank in Paris and to issue notes in the name of his enterprise. Law's first step was to "guarantee" publicly that the notes issued by his bank would be redeemed not only in coin on demand, but in *amounts current at the date of the note's issue.* He also prominently announced that in his opinion any banker who issued notes in excess of the amounts he could redeem deserved to be put to death. These were shrewd strokes; by making his notes seemingly "depreciation proof," they became much in demand and were soon circulating at a large premium over the constantly depreciating coin and notes issued by the state.

The Regent was astounded at Law's phenomenal success and gradually began to accept the idea that paper money not only could be an auxiliary to metallic currency, but could eventually replace it entirely. He eagerly accepted Law's next proposal, which was to establish a joint stock company that would have exclusive rights to all trade and commerce on the Mississippi River and in the rest of France's vast Louisiana Territory. The Louisiana lands were as yet an unsettled, almost uncharted, wilderness, but Law represented them to the public as a vast treasure house of wealth, literally bulging with deposits of gold and other minerals. A frenzy of speculation developed as everyone sought shares in the new golconda. The Regent and all the court were even further borne away by the enthusiasm, and every day additional privileges were heaped upon Law and his bank. First they were given the monopoly of all trade in tobacco, then the sole right to refine gold and silver, and finally Law's bank was officially proclaimed Royal Bank of France.

Intoxicated with success, Law apparently forgot his earlier dictum that any banker who issued paper money beyond his capacity to redeem it was deserving of death. Now that the bank was a royal establishment, he felt no need to object when the Regent proposed a new issue of paper money amounting to 1,000 million *livres*. An illusion of prosperity swept the country as a result of the inflationary impact of the huge note issue and the booming rise in the price of Mississippi shares. Soon Law was to realize, like Keynes two centuries later, that once politicians become enamored with their own imperfect grasp of another's economic theory, they are apt to exploit it without limit or reason. In a very short time, France was being inundated with an unquenchable stream of bank notes gushing from the Royal Bank.

In 1719 another edict gave the Mississippi Company exclusive rights to all trade and commerce in France's possessions in the South seas and the Far East as well. The result was another vast issue of stock and another spate of bank notes, supposedly deriving their value from the yet untapped wealth of the French colonies. Soon Law was the most influential man in France and hailed as the savior of the country. As for the Regent, knowing nothing of economics, he reasoned that if 1,000 million *livres* of paper money had apparently done so much good, 2,000 million would do even better. Furthermore, as the stock of the Mississippi Company, which was the bank's chief asset, rose in value, new notes could be issued against it.[9]

Early in 1720, the more astute speculators began to suspect that the end was not far off, and began cashing in their stock and bank notes for gold—which they immediately and prudently smuggled out of the country for safekeeping. It was not long before the Royal Bank's feeble reserve of specie was approaching exhaustion. A council of state was called, and upon Law's recommendation an edict was published depreciating the value of coin 10 percent below the value of paper currency and restricting the bank's payouts to a maximum of 100 *livres* in gold and 10 in silver per transaction. Soon after, another edict followed, this one forbidding the possession of more than 500 *livres* in coin and the export or hoarding of gold or silver.

But despite these and other edicts, and the most odious police measures, gold and silver continued to flee the country. The value of shares in the Mississippi Company fell rapidly as they were thrown on the market for whatever they would bring. Coin and bullion rose sharply in value despite every effort to prevent it. In February 1720 still another royal edict ordered that payment of all debts had to be made in paper only, and further authorized the issue of an additional 1,500 million *livres* (about $300 million) in paper bank notes.

It was all of little use. In May the bank was forced to suspend payment in specie entirely and the whole country found itself in a state of ruin far worse than when Law and the Regent had undertaken to save the nation through the magic of paper money. The royal treasury was stripped, good coin and all other gold and silver objects had entirely disappeared from circulation, the enormous issues of stock in the Mississippi Company were without value, and 2,700 million *livres* in paper bank notes remained outstanding and unredeemable. All that remained was the melancholy task of liquidating a national bankruptcy. By a further series of decrees, the outstanding bank notes and stock certificates were officially depreciated to their actual worthlessness, withdrawn from circulation, and publicly burned.[10] Future contracts were required to be settled, once more, in gold and silver. Law and his family had to flee for their lives, and all his valuable properties and estates were confiscated. He died in Venice in 1729, virtually penniless.

In January 1721 a rash speculator purchased with a single gold *louis*, with a face value of forty-five *livres*, a block of stock that had sold a year earlier for 20,000 *livres* in paper money. Thus ended the first great paper-money experiment.

Despite the shocking experience of John Law and his bank notes, an experience from which the French monarchy never completely recovered, it was the French again who underwent an even more radical experiment in "managed" economics just seventy years later. In 1789, on the eve of the French Revolution, the nation once again found itself embarrassed by an unmanageable debt and a consequent economic depression. Once more there was the search for some shortcut to prosperity, and once more the idea was put forth that the great need of the country was for more circulating currency, more "purchasing power."

As the condition of the country worsened, the oratory in the National Assembly grew more fervent for the issue of irredeemable paper money. The arguments against it, led by Necker, the finance minister, and a few of the wiser members of the assembly, increasingly fell on deaf ears. In vain did one old gentleman wave one of John Law's ancient bank notes before the assembled notables and invoke the frightful memories it recalled.

The opportunity came at length when in 1790 the Revolutionary Government confiscated all lands and properties of the church. It was immediately proposed that paper money be issued based on the value of these lands (which in their entirety amounted to almost one-third of all the real estate in France). In April 1790, 400 million *livres* in new paper bills were issued under the name of *assignats* ("mortgage notes"). These new notes theoretically could be presented at any time for the purchase of state lands at fixed rates. Furthermore, they bore interest at the rate of 3 percent per year. As Andrew Dickson White put it, "No irredeemable currency has ever claimed a more scientific and practical guarantee for its goodness."[11]

Unlike John Law's notes, which were ultimately backed only by the mythical assets of the Mississippi Company, the new *assignats* were convertible at any time into agricultural land—what greater security could there be than a first mortgage on productive real estate? Furthermore, as the notes bore interest, they would grow ever more valuable if left to circulate—at least that was the theory.

The initial result of the *assignats* was all that could be desired. The public debt was substantially reduced, ordinary government expenses were met on time and trade began to revive all around the country—all difficulties seemed on the way to complete solution. But a short five months later, the government, having spent all its new *assignats*, found itself once more in financial distress. Throughout the country the cry arose again for more "money" to solve the problems of an increasingly deteriorating economy.

Now at the time of the first issue, the opponents of paper money unrelated to specie had charged that once started there would be no limit to the downward spiral of inflation, and that further issues would follow just as sure as night follows day. The supporters, however, had insisted that *the people* were finally in control of their own destiny and, unlike the failures of corrupt royal governments in the past, currency could now be successfully managed to suit the "needs" of the nation.

It was officially ruled that the first issue of *assignats* had proved a success and therefore a new issue of 800 million more *livres* would be made. It was also argued that any excess paper money over the requirements of trade would be withdrawn automatically through the purchase of state lands. Inexorably, however, gold, silver and even copper coin began to disappear from circulation. To supply more metals for coinage and to hold it in circulation, all forms of desperate measures were tried. Silverware and jewelry were confiscated, the gold and silver plate of the King's household was sent to the mint, and churches were ordered to surrender all gold and silver vessels except for the bare minimum required for public worship. The church bells were melted down to obtain bronze for small coin. Still, metallic currency continued to go into hoarding or flee for safety beyond the borders of France.

In June 1791 another 600 million *livres* of *assignats* were placed in circulation. The Revolutionary Government was now irrevocably committed to inflation, and the delusion, born of desperation, that inflation was prosperity swept France. More issues followed, but the country grew ever more unstable. In 1792 there were new riots in Paris, the King was arrested and the monarchy abolished. In 1793 the hapless royal family went to the guillotine and the Reign of Terror began. The Revolutionary Tribunal imposed stringent price controls, forbade all further dealing in specie, decreed the death penalty for violators and hoarders, and placed another 1,200 million *livres* of *assignats* in circulation. By 1794 the Reign of Terror reached its bloody climax; Robespierre was elected president of a new National Convention and 3,000 million more *livres* of *assignats* were issued.

By the end of 1795 all France was in unprecedented misery;

anything resembling normal business or commercial activity had long since collapsed. Shortages of food and of all other necessities were critical, and public rioting and disorder were common. The total number of *assignats* in circulation reached 35,000 million *livres* ("francs," as they came to be called by the Revolutionary Government). But through it all, the *louis d'or*, the old standard gold coin of France, originally valued at 25 *livres*, remained the unshakable measure of value. On August 1, 1795, the gold *louis* brought 920 paper francs; on September 1, it commanded 1,200 francs; on November 1, at least 2,600 francs; and on February 1, up to 7,200 francs.[12] The burden of this catastrophic depreciation fell mainly, as might be expected, upon the working classes. The wealthy and sophisticated kept their wealth in stores of goods, in land, or even in gold, despite edicts threatening the death penalty for large holders of coin or plate. By December 1796 the gold *louis* was being quoted at 15,000 francs in paper.

In 1796 a new plan was devised, which would have been ludicrous but for the tragedy of starvation and death that stalked the land. It was determined that a new paper money should be issued to replace the now worthless *assignats*. The new notes were to be called *mandats*, and they were to be made "as good as gold," or so it was said. The issue of *mandats*, it was promised, would be strictly limited and, as with the *assignats*, choice government land was reserved for their backing. But before the new *mandats* could be passed from the bank windows, they had already depreciated 30 to 40 percent from their face value, and by the end of the year they too were virtually worthless.

Finally, in early 1797, reality was reluctantly faced, and it was decreed that the issuing of all paper money would cease and that the printing presses and plates would be broken up in public. All paper notes were eventually declared no longer legal tender, except that old debts due the state could be paid with paper at the rate of 1 percent of its face value. Outstanding at the final declaration of bankruptcy were 40,000 million francs in *assignats* and 2,600 million in *mandats*.

At first it was feared that with all paper currency voided and coin entirely in hoarding, the country would be completely without a purchasing medium. But as the journalist, M. Thibaudeau, shrewdly observed, "There will always be money," and coin gradually came back into circulation as it was needed.

Nonetheless, when Napoleon came to power in 1799, France was still almost totally prostrate economically. The armies engaged in the war on the Rhine and in Italy had not been paid for months, the treasury was still bankrupt, and an enormous debt continued to burden the government. The country was stripped; collection of any new taxes was impossible. At the first meeting of the new Council of State, Bonaparte was pressed to issue some new paper money. "Never," he replied, "I will pay cash or nothing"—and he conducted all his future operations on that basis.

Under Napoleon's financial direction, specie payment was resumed whenever possible. New gold coins were minted as rapidly as gold became available (eventually bearing the likeness of Emperor Napoleon). As with Byzantium, as soon as France was placed on a sound and determined gold basis, she had surprisingly little trouble commanding all the gold that was needed.[13] In a very short time Napoleon restored France to stability and greatness—no wonder the French followed him literally to the death.

But at last, the inevitable reverse came to the overextended Napoleonic Empire, and the Emperor found himself hard pressed, financially and militarily, by the weight of the great coalition formed against him. Once more he was importuned to issue paper notes, but again he refused. "While I live," he wrote his finance minister, "I will never resort to irredeemable paper." He never did. After Waterloo, when France was invaded by the allies and had heavy indemnities levied against her, she experienced no prolonged distress. If nothing else, the legacy of Napoleon had finally given France a sound monetary structure resting on a full specie basis.

More than fifty years later, France again suffered a stinging defeat in the Franco–Prussian War, and once more her sound monetary system and ample reserves of gold assured her a speedy recovery. The ruler of France's Second Empire, Napoleon III, was, like his uncle, a firm believer in good gold coin, and his impression on the 20-franc "napoleon" survived to benefit Frenchmen long after he himself was carted off a prisoner of the Prussians at Sedan. The contemporary Frenchman's affinity with gold is understandable in the light of his past history—but the events of modern times have done still more to reinforce this lesson.

Notes

CHAPTER III

1. See for example, Dickson G. Watts, *Speculation as a Fine Art* (reprint ed., New York: Trader's Press, 1965).
2. Groseclose, *op. cit.*
3. Theodor Mommsen, *History of Roman Money* (Paris, 1873), as quoted in Groseclose, *op. cit.*
4. The Greek heritage of the gold *bezant* can be seen in its weight, which conforms very nearly to that of the silver *drachma* of Athens (66 grains), the standard coin of the older Hellenic world.
5. The actual and would–be assailants of Byzantium were not entirely repulsed by force of arms; the military incompetence of Byzantine armies was notorious. But those enemies who could not be fought off were invariably bought off. Even the most brutal of barbarian chiefs were not immune to the lure of the *bezant*.
6. Actually a whole series of manuscript folios that have become an important primary source for historians of the early Middle Ages. Quotation from Groseclose, *op. cit.*
7. An interesting comparison with the current practice of selling bonds and then redeeming them at maturity with inflated paper currency. (A U.S. Treasury bond sold in 1940 could be redeemed now for 40 cents on the dollar.)
8. The *dinar* conformed exactly in weight and style to the *bezant*, and the Arabs obviously borrowed their attitudes toward money from the Byzantines as well. (The imperial Arabs were also great admirers of classical Greek philosophy.)
9. At present in the U.S., Treasury bonds are deposited in the Federal Reserve Bank and notes are issued against them.
10. The actual legal steps in the bankruptcy of the Mississippi Company were tedious and complex, but the eventual end was as noted. See Mackay, *op. cit.*

11. Andrew Dickson White, *Fiat Money Inflation in France* (reprint ed., New York, 1959).

12. *Ibid.*

13. Of course, it can be charged, with some accuracy, that Napoleon was not above looting, but it must also be remembered that force cannot compel gold to circulate—the guillotine of the Directory failed in that.

IV

Gold and Money in the Modern World

"It may well be doubted whether all the misery which had been inflicted on the English nation in a quarter century by bad kings, bad ministers, bad parliaments and bad judges, was equal to the misery caused by bad crowns and bad shillings."
—THOMAS BABINGTON MACAULAY,
The History of England

IN SPITE OF THE 3,000-YEAR TRADITION OF THE USE OF GOLD AS the most successful universal money, a true international gold standard is a relatively recent development. Before 1800, the nations of Europe had allowed their monetary systems to grow haphazardly into a confusing hodgepodge of bimetallism and credit money. Gold and silver coin, coin certificates, bank credit notes and government fiat paper were all issued and sometimes circulated simultaneously, with few successes in various and erratic attempts to coordinate and stabilize them. (These conditions not only existed in the United States, but continued to plague us through most of the nineteenth century.)

As a result of this international instability, gold remained scarce in most countries and gold coins were constantly hoarded, in response to Gresham's Law. The situation was further aggravated by the repeated export of gold to finance international trade. Consequently, silver often became the *de facto* if not the official standard of value in many parts of the world. Countries such as Mexico and China preferred to use silver because of their large domestic sources of that metal. Foreign trade, such as existed in those days, had to be conducted on the basis of intrinsic value by weight of the various gold and silver coins offered. And without fixed and reliable exchange rates, such negotiations were often tedious and unsatisfactory.

The rapid industrialization of the West and the great expansion of international trade in the nineteenth century demanded a new appraisal of the world's inefficient monetary arrangements. Great Britain took the lead in 1816 by making all its money—silver and paper notes—fully convertible into gold sovereigns at a fixed rate, and by redefining the pound in terms of a fixed amount of gold. This made all British currencies, whether held by citizens or foreigners, "good as gold."

The move was extremely successful and further enhanced Britain's dominant position as the center of a vast colonial and trading empire. The 100 percent gold-backed pound sterling (ironically, initially based on a pound of silver) became the most important currency in the world, and London the heart of the international banking system. By 1875 nearly all Europe had adopted the new "gold standard" and had tied their currencies to a fixed gold parity.

As for the United States, although our gold coinage had been minted at a fixed standard since 1834, we continued to experiment unsuccessfully with bimetallism for the remainder of the century. It was not until 1900 that the Gold Standard Act was passed, putting the U.S. on a full gold-coin standard.

The international gold standard did not last 100 years. In 1914 most nations were forced to abandon gold convertibility in order to allow for the huge expansions of credit money necessary to finance World War I. After the war a return to the full gold standard was impossible for most countries. Prices had risen too high and the tremendous amount of paper credit money in circulation could not foreseeably be offset by new gold production. Among the major countries, only the United States was able to continue full domestic and international convertibility for its currency. Great Britain, however, did eventually return the pound to its prewar parity in spite of the inflationary conditions of the postwar world.

Other European nations also attempted some sort of fiction to demonstrate that their vastly inflated currency and credit structures were still related to gold.

It was a gigantic blunder. By not universally devaluing the pound, the dollar and other inflated paper money (raising the international price of gold), and by thus maintaining the charade that most of the unrestricted wartime issues of paper and credit were still "good as gold," the stage was set for the unprecedented spending and gambling spree of the twenties. This postwar monetary system was termed the "gold exchange standard." It differed from the old gold standard in that only the U.S. maintained full convertibility and continued to mint gold coins; other nations were not required to keep their reserves or settle international balances in gold, but could use dollars, pounds, or other paper currencies or credits, since these currencies were supposedly "good as gold."

The result was a huge inverted pyramid of inflated paper notes and credit balanced precariously on a grossly inadequate base of gold. The world never really recovered from that inflationary binge of the twenties, even though the orthodox central bankers of that era had no intention of cutting the ties to gold; they just thought it was a splendid idea to stretch them a bit and "conserve gold." Unfortunately, they stretched them to the breaking point.

The events that followed the failure to return honestly to gold and the consequent excesses of the 1920s unfolded with the inevitability of a Greek tragedy. Stock market crashes, bank failures, and economic collapse in one country after another were triggered and accelerated by the growing awareness that the bankers themselves were bankrupt, that most of that astronomic debt could never be paid, and that not all the gold in the world could redeem even a fraction of the ocean of paper money. Great Britain was forced to suspend gold sales in 1931. In 1933 and 1934, in the midst of economic chaos and staggering unemployment, the U.S. played out the final act in the golden age by nationalizing its gold, confiscating all outstanding gold coins and bullion, abandoning domestic convertibility, and devaluing the dollar from $20.67 to $35.00 to the ounce of gold.

But the worst was yet to come: subsequent years brought further devaluations in other countries, rampant protectionism, drastic declines in international trade, and the rise of hysterical nationalism. The Great Depression became the spawning ground for another vast insane war even more frightful than the first. And the ultimate result of World War II, over and above the immediate desolation and misery it caused, was the loss of half of Europe and most of Asia to Marxist socialism.

In 1944 the Allied nations met at Bretton Woods to plan a new monetary system for the postwar world. The expansionists and inflationists, undaunted by the events of the preceding years, were more firmly convinced than ever that the gold standard was a monetary straitjacket. They proposed that only foreign central banks should be allowed to convert their money into gold, and then only when presented for redemption by other central banks. This would "economize" the use of gold and still allow the establishment of gold parities for all currencies. At the same time it would permit great flexibility in the manipulation and expansion of domestic currencies. Clearly, this line of argument merely advocated a more formal version of the old gold exchange standard that had failed so drastically in the thirties.

But to the believers in the "New Economics" led by John Maynard Keynes, any sort of restriction on a government's economic freedom was intolerable. Why shouldn't each country be allowed to manipulate its money supply and its price levels according to its internal "needs"? Why should it have to maintain its currency on a fixed parity with gold or any other currency? Keynes (obviously a man ahead of his time) went so far as to propose that a new international paper money be established under the control of the International Monetary Fund or some similar agency, and that this new money or "credit" could be used to settle international payments in lieu of gold. Then the ties that had bound men to gold for so many centuries could at last be cut forever.

Ironically, it was the United States that objected most strongly to the prospect of a goldless economic world. The fortunes of war once more had made the U.S. "rich" in terms of gold. The major

part of the world's supply of monetary metal, the gold that had
fled Europe and Asia in the face of disaster, resided safely in Fort
Knox, and we were not about to "demonetize" $20 billion worth
of our good hard cash.[1] And so at Bretton Woods a compromise
was agreed upon: only one central bank, that of the rich United
States, would have to convert its money into gold, and then only
when presented by foreign central banks. All other currencies would
maintain their parity only in terms of dollars. The dollar would
become the new international currency. With all currencies tied to
the dollar and the dollar anchored to the world's largest gold pile,[2]
the role of gold in international affairs would be minimized, and
all countries would be able to pursue their internal monetary
policies relatively free of its irksome discipline. It was, of course,
just another variation of the old gold exchange standard, except
that its inflationary potential was even greater.

The "solution" to the gold problem arrived at in 1944 obviously
provided no final answers to the historic questions concerning the
nature of money: is money intrinsic, i.e., an actual commodity like
gold or silver, or is it merely conventional—a bookkeeping entry—
nothing more?[3] Or is it a combination of convention and intrinsic
value? Does paper money always need gold backing to remain
stable? And if so, what percentage of gold is required in relation to
total money supply? Pondering these questions brings to mind an
observation attributed to the legendary Baron Rothschild. The
wizard of international finance is said to have remarked that there
were only two men in the entire world who really understood the
true monetary function of gold—an obscure clerk in the Bank of
France and a director of the Bank of England. "Unfortunately,"
he concluded, "they disagree."

Apparently the bankers, economists and politicians who met at
Bretton Woods in 1944 also disagreed. They seem to have wanted
it both ways. Obviously they thought it prudent to establish,
theoretically at least, that their paper currencies were still "good
as gold," and yet they also wanted to be free to manufacture unlimited quantities of fiat money and credit according to their
"needs." They said in effect: the tie to gold is necessary—but not

important. Yet while the Keynesian academicians and their political disciples continued to look forward hopefully to their utopia, where gold would be banished forever and endless credit manufactured by computers, events in the postwar years followed a rather familiar pattern.

The Age of Inflation

The first and most significant feature of the post–World War II years was inflation. Jacques Rueff, the distinguished French economist (the only economist chosen to be a member of the elite French Academy) who was President de Gaulle's economic adviser, observed that future historians might well characterize these years as the "Age of Inflation."[4] How sadly true it is. Inflation has literally ravaged the economies of the greater part of South America, utterly destroyed any semblance of economic order in most of Asia and caused serious losses of wealth and savings in Europe and the United States.

The Brazilian *cruzeiro*, for example, once a reasonably strong currency, plummeted from .0544 cents in 1959 to .00035 cents in 1967, or from approximately 18 to the dollar to 3,500 to the dollar in just eight years. Similar, although not quite so drastic, declines have affected the Argentine and Chilean pesos and many other Latin American currencies.

One of the most destructive inflations in modern times was that which affected Nationalist China before its defeat by the Communists. The mainland Chinese economy rapidly disintegrated in a wild postwar inflation until the Chinese paper dollar or *yuan* traded with the U.S. at a 5,000-to-10,000-to-1 ratio. The immediate cause of this debacle was the attempt of the U.S. and the Chinese Nationalist government to finance the 1946–1949 Nationalist-Communist war with printing-press money. The appalling stupidity of this policy can be realized from the fact that the Communists themselves were careful to pay their own troops with hard money whenever they could, and that they continually bought off Nationalist troops with the promise of four Chinese silver dollars per month (equal to two U.S. dollars). The tragedy is compounded by the knowledge that the Nationalist government had nearly $300 million worth of gold and silver bullion safely hidden in Taiwan, but none was ever coined and allowed to circulate.[5] The U.S. at that time had more than 2 billion ounces of silver and $24 billion worth of gold bullion. It is possible that by coining even a small fraction of this hoard and by allowing it to circulate freely in China, the world's most populous nation might have been saved from Communist dictatorship.

The experience of Europe after World War II was very similar to what occurred after World War I. In Germany and Eastern Europe the prewar currencies were virtually wiped out for the second time in a single generation. In Hungary, perhaps the most incredible inflation yet recorded in history took place—even exceeding the insane orgy of note issue that Germany experienced after the first war. Hungarian bank notes with denominations as high as *one hundred sextillion pengo* were in circulation in 1946. Ironically it was the Communist government that finally ended the catastrophe by voiding all outstanding currency and introducing a new series that was backed by, or at least tied to, monetary gold. It was not the first time a Communist government resorted to gold to halt inflation.

In the early days of the Soviet Union, the Bolsheviks had characteristically attempted to finance their way with printing-press money. The result was, predictably, runaway inflation and economic chaos. Lenin, ever the realist, knew what had to be done to halt the disastrous degeneration of the paper *sovznaki* rouble. Forgotten were the boasts that gold was just another capitalist snare, which would be completely unnecessary in the worker's paradise; fiscal orthodoxy and the capitalist gold standard were called upon to save the revolution.

Late in 1921, over the protests of his own Marxist theoreticians, Lenin rammed through a decree requiring, among other things, balanced government budgets, the reestablishment of a normal banking system based on the central bank concept, and the introduction of new bank notes with a fixed gold basis. The monetary unit provided by the new law was the *chervonetz*, having a gold value of 10 prerevolution gold roubles, or 119.4826 grains (.2489 troy ounce) of fine gold. All new bank notes were to be secured by at least 25 percent gold or gold-backed foreign exchange on deposit.

These moves were entirely successful. Thus the Soviet government secured economic stability only by returning to the proven principles of balanced budgets, sound banking and a fixed gold standard, putting it, for all practical purposes, on the same fiscal basis as the most conservative Western nations of that era. In 1923 the Soviets further demonstrated their new-found financial orthodoxy by minting the only known Soviet gold coin, the 10-rouble *chervonetz* (Friedberg No. 142). Mintage figures for this coin are unknown, but today they are quite rare, having a value of about $375.

Again, what irony there is in history; a half century after the Bolshevik Revolution, we still find the fiscal arrangements of the Soviet Union under the control of tightfisted orthodox money managers, who demand balanced budgets and strict accounting, while the banking and monetary systems of the U.S. and Britain are dominated by Keynesian-oriented, credit-happy, fiat money, New Economics spendthrifts.

In Germany, with the currency depreciated to almost zero for the second time within the memory of most Germans, the Bonn government began in 1948 the painful process of economic and monetary reform under the direction of its new Economics Minister, Ludwig Erhard. Understandably they voted overwhelmingly for sound money and no budget deficits; they emphatically rejected the neo–Keynesian banking and fiscal devices that some of the economists and administrators of the Allied governments were still trying to force upon them.[6]

The stability of the German *deutschmark* eventually became second only to the Swiss franc. The *deutschmark* holds the distinction of being the only major currency in modern times that was revalued upwards in terms of foreign exchange. The only thing miraculous about the "German Miracle" was that they were able openly to proclaim their adherence to a free market noninflationary economy (it is unconstitutional for a West German government to run a budget deficit) while still under the domination of Allied governments obsessed with Keynesianism, socialism and neosocialism.

Unfortunately, however, despite their admirable banking and credit policies, neither the Germans nor anyone else in Europe, not even the Swiss, have been immune from the cost-push kind of inflation primarily generated by the gold exchange standard and the resultant outpouring of American paper dollars all over the world. The "cost of living" rises everywhere, apparently to continue forever; the price of monetary gold is supposed to remain static. (But the price of gold coins has not!)

France after World War II became for a time the victim of the same self-serving political stupidity that had caused her ruin prior to the war. With a surplus of political parties and a constitution too weak to control or restrict the demagogues, France was helpless to prevent its legislators, many with socialist or Communist ties, from repeatedly voting socialist benefits for the public, and then from failing to raise taxes or curtail other expenses to pay for them. The French also tried to fight two disastrous losing wars during this period, one in Indochina (Vietnam) and another in Algeria, without imposing the required financial sacrifices on their tired and restive citizens.

As a result, the franc skidded from the already inflationary wartime ratio of 50 to the dollar in 1944 to 500 to the dollar by 1958. When Charles de Gaulle came to power in 1959, he immediately moved, with the help and guidance of his distinguished economics adviser, Jacques Rueff, to reestablish a sound monetary system for his beloved France. Inflation was halted by eliminating the wasteful deficit expenditures. The unhappy war in Algeria was concluded by negotiation and withdrawal. The franc was revalued: 100 old francs were exchanged for one new franc. With internal deficits curtailed, France's gold and foreign exchange reserves began a rapid recovery.

By 1967 de Gaulle was finally able to restore the franc to full international convertibility and to allow free and unrestricted gold trading on the Paris bourse. Until the surprise "revolution" of 1968, the franc under de Gaulle was regarded as one of the world's soundest currencies. But as a result of this difficult period, the future of the franc, along with the pound and the dollar, is now subject to considerable uncertainty.*

The British pound, subsequent to its initial devaluation in 1931, has been officially devalued three more times. After first being allowed to "float" for a while, the pound finally stabilized at a rate of about $4.90 in terms of the devalued 1934 American dollar. But in 1939 the pound was again formally devalued to a new fixed $4.03 ratio. In 1949 it was reduced once more, this time to $2.80, and finally in November 1967 the exchange rate was lowered to the $2.40 level. At this writing there is some question whether the $2.40 rate can be maintained for long.

It must also be kept in mind that the pound, along with all other major currencies under the operation of the gold exchange standard and the International Monetary Fund, is irrevocably tied to the dollar. If the dollar is to be devalued, or its gold parity eliminated completely, obviously the pound and all other currencies will be drastically affected. The past is instructive: in 1934 when the dollar was last devalued, even the redoubtable Swiss franc was forced into a parallel devaluation.

The United States dollar has so far narrowly managed to avoid a formal devaluation in the postwar years, but it has suffered a serious erosion of its domestic purchasing power. Since the euphoria of Bretton Woods, the paper dollar has lost more than 50 percent of its pocketbook value. The following table (Fig. 2), prepared from the U.S. government's official index of consumer prices, illustrates this apparently irresistible trend, running through Democratic and Republican administrations alike. It also appears that the pace is accelerating.

---

* Indeed it is; on August 8, 1969, the franc was devalued again, this time by 12½ percent. This move, found necessary only three months after the resignation of President de Gaulle (who managed to keep France and the franc intact for a decade), may have temporarily saved France from national bankruptcy, but it will hardly inspire confidence in the long-term outlook for the franc.

Fig. 2

PURCHASING POWER OF THE U.S. DOLLAR
1944–1969

Based on Consumer Price Index, U.S. Dept. of Labor
(Using 1944 as Base)

Year End		Value
1944	....	$1.00
1945	....	.97¾
1946	....	.82¾
1947	....	.75⅞
1948	....	.73⅞
1949	....	.75½
1950	....	.71⅛
1951	....	.67¼
1952	....	.66⅝
1953	....	.66¼
1954	....	.66⅝
1955	....	.66⅜
1956	....	.64½
1957	....	.62½
1958	....	.61½
1959	....	.60⅝
1960	....	.59⅝
1961	....	.59⅜
1962	....	.58⅝
1963	....	.57⅝
1964	....	.56⅞
1965	....	.55¾
1966	....	.54⅛
1967	....	.52½
1968	....	.50⅛
*1969	....	.47¼

* Estimated

The American Gold Crisis

The second outstanding economic feature of the postwar years was the drastic decline in what Keynes had once referred to as the "impregnable liquidity" of the United States; in other words, our gold stock went down while our debt liabilities went up. The first serious signs of this weakening in the world monetary structure, jerry-built at Bretton Woods in 1944, occurred in 1958. Just ten years earlier, the U.S. gold stock had reached its historic peak of $24.4 billion, and at that time (1948) the potential net foreign demand claims (under the gold-dollar exchange standard and IMF rules) were only a little more than $7 billion. Also a claim on this gold supply, even if only a theoretical one, was a total domestic purchasing media (currency and checking accounts) amounting to $68 billion. Altogether, from any banker's point of view, a highly liquid and indeed seemingly "impregnable" position. But in 1958 the first sizable cracks began to appear.

Our liquidity position, however, was still strong in 1957, with $22.6 billion worth of gold in Fort Knox, although foreign demand liabilities had risen to $12.6 billion and domestic purchasing media had jumped to $115 billion.[7] But in 1958, a sharply increased balance-of-payments deficit was incurred by the United States; European recovery had reached a point where Europe was no longer a helpless economic dependent but a vigorous international competitor. As a result, a good many dollar credits were presented at the Treasury window for redemption in gold. By 1959 our gold supply had skidded to $19 billion.

The response of the Eisenhower Administration (seemingly setting the pattern for all subsequent administrations) was too little, too late, and directed at the wrong target. Some dependents of American servicemen overseas were ordered home, and Post Exchange stores at American military bases abroad were instructed to limit their sales of foreign merchandise. Still the monetization of U.S. debt into money continued unchecked at home and massive government spending on grandiose military and "aid" projects abroad went merrily on.

By 1961, net foreign claims outstanding exceeded our actual gold supply. The reaction of the Kennedy Administration was, like that of its predecessor, neither sustained nor effective. A few more American offices abroad were closed or cut back, but on the other hand aid to Vietnam and other parts of our troubled world was stepped up. In the United States, the economy was encouraged to start "moving again" by tax cuts and another massive infusion of credit (debt) money. The total domestic money supply reached $130 billion.

At the beginning of 1965 the situation had evolved from serious to desperate. America's gold stock sank under $15 billion while potential foreign claims continued to expand, in spite of massive gold redemptions, to the point where they reached $27 billion. The Johnson Administration and Congress met that emergency by voting to repeal part of the law in effect since 1946, that reserves of gold must be held by the Treasury equal in value to 25 percent of the total of Federal Reserve Bank deposit liabilities and 25 percent of the amount of actual currency (Federal Reserve notes) in circulation.[8] They eliminated the provision requiring a 25 percent "cover" on Federal Reserve deposits, in order to have more gold legally available to meet foreign claims (and consequently less to restrict the expansion of the domestic money supply).

Secretary of the Treasury Fowler "promised" that the government would eliminate its chronic deficit at some future, but unspecified, date. Meanwhile, a 15 percent tax was levied against the purchase of foreign securities by U.S. citizens, and pressures were exerted on U.S. businessmen to curtail "voluntarily" other types of overseas investment.[9] Interest rates were raised to the highest levels in forty years. Treasury officials began "arm-twisting" visits abroad to persuade and implore creditor nations to keep their surplus dollars and not cash them in for gold. West Germany was induced to accept four-year Treasury bonds in lieu of gold for her excess dollar profits.[10] It was all of little use; the "gold drain" became a hemorrhage. Too much of it was going to nervous private citizens anxious to avoid the impending bankruptcy of the dollar (and the pound and the franc) and they could not be bullied or bribed like foreign central banks.

By 1968 the gold "problem" had become the gold crisis. Once again the government moved, this time to strike down the remaining 25 percent gold cover on Federal Reserve note currency, putting the United States internally on a pure fiat money system. There was no gold left to back our currency (even theoretically). There was no silver either; the last of it was being sold over the Treasury counters in a futile and unnecessary attempt to hold down the price of that metal. Our coins had been reduced to cupro–nickel slugs since 1965. The U.S. gold reserve had fallen to $10 billion— a level last seen in 1936—and we were technically liable for three times that amount at the request of foreign creditors. And to top it off, our total outstanding purchasing media (currency and checking accounts) soared past $200 billion—without a single ounce of free gold or silver to anchor or support them.

The privately owned gold of American citizens was confiscated in 1933, partly on the theory that a wise government could more efficiently manage our monetary system if gold were made a national monopoly. How well it has done is illustrated by the following chart (Fig. 3):

The reader will note that after plunging precipitously to a low of $10.4 billion in July of 1968, the U.S. monetary gold stock appears to have stabilized somewhat. It is the author's opinion, however, that this apparent levelling-off will prove illusory. It can be completely accounted for by the heavy European investment in the U.S. stock market, which occurred in 1968, and by the massive borrowing abroad by U.S. corporations during 1968 and 1969. Both of these factors are far in excess (in dollar value) of the minor recovery in the U.S. balance of payments that occurred during the first half of 1969.

Furthermore, during the same period our once very healthy balance of trade has been reduced almost to the vanishing point. Therefore, the true gold situation of the U.S. has in reality continued to deteriorate despite the apparent 1969 stability in our monetary gold balance. Any prolonged weakening of the American securities markets or any substantial decline in short-term interest rates will unquestionably result in a renewal of the decline, as this "hot money" returns to Europe and becomes an even greater pressure on our gold supply than has previously occurred.

There is not room here to detail the extraordinary events of the gold crisis of 1967–68. There were the waves of bullion speculation on the London and Paris gold markets, the avalanches of gold smuggling, and the frantic monetary meetings in Washington, Lon-

FIG. 3

U.S. MONETARY GOLD SUPPLY
1944 - 1969
(BILLIONS OF DOLLARS)

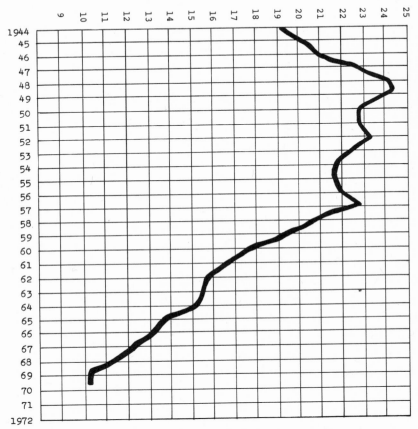

10.367 BILLION DOLLARS, AUG. 30, 1969

Fig. 3

10.367 billion dollars, Aug. 30, 1969, does not include approximately $787
million in the Exchange Stabilization Fund, but does include $1.6 billion pledged
to the IMF, about $1 billion in collateral pledged for miscellaneous foreign cur-
rency loans and $500 million in gold guarantees for Bundesbank holdings of U.S.
Treasury bonds. Taking all factors into consideration, the actual U.S. monetary
gold reserve is probably closer to $8 billion than to the officially quoted $10.367
billion. Dr. Franz Pick, the noted world currency authority, estimates it to be as
low as $7.4 billion.

don, and Zurich. Then the collapse of the pound shocked the world, and this event was soon followed by the worldwide gold panic of March 1968, the establishment of a "two-tier" gold-price system, and the "blow-off" rise and collapse of gold-mining stocks on the New York and London stock exchanges. Finally, there was a sudden awakening on the part of many Americans to what Europeans have known for centuries—that gold coins are an exciting investment—and a consequent wild spurt in the price of gold coins.

What are most significant, however, and must be examined here at least briefly, are the almost hysterical statements and actions of those charged with regulating and managing the monetary system of the United States during this period. Having failed so decisively in their responsibility to maintain the integrity of the dollar, the money managers rushed to embrace, with inordinate haste, the philosophy of the neo-Keynesian money doctors that gold is an anachronism in a world of laser beams and space ships. No less a personage than the august chairman of the Federal Reserve Board, Mr. William McChesney Martin, passed his now famous curse upon gold as a "barbarous relic,"[11] while Secretary of the Treasury Fowler went about pleading for the creation of a new IMF paper currency to replace gold in international payments. "Paper gold" suddenly became the obsession of and the holy grail of salvation for the Treasury.

Other bankers (in and out of the Treasury) threatened darkly that if those greedy foreigners didn't quit cashing in their perfectly good dollars, we would stop paying out gold altogether; we would demonetize gold completely rather than break our vow never to devalue the dollar. (A ludicrous notion that if you can't pay your debts in full you are justified in repudiating them altogether.) Chairman Martin, however, contrarily insisted that we would pay out our gold "to the last bar," and that the American people would be better off once they had seen the end of it.

The head of the State Department's International Finance Division argued that the dollar was better than gold and that the U.S. should threaten to stop buying gold at $35 per ounce, and thus force the price down (overlooking the fact that the Treasury had not been able to buy an ounce on net balance since 1956). He went on to insist that the complete separation of the dollar from gold would "precipitate gold's demise as money."[12]

At last a compromise was put forward by the Treasury and the IMF, whereby a limited amount of "special drawing rights" (SDRs) would be granted by the IMF to debtor countries (such as the U.S.). These SDR certificates could then be used instead of gold; they would be negotiable for the settlement of international payments. The proposal awaits ratification by the 107 IMF member nations. The U.S. hailed this scheme as a great victory for the dollar over gold—which has apparently joined the ranks of our enemies.[13]

Meanwhile, a cynical world looks on, still preferring the reality of gold to the empty promises of politicians, who have deceived too often before, and apparently believing with Elgin Groseclose that gold is "the only cash with universal validity." Perhaps one can also conclude with Dr. Groseclose that "a better grasp of the monetary problem [can] be gained by more reading of historical experience, more familiarity with actual business and less with monetary theory, particularly current monetary theory."[14] Whatever the cause, private interests continued to buy more gold than was produced by the mines in 1967 and 1968, and gladly made up the difference by taking all that was offered by the Treasury and other central banks.

If the United States does succeed in getting the SDR scheme accepted, and "paper gold" becomes the basis for the settlement of international balances, the long-run inflationary impact on the world's monetary structure will be, in the author's opinion, absolutely disastrous. For the basic cause of inflation and monetary instability, on an international basis, is not a "lack of liquidity," or an *insufficiency* of monetary instruments, as the United States Keynesian money managers contend, but a serious *lack of quality* (i.e. convertibility) in the international monetary system now in use. Adding more nonconvertible paper to the system, in the form of SDRs, will only decrease the quality of the world's money still further, and feed the fires of inflation more vigorously than ever before.

Some Lessons from the Recent Past

There is an old aphorism to the effect that those who do not learn from history are condemned to repeat it. For those of us who wish to avoid as much as possible the unhappier phases of such repetition, there are some rather pointed lessons that can be learned from the recent past. The first and most obvious is that the citizens of the world who have kept most or all of their long-term capital in the form of bank deposits, bonds, mortgage notes, or any other kind of fixed-income credit money instruments during this "Age of Inflation," have suffered anywhere from a severe to a catastrophic loss of accumulated wealth.

The second observation one can make is that, financially speaking, we in the West are all in the same boat. The mechanics of the IMF and the gold-dollar exchange standard make it too easy for the United States to spend its credit dollars abroad, and for these same dollars to be "earned" and consequently added to foreign central bank reserves, where they become monetized into excess purchasing media. This becomes one of the causes of the endless rise in the price levels of every country—even of those with an apparent devotion to fiscal orthodoxy. (It was also a source of constant irritation to de Gaulle!) The United States, in the words of Jacques Rueff, has been "exporting" its domestic inflation since 1958.[15] And we will probably do our best to retain this monetary "freedom" one way or another for as long as we can, regardless of the final consequences. Thus we clamor for the SDRs.

Another major source of inflationary pressure is the constantly rising expectation of the world's masses for a higher standard of living and a greater share of their countries' wealth. These understandable ambitions are all too frequently encouraged beyond reason or possibility by demagogic politicians seeking office through the deplorable but time-honored method of bribing the electorate with illusory promises. And we must add to this problem the enormous monopoly powers of big labor unions, which have proved quite willing at times to use their powers to extort exorbitant and unwarranted wages.

It appears then that inflation and economic instability in the modern age are permanent facts of life. As a consequence, investment of surplus capital is not just a matter of choice or inclination but a necessity of economic survival. From the European point of view, direct investment in gold or in gold coins has always been popular. This kind of investment has proven highly reliable and successful, not only as a hedge against currency depreciation and devaluation, but as a protection against calamity as well. I have been told by European friends that during the wartime occupations a few gold coins could sometimes buy oneself, a relative or a dear friend immunity from deportation or even from a concentration camp—something no amount of paper francs or marks could do.[16]

At any rate, the Frenchman contemplating his little rosewood collector's box of *louis d'or* and napoleons knew that his modest investment capital was as secure as anything could be in this world. If he were able to hold his position or add to it throughout the debacles of the Third and Fourth Republics, he not only maintained his wealth intact, but made a handsome profit besides. He did not suffer from the worry and harassment that befell those who put their surplus funds into real estate, which was subject to confiscations, rent and price controls, and excessive taxation.

Nor did holders of common stocks have an easy time. Dividends were cut or dropped, excessive taxes were imposed on corporations, some industries were nationalized, and in others powerful unions, strikes and exorbitant wage settlements destroyed operating efficiency. Government controls also distorted production, and venal politicians extorted graft and payoffs. In short, erratic and generally unprofitable performance is typical for all kinds of industry and enterprise during periods of great economic and political disorder.

Contrary to popular opinion, the records show that even in peacetime stock markets have a pronounced tendency to *decline* during periods of rampant inflation. For example, from 1946 to 1949 the U.S. experienced its sharpest price-level advance of the postwar years, but during this time the U.S. stock market, as represented by the Dow Jones Industrial Average, declined 25 percent. To illustrate similar cases, the following table shows the action of some foreign stock markets from 1962 to 1966 as compared with the rise in the consumer price levels during the same period:

Fig. 4

Country	Cost of Living	Stock Market*
France	up 14%	down 35%
Germany	up 13%	down 22%
Italy	up 21%	down 24%
Netherlands	up 26%	down 19%
Belgium	up 15%	down 24%
Japan	up 28%	up 4%

(Source of Data: International Monetary Fund)

* Most popular average

Furthermore, neither real estate nor securities offer any immediate protection against devaluation. Typically, devaluations are followed by a government-decreed period of austerity in an attempt to make them effective. Extremely high interest rates, wage and price controls and stiff tax increases are often a part of these programs, and are intended to hold the internal price of *everything but gold* at its predevaluation level. After each devaluation of the British pound, a long period of such austerity was imposed. The case of the American dollar, devalued in 1934, was somewhat different in that the U.S. government was actually trying to promote inflation rather than restrain it, in hopes of counteracting the Depression. Nevertheless, price levels in the U.S. generally remained static until the eve of America's entrance into World War II.

The effect of devaluation on gold or gold-related investments, however, is immediate and salutary; the price goes up. The inflation chart (Fig. 5) at the end of this chapter shows what happened to the price of gold in terms of currencies as a result of devaluations and inflations since 1923.

To sum up the meaning and importance of gold in the modern world and the potential of gold and gold coins as investments, the following assumptions appear valid:

1. *Inflation is permanent.*

   This feature of the modern world economic system will continue with only brief interruptions and perhaps soon increase in velocity as long as:

   a. the gold-dollar exchange standard or any variation of it (such as SDRs or "paper gold") exists and allows paper notes, bonds, or certificates to be used as central bank reserves instead of real gold.

   b. massive military expenditures continue to be necessary for our defense.

   c. the unjustified power of certain labor organizations and similar economic pressure groups remains unchecked.

   d. political parties and politicians are inclined or forced to buy their elections with something-for-nothing promises and schemes.

   e. popular unrest and disorder, often a result of inflation, continue to be a part of the vicious circle leading to its cause.

2. *None of the preceding is likely to change.*

   We will, in all probability, not abandon the present course until a complete economic or military disaster has destroyed entirely the existing monetary system; the only thing we really seem to learn from history is that we never learn from history.

3. *Devaluation of the dollar is inevitable.*

   The dollar will be devalued, that is, the "official" price of gold will be substantially raised by the U.S. The dollar may not be formally devalued at first, but allowed to "float" in terms of gold for a while, as was the case with the pound in 1931. In either event, the result will be the same—the price of gold will go up:

   a. as a result of items one and two on this list.

   b. because of the drastic decline in the gold reserves of the United States and the huge increase in the amount of fiat paper money and credit in circulation.

4. *Gold and gold-related investments offer protection.*

   They provide one of the most reliable and historically successful methods of protecting capital against both price-level inflation and devaluation.

5. *Gold coins offer certain definite advantages over other types of gold investment because:*

   a. Gold bullion may be and has been subject to government confiscation, as it was in 1934. (It is at present illegal for private citizens to possess gold bullion in the United States and Great Britain.)

   b. Investors in gold-mining stocks must assume certain risks. Excessive taxes may be levied against profits gained from a higher price of gold. The gold-mining industry may, in some cases, be nationalized or operated under strict government control. Political disturbances, labor troubles, racial unrest, or war may also interfere with mine operations and profits in some countries.

   c. Gold coins have a numismatic value in addition to their intrinsic value, and a properly selected collection can enjoy the benefits of a rise in both types of value.

   d. The owner of gold coins experiences esthetic pleasures and satisfactions denied the average investor in stocks or real estate. His "investment" may bring him years of constant enjoyment, while the owners of real estate and common stocks invariably suffer periods of acute anxiety. (Their only real pleasure comes from that brief moment when they can sell at a profit.)

   e. The owners of gold-coin collections can more easily remain anonymous, while the holders of real estate and securities are always legally recorded—and consequently fair game for the tax collector, the thieving politician, and the socialist-collectivist.

   f. In general, those who have kept a portion of their wealth in coins, works of art, antiques, rare books, and similar items have enjoyed, for that part of their wealth, more freedom from official harassment in times of war and great economic and political stress than was experienced by those with other kinds of investment.

6. *Gold is depression-proof.*

Gold is the only investment that offers protection against inflation *and depression,* because the panic and uncertainty of economic collapse cause people to cling more tightly to the historic security of gold. Also, devaluations are sometimes resorted to during depressions as a stimulant to "reinflation" of the economy. This was the case in 1934 in the United States.

7. *It is worthwhile to try to preserve capital.*

History shows that no matter how desperate the human condition becomes during the frequent low points in its violent cyclical evolution, recovery and eventual return to prosperity are inevitable. Preserving capital means always having something for a fresh start.

Fig. 5

INFLATION CHART 1923–1969

YEAR	ENGLAND		FRANCE		GERMANY	
	Pound in U.S. Cents	Gold Value of 1,000 Pounds	Franc in U.S. Cents	Gold Value of 1,000 Francs	Mark in U.S. Cents	Gold Value of 1,000 Marks
1923	457.5	223.	6.08	2.94	Old Mark	Worthless
1924	441.7	213.	5.24	2.53	23.00	11.14
1925	482.9	234.	4.77	2.30	23.80	11.50
1926	485.8	234.	3.24	1.56	23.80	11.50
1927	486.1	235.	3.92	1.89	23.76	11.48
1928	486.6	235.	3.92	1.89	23.86	11.53
1929	485.7	235.	3.92	1.89	23.81	11.51
1930	486.2	235.	3.92	1.89	23.85	11.53
1931	453.5	219.	3.92	1.89	23.63	11.42
British Pound Devalued						
1932	350.6	169.	3.93	1.90	23.75	11.48
1933	423.7	121.	5.03	1.44	30.52	8.73
* U.S. Dollar Devalued from $20.67 to $35.00 Per Ounce of Gold						
1934	503.9	144.	6.57	1.88	39.38	11.25
1935	490.2	140.	6.60	1.88	40.26	11.49
1936	497.1	142.	6.11	1.75	40.30	11.50
1937	494.4	141.	4.05	1.16	40.20	11.48
1938	488.9	140.	2.88	.824	40.16	11.47
1939	443.5	127.	2.51	.717	40.06	11.44
British Pound Devalued			Franc Devalued		World War II Begins	
1940	383.0	109.	2.08	.595	40.02	11.43
1941	403.2	115.	France Under German Occupation		U.S. at War with Germany	
1942	403.5	115.				
1943	403.5	115.				
1944	403.5	115.				

INFLATION CHART 1923–1969 *(Continued)*

	ENGLAND		FRANCE		GERMANY	
YEAR	*Pound in U.S. Cents*	*Gold Value of 1,000 Pounds*	*Franc in U.S. Cents*	*Gold Value of 1,000 Francs*	*Mark in U.S. Cents*	*Gold Value of 1,000 Marks*
Bretton Woods Conference—International Monetary Fund Begun						
1945	403.0	115.	1.97	.573	World War II Ends	
1946	403.4	115.	.84	.240	German Mark	
1947	403.4	115.	.84	.240	Virtually	
1948	403.3	115.	.30	.086	Worthless	
British Pound Devalued			Franc Devalued			
1949	280.1	80.0	.288	.082	German	
1950	280.5	80.0	.286	.082	Economic Reform	
1951	279.9	80.0	.286	.082	Begun	
1952	279.5	80.0	.286	.082	23.00	6.57
1953	281.1	80.0	.286	.082	23.84	6.82
1954	278.4	80.0	.286	.082	23.84	6.82
1955	280.3	80.0	.286	.082	23.74	6.79
1956	278.3	79.6	.286	.082	23.74	6.79
1957	280.3	80.0	.239	.068	23.82	6.81
1958	280.3	80.0	.239	.068	23.91	6.83
1959	280.4	80.0	.204	.058	23.97	6.86
			Franc Revalued 100 Old Fr.–1 NF			
1960	281.6	80.4	20.25	**.058	23.98	6.86
1961	281.6	80.4	20.55	**.059	24.98	7.13
1962	280.1	80.0	20.41	**.058	24.96	7.13
1963	279.8	80.0	20.41	**.058	25.14	7.18
1964	278.4	79.6	20.41	**.058	25.14	7.18
1965	280.4	80.0	20.41	**.058	25.00	7.15
1966	278.7	79.7	20.24	**.058	25.16	7.19
1967	277.6	78.6	20.34	**.058	25.20	7.20
British Pound Devalued						
1968	238.4	68.1	19.93	**.057	25.18	7.19
			Franc Devalued			
1969	238.2	68.0	18.04	**.051	25.15	7.18

Notes:

Gold values are expressed in troy ounces of gold.

U.S. gold price of $20.67 per ounce is used from 1923 through 1932, and $35.00 per ounce from 1933 to 1969.

* The devaluation of the U.S. dollar in 1934 caused a *de facto* devaluation of all other currencies tied to the U.S. dollar via the gold exchange standard, even though they temporarily appear stronger *in terms of the devalued dollar.*

Foreign exchange rates are taken from various issues of the *World Almanac* and the *Wall Street Journal.* Prior to 1939, averages for the year are given; after 1939, year-end values are used. Figures for the pound in 1967 are for the period prior to the November 25 devaluation. (All 1969 figures are as of August 30.)

** Gold values after revaluation of the franc in 1959 are for 10 new francs in lieu of 1,000 old francs in order to present true value consistently.

Because of their number, not all of the officially announced devaluations of the franc were specifically noted. But it will be obvious to the reader that despite occasional periods of stability, the long-term course of the franc has been one of repeated and drastic decline. So far, de Gaulle established the best record of the modern era, having maintained the gold value of the franc for ten years. An impressive feat in our "Age of Inflation" perhaps, but hardly so when compared to the more than 100 years of fixed gold value in Napoleon's franc, which was carefully preserved by all the succeeding governments of France until 1914. To his credit, however, de Gaulle steadfastly refused unilaterally to devalue his "New Franc" despite the pressures caused by the repeated monetary crises of 1968–69. He openly rebuffed every suggestion of such devaluation, and branded the idea "an absurdity." But scarcely three months after de Gaulle had left office, the "absurdity" was committed (in great secrecy) by his successor—and promptly hailed by the Keynesians in Washington and London as a "constructive" measure that would "strengthen" the existing international monetary system.

Notes

CHAPTER IV

1. Historically, "cash" has always meant specie or metallic currency. Paper notes were regarded merely as receipts for specie (whether as coin or bullion).

2. Equal to $24.4 billion in the U.S. out of a world total of only $36 billion. (In 1968 the figures were $10.4 billion for the U.S. out of a world total of $43 billion.)

3. I think the following is as good a description of money as can be arrived at: "Throughout history the value of money has been a compound of intrinsic worth and the authority of the issuing

agency. Remove the latter and barter results; remove the former and monetary chaos follows" (Elgin Groseclose, "The Case Against De-emphasizing Gold," *Wall Street Journal*, May 22, 1967).

4. Jacques Rueff, *The Age of Inflation* (Chicago: Henry Regnery Company, Gateway Editions, 1964), p. 1.

5. John Leighton Stewart, *Fifty Years in China* (New York, 1954), p. 288.

6. *Twentieth Century Common Sense and the American Crisis of the 1960's* (Great Barrington, Mass.: American Institute for Economic Research, 1960), p. 65.

7. Data on domestic purchasing media from publications of the American Institute for Economic Research, Great Barrington, Mass.

8. Before 1946, the reserve requirements for gold were 40 percent against Federal Reserve notes and 35 percent against member bank deposits.

9. When asked how the Federal Reserve System could so easily secure such "voluntary" compliance with its requests, Chairman Martin is said to have replied, "Because we have the gun in the closet right behind us" (*Wall Street Journal*, February 26, 1968).

10. But only after a "gold clause" guaranteeing eventual redemption in gold was included.

11. Not exactly an original observation; Keynes said it first. See *General Theory*, etc.

12. John Parke Young, "Should the U.S. Change its Gold Policy," *Wall Street Journal*, May 9, 1967.

13. Nevertheless, the international bankers in the IMF have "defined" the SDR credit as being (very precisely) equal to .888671 grams of fine gold.

14. Elgin Groseclose, "The Case Against De-emphasizing Gold," *Wall Street Journal*, May 22, 1967.

15. Rueff, Interview, *U.S. News and World Report*, October 17, 1966.

16. The author remembers that in 1943, rewards in gold were offered and paid for the assistance and safe return of American fliers forced down in the North African desert. As I recall, the amount was equal to $1,000. Things have apparently not changed much; in 1967 American planes dropped millions of gold-colored leaflets over North Vietnam. The leaflets were captioned, "Reward—Fifty Taels of Gold—Reward," and explained that anyone helping a downed American flier escape could obtain this reward—about $1,760 in gold bullion (*New York Times*, July 16, 1967).

V

Investment or Speculation?

"Money is always on the brain—if the brain is in reasonable order."
—SAMUEL BUTLER

THE MONETARY HISTORY OF THE WEST IS OBVIOUSLY NOT VERY comforting. As for the most recent events and what they portend for the future, it is plain that the damage already done to the dollar, the pound and the franc by riots, devaluations, reckless and irresponsible monetary management, the mindless greed of certain labor organizations, and an insane credit binge is so bad that it would take years of financial stability and fiscal responsibility to restore confidence and relieve the present worldwide fears of further inflation and devaluations. Patently, the chances for any such broad stability developing in world economic and political affairs, for any length of time, are so remote as not to be worth serious consideration.

However, before we conclude once and for all that man, after 3,000 years of experiment, has failed to master the money mechanism, we should define what constitutes a successful money system. Money, as historically conceived and theoretically considered, ideally performs three main functions:

1. *A medium of exchange,* whereby goods and services are paid for and contracts and debts discharged.

2. *A unit of account*, in which records are kept, costs are computed and values compared.
3. *A store of value*, to serve as a reservoir of future purchasing power.

Now it must be conceded that the present monetary system of the United States, at least up until 1968, has had the best record of any modern currency in the overall performance of these vital functions—but the best has hardly been good enough. True, the dollar has been officially devalued only once in 135 years (although the next devaluation is very close), but if official devaluation can be postponed for a considerable time by substituting credit inflation for outright currency depreciation, the effect on the price level cannot. The result of such concealed currency depreciation through credit inflation since the last official devaluation of the dollar in 1934 shows the following staggering loss in the *store-of-value* function of the "almighty dollar":

Year	Official Value of 1 Oz. Gold	Purchasing Power of Paper Dollar
December 1934	$35.00	$1.00
July 1969	$35.00	.36½ ¢

Sooner or later the "official" U.S. price of gold will be adjusted to the realities of the present; the longer it is postponed, the more drastic such an adjustment will be. Considering that the general price level has risen by 250 percent since 1934, the price of gold would have to be raised to $87.50 per ounce merely to stay even. If, or more properly when, we find it necessary to liquidate a part of the enormous international and domestic debt we have accumulated, the price of gold will have to be raised much higher. No one can realistically guess at what level a new gold dollar will one day be fixed, but considering the length and excesses of the inflationary period we have already been through, and the even more violent era of economic instability that is sure to come, a future gold price of $150 per ounce seems entirely possible.

It must be remembered that no future devaluation will become final as long as the modern credit inflation economy continues to be practiced. No amount of gold will ever suffice to stabilize the monetary structure under these conditions, for as fast as it can be added to central bank reserves, new bank credit will be monetized and pyramided upon it.

As a medium of exchange, no doubt the paper dollar will continue to function adequately; after all, the Brazilian *cruzeiro* continued in use when it was valued at 3,500 to the dollar. Moreover, as a unit of account it will probably remain acceptable, although it will continue to be somewhat of a burden to bookkeepers and accountants (perhaps we will all become better mathematicians by constantly dealing in larger numbers). But as a store of value the dollar and most other major currencies have proven, and will very likely continue to prove, highly unsatisfactory.

The problem remains: to find media that will provide not only a stable store of value, but methods of increasing the surplus earned by honest toil. We have already reviewed the major virtues and advantages of gold coins in this area, but before going on to our specific review of collector's gold coins it will be advantageous to examine briefly the two general approaches to preserving and increasing wealth by dealing in stores of value other than currency. These two general approaches are categorized as *investment* and *speculation*. As both ideas are often subject to some semantic confusion, a preliminary examination of terms is in order. I find the dictionary definition sufficiently precise:[1]

> *Speculation:* to buy and sell with the expectation of profiting from fluctuations in price.
>
> *Investment:* to lay out money with the view to obtaining an income or profit, or to convert money into some form of wealth other than money.

The object of both ventures is the same: profit. But there are important differences, even though we must concede that all financial transactions contain some elements that are more or less speculative.

First there is the degree of risk undertaken. The dynamics of speculation are simple: the longer the chances of success (odds), the greater the potential reward—or loss. When one attempts to anticipate fluctuations in the price of a medium that is subject to such fluctuations, one assumes risk. The greater the possible range of such price changes, the greater the risk. Converting money into some other form of wealth, however, if undertaken with reasonable care and knowledge, can provide profits and security with little or no risk at all.

Second, although it is not specifically stated in our definitions, a time element is indeed implied. The speculator generally aims for the short term; prices that fluctuate do not, by definition, continue a trend indefinitely. Ideally, then, a good investment is a *long-term store of value* that not only maintains itself but contains factors that increase its worth with the passage of time.

Time, Often the Enemy of the Speculator, Is the Investor's Formidable Ally

We have learned from the clever Lord Keynes that "in the long run we are all dead." But Keynes was no Keynesian. In the long run he managed the Bank of England, directed insurance companies, wrote books, taught school, and made a fortune. Like the rest of us, he was a hopeless optimist and never hesitated to pledge his energy and his money to the future.

Generally, the short-term fluctuations in the prices of coins and other antiquities do not offer sufficient opportunities for speculative profits. Furthermore, successful speculation requires considerable personal commitment (and agility) on the part of the speculator. All speculative markets, including the coin market, are dominated by professionals—and they are apt to possess the sharpest minds found anywhere. Anyone going to play in their league had better be prepared to give it his undivided attention; too many amateur traders have been pulverized in the stock and commodity markets to believe otherwise. My advice is definite on this point: leave speculation in coins to dealers and other specialists. Do not buy gold coins merely as a short-term speculation during some momentary gold panic. Do not buy them in the hopes of making a quick killing from an early rise in the price of gold. Do not consider buying gold coins unless you are prepared to hold them as part of your long-term store of value.

Gold coins are generally a highly liquid investment, that is, they can be bought and sold readily, but they are hardly liquid enough to accommodate quick speculative profits. The essence of successful speculation is timing. You not only must trade in the right commodity but you must buy and sell at the right time. The coin market, even with its teletype quotation service and other aids, is still too loosely organized to permit the fast timing and execution of orders so necessary in any true speculative operation. For those so inclined, there are more than enough opportunities for speculation in the stock and commodity markets. If you are going to take the risks of speculation, at least give yourself the advantage of operating in markets specifically organized to accommodate the requirements of speculators.

Gold Coins and Gold Speculation

The events of March and April 1968, during the "gold pool" crisis, brought a new wave of speculative buying in gold coins. But judging from the reports of dealers, few of those "speculators" had much opportunity to profit from their venture. Most found themselves with a substantial short-term loss within a few days. (And if they were typical of most amateur stock market speculators, many of them after buying at the peak price sold out in panic as soon as prices began to fall off again.) The following press report is revealing:

> *Gold Coins Join Price Spiral*
> NEW YORK (AP) (3–21–68)
> "Ten years ago the wholesale price for a $20 gold piece was $38," says coin dealer Dan Messer. "Now it's . . . take your pick, guess."
> The speculative fever that has swept the world's gold markets

in recent weeks has spilled over into the coin dealer's world and has driven the retail price of gold coins up and up. Dealers have been offered $80 and more for a $20 gold piece, although the current price is ranging between $73 and $75.

"We've had some rather heavy demands on gold coins," says Messer, of New York's Coen-Messer Co. "In the last couple of weeks their prices have followed the rise of gold generally on the European market."

Messer attributes the increased demand for coins in part to a desire to guard against inflation.

"Gold coins are one type of hedge against inflation American citizens are entitled to deal in," he says. "That's because the only gold they can own is gold coins or *in* manufactured gold, such as jewelry.

"The person who wants gold is going to pay a higher premium for manufactured gold than he is for coins. That's the reason coins are so popular.

"WHEN gold coins were being minted in the United States they circulated as $1, $2.50, $5, $10, $20, and $50 pieces.

"But the big trading now is in the $20 piece.

"The trading was spilled over into the $5 and $10 pieces, but the predominant trading is in the area of the $20 coin," says Benjamin Stack of Stack's Coin Co. in New York.

"The $20 piece is the lowest-priced coin in proportion to the amount of gold contained in it," Stack says. "It contains an ounce of gold, compared to the $10 piece, which contains half an ounce of gold but sells at only about $10 less than the $20 coin. There are more rarities among the $10 piece than among the $20, which boosts their price up."

STACK'S company briefly stopped selling gold coins because of the "insane prices" but now is selling single coins.

"We are not selling quantities," Stack says. "We will sell one $20 gold piece to a customer at $75. I just had a call from a man who wanted 500 of the $20 pieces at $80 each, and I turned him down. We do not want to be a part of this wild frenzy. We have a name to uphold. We could very easily sell right out to the bare walls, but if we sold out to the speculators we couldn't supply our regular customers—the collectors—and they might not come back."

MESSER cited the "European feeling" as being behind much of the desire for holding gold coins.

"Having gold in Europe is very important," he says. "A lot of people got out of Nazi Germany because they had gold coins to use as barter. This feeling of having gold coins in one's possession represents a certain security. And the time may come when an American can use a gold coin to buy something while his paper money is worthless. A lot of people are buying them as hedges against runaway inflation."

It has been illegal since 1933 to hold gold bullion, although the "Gold Act" later was modified to exclude gold coins.[2]

Another newspaper story, also indicative of the times, was this one concerning one of the country's nationally known dealers in gold coins who operates in the South:

Dantone Sells Half–Million In Gold Coins In One Week
ATLANTA, GA. (4–14–68)

Atlanta, Ga., coin dealer Blaise J. Dantone, operator of Peachtree Coin Shop, sold half a million dollars in gold coins in a single week during the recent rush by speculators to the precious metal.

Dantone said this business amounts to 10 to 20 times more than he normally does in an average week.

Most of his customers, the Atlanta dealer said, wanted U.S. double Eagles and paid up to $80 for them, buying in lots of 100 or more. For the greater part, he said, they were not coin collectors but professional people and business executives who were speculating.

Dantone's experience with speculator demand was paralleled by that of other Eastern dealers' experiences, reported from New York and Springfield, Mass. Both the Springfield dealer, Tatham Stamp and Coin Co. and Stack's in New York, however, were turning down speculators' orders for large quantities of gold coins.

Benjamin Stack expressed skepticism about the chances of gold hoarders making a fast profit on their speculation. "The average man coming in with his savings and buying $20 gold coins at $82, probably will not get it back," he said, adding: "We felt we had no right to encourage gold hoarding."

While admitting that he entertained some doubt about selling to speculators, Dantone said he felt an obligation to do it, in order to maintain his "national reputation as a dealer in gold coins."[3]

Despite the hasty generalizations and contradictions inevitable in spot news reporting, these articles accurately present the tenor of the time and reveal something of the emotional atmosphere that is always typical of intensely speculative periods. If there is one thing that is necessary for success in any financial venture, it is to proceed logically and analytically without judgment being distorted by emotional exaggerations such as greed and fear.

To complete the story, the author personally interviewed the larger coin dealers in Chicago during and after the April 1968 panic buying and found that the price of common–date double Eagles (U.S. $20 piece containing approximately 1 ounce of fine gold) had soared to $85 during one hectic week. Three weeks later calm had returned and these dealers were offering $60 to $65 for the same coin. In all fairness to these dealers, it must be said that most of them did their best to restrain the avarice of some of their customers. The following was told to me by a good friend who is one of Chicago's major dealers:

My place looked like a LaSalle Street grain broker's office. Complete pandemonium—I tried to tell them to wait a few days and let things cool down a bit, but nobody listened. They wanted *gold* and they wanted it right away. They were desperately determined to convert their savings into gold before what they thought was an impending devaluation.

I had been through these gold panics several times before, and even though this was the worst one yet, I still expected things to run true to form and prices to come back to a more reasonable level in a few weeks. I tried to tell these customers, most of whom I'd never seen before, to take it easy and not chase the prices, but it was like trying to reason with a herd of buffalo.

Even if the dollar was really going to be devalued this time, prices had already gone up enough to discount most of it, and besides, after any devaluation was announced there would probably be at least a temporary slump in gold prices as well, as all the short–term speculators tried to unload at the same time and take their "profits."

You know, except for the increased volume of business we were not making any great killing on the operation; we were forced to bid the same high prices to get coins to fill the customer's orders, and our mark-up was very little higher at $80 per double than it was at $60.

But right in the middle of the worst of it, this fellow comes in waving a cashier's check for $20,000 and saying he wanted to spend it all on gold right away.

"We will get massacred," I told him, "putting in an order of that size in a market as tight as this." But he was adamant—he wanted $20,000 worth of gold coins and he wanted them at once. "OK," I said, "it's your money, but we won't be able to supply you here; we will have to get offers via teletype from out-of-town dealers all over the country."

Well, we filled that order, but it cost him up to $90 an ounce for some of the gold he got. A month later he was back, disgusted and angry, wanting to sell some of his doubles, and the best I could give him was $60 each—a 33 percent loss.

Like most dealers, my friend had little respect for the talents of outside coin speculators.

"Very few of them really make worthwhile money," he confided. "Their timing is nearly always bad; they buy when they should be selling and sell when they should be buying."

"Precisely," I agreed, "it is the same on Wall Street with stocks and on LaSalle Street in commodities."

It is part of the lore of Wall Street that the really big money is made by those who can recognize the *primary* trend of a stock and then stay with it as long as that trend continues. I firmly believe this to be true, even though I have at times made my living as a professional trader. In sum, most of the stock market losses are racked up by short–term traders and speculators—and so it is with the coin market.

Those who have accumulated and held quality coins for a reasonable time have enjoyed, for that part of their capital, complete immunity from our chronic and apparently incurable monetary erosion. It does not matter if they acted for profit or pleasure or both (the ideal combination); if these collectors proceeded with even a modest amount of numismatic knowledge, success was assured. If they also had a bit of investment sophistication, they would by now have made a good profit.

Going to Market

Actually the term "coin market," like "stock market," is a broad generalization for a number of related activities. The coin market, like the stock market, is a continuous auction, involving dealers and their clients and all other interested parties, in which prices are established (theoretically at least) solely in response to the laws of supply and demand.

The various types who make up the coin market include numismatists, collectors, accumulators, hoarders, dealers, investors, and speculators. It is perhaps paradoxical that the genuine numismatist or serious student of coins and medals accounts for only a small percentage of the total coin market. The more casual coin collectors and the haphazard accumulators (who simply buy anything that strikes their fancy) are far more numerous, but much less influential in affecting the trend of coin prices. As for the hoarders, although they have little effect on the traditional numismatic market, their operations are of course strongly felt in the area of common gold and silver.

It is the scholarly research of the dedicated numismatist that does most to *identify* the rare qualities, historic associations, scarcity, artistic merit, and other tangible and intangible factors that give uncommon value to certain coins. The role of the investor is to consider these pure numismatic values as they are, or will be, influenced by general economic conditions and various historic and cultural trends. By emphasizing the economic aspects of the whole field of numismatics, the investor helps provide continuity and stability for the coin market. The dealer naturally is the middleman, the professional arbiter of supply and demand.

It is the speculator, however, who provides the fireworks (and suffers most of the burns) in any auction market. He is the primary cause of the cyclical nature of markets.

Obviously the coin market is difficult to characterize as a whole. To be successful, a coin investor must develop more than a passing interest in numismatics, and numismatics can be much more enjoyable if you know you are acquiring a profitable investment at the same time. But if you are a speculator in coins, you will need a lot of luck—even if you are also a dealer.

If gold coins are a hedge against currency devaluation because of their intrinsic value (which they are) and if gold coins have numismatic value that derives from their scarcity, history, and beauty (which they have), then an ideal approach to collecting would be one that combines these values. That is the program of collecting that the author basically recommends.

The balance between these two values should be based generally on the amount of money invested. If the total is modest, then lean primarily towards coins of high intrinsic (bullion) value. If you have a generous amount to invest, the emphasis should be on coins of high numismatic value, which have demonstrated a long-term rising price trend. But any investment collection should contain elements of both types of value. I would not recommend that even the most modest collection be all bullion, nor would I suggest that those who can afford the most generous investment ignore intrinsic value completely. (The model portfolios presented in Chapter XIII suggest and illustrate typical collections designed to accommodate various investment brackets.) But by using this general guideline, the more modest collections will contain a higher overall percentage of intrinsic value and therefore enjoy a greater degree of safety (and possibly the greater opportunity for short–term gain from devaluation). However, do not hesitate to give consideration to your personal desires and instincts in this matter—this book is intended only as a guide.

As to the total amount of investment capital that should be put into gold coins, that too is a personal decision. Obviously one should not use money that is required, or will shortly be required, for family or personal needs. Money that goes into gold coins should come out of earned surplus—money available for the purchase of stocks, real estate (but not your own home), antiques, and similar investments. Another good way to look upon your coin collection is as an insurance policy, as a long-term asset to which you contribute on a regular basis, an asset that will be sold only when you really need the cash, and all other sources have been exhausted.

If you begin selling things as soon as you have a little profit in them, you will never achieve success; you will never build up a worthwhile asset. Invariably you will sell too soon, only to find in a few months that a higher price will have to be paid to get the same item back.

Hold your position and add to it whenever you have the opportunity. Don't sell unless you absolutely must have the money. After all, one doesn't cash in an insurance policy as soon as it acquires a little surrender value.

As soon as one begins to acquire a gold-coin collection of significant value, there is one very basic point to remember: Do not keep your gold-coin collection at home! It belongs in a safe-deposit box. A very valuable collection of gold coins can fit into a typical safe-deposit box, and larger boxes can be rented at a modest increase in fee for the big-time operators. It may seem a little inconvenient to have to go to the bank to see your collection, but it's really not that bad. A half hour or so on a Saturday morning spent in the tranquility of those little coupon rooms next to the bank vault can be very refreshing.

There is only one minor problem connected with storing your collection at a bank; generally the contents of safe-deposit boxes are not insured by the banks themselves. True, robberies of safe-deposit vaults are quite rare, but they have happened. So for your own peace of mind and safety, have your collection insured by your own insurance agency—the fee will be quite modest. Make a list of your coins and keep it up to date. Give a copy to your insurance man if you like, or if he requests it, and keep another in a safe place (but not in the safe-deposit box) for yourself.

If you want to show your collection to a friend, arrange to meet him at the bank. If you want to show your gold coins to guests in your home, bring only a few selected pieces at a time. Don't advertise to every stranger or mere acquaintance that you have a valuable collection of gold coins. Be discreet, for there is one generalization that can always be made about thieves: they have an infallible sense about what is valuable. They are strongly attracted to coin collections and particularly gold coins, not only because they recognize their value, but because they can be sold so easily. So don't keep your coins at home and don't talk about them with anyone but trusted friends—a thief may not get the part of the story that you always keep your coins in the bank.

If you are thinking about installing a safe in your home, I would advise against that too. Far from being a deterrent, a safe in a home is usually an irresistible invitation and a challenge to a professional thief. No matter how carefully the safe is concealed, there is always the possibility that the knowledge of it will find its way to the wrong ears. If you are not home, burglars may tear half the house down looking for it or trying to get it out. If someone is home— well, there are too many accounts in the newspapers of the despicable brutality employed by thieves to force someone to open a safe. So I repeat, the best place to keep your coin collection is in a safe-deposit box in a good bank.

If you are one of those fearful of a total military or economic disaster about to engulf the country or the world, then divide your gold into two or more banks, widely separated—although I am inclined to believe that this is an exercise in futility. If the time ever comes when the government's currency is totally repudiated and private gold is the only acceptable money, it will probably be too dangerous to use it as such. (It was during the Reign of Terror in France.) You would have to risk being robbed by bandits or shot by the government for possessing it. Against such total calamity only God can protect us; if we are to be so unfortunate as to be exposed to such an era, all we will be able to do is wait until things get better and hope to survive in the meantime. But if it makes you feel more secure to have gold stashed away in several places, go ahead. Just don't keep it at home.

All of the preceding concerning the storage of a gold–coin collection is by no means intended to imply that possessing gold coins is in any way hazardous. I merely suggest that one should use a little common sense in this matter. One does not prudently keep stock and bond certificates, deeds, insurance policies and other valuable papers in the home; the best place for them is in your safe-deposit box, and a safe-deposit box is also the best place for your gold-coin collection.

There remains one final observation regarding investment and speculation. If, in spite of all that I have said concerning the advantages of building a balanced collection over a period of years, you still regard gold coins merely as a one–shot speculation on devaluation, then your operation is simply one of buying and holding coins that have the highest intrinsic value at the least price per ounce of gold. A careful reading of the second part of this book should offer adequate suggestions for coins suitable for this limited objective.

But I must add that I feel the time is growing quite late for large profits to be made in this limited kind of investment. Those who acquired common–date gold coins before 1967 generally paid (if they were careful shoppers) between $45 and $50 per ounce of gold for them.[4] A devaluation to $70 per ounce of gold would make pre-1967 holders a nice profit. Those who bought common-date gold in recent months paid at least $65 per ounce for it—not much room for profit, even with a doubling of the present price of gold to $70 (which would probably be the minimum for any near–term devaluation). However, a gold price of $100 would allow significant speculative profits, and no one really knows how high the price of gold will go eventually. I must concede this: even paying the equivalent of $70 to $80 per ounce for gold in coin form would preserve capital whether it made a paper–dollar profit or not. It would prevent a loss, and that in itself can sometimes be a major financial accomplishment.[5]

Those who feel that a devaluation of the U.S. dollar (and consequently the further devaluation of all other world currencies) is quite near (and I am one who does) might also consider a speculative commitment in gold-mining stocks. As these shares can be extremely volatile at times, they should satisfy the requirements of the most active speculators. They also might be good long-term holdings. Your broker can give you further information on this matter. But our business here is gold coins, and it is the author's opinion that:

1. They are safe and sure protection against inflation and currency devaluation.
2. They can serve as a successful long-term store of value.
3. They provide unusual opportunities for profitable investment.
4. They offer a great deal of pleasure, satisfaction and education.
5. The numismatic values of many gold coins have been greatly underestimated in the past and they still have great potential ahead of them.

Therefore, we will take a look at gold coins in detail in the second part of this book.

Notes

Chapter V

1. *Webster's Collegiate Dictionary*, 5th edition, G. & C. Merriam Co., Springfield, Mass., 1947.
2. *Chicago Daily News*, March 21, 1968.
3. *Coin World*, April 17, 1968.
4. These prices assume the purchase of uncirculated coins. Prices would be still lower if circulated or worn coins were purchased, and these of course would be adequate for purely a bullion speculation.
5. We are considering coins hypothetically here, solely in the matter of intrinsic value, and are leaving out any numismatic values— although in reality it would hardly be prudent to overlook the latter.

PART 2

BUILDING

YOUR GOLD-COIN

COLLECTION

VI

A Technical Review

"It is much better to have your gold in the hand than in the heart."
——THOMAS FULLER

THERE IS AN OLD TRUISM, PART OF THE LORE OF THE PROFESsional investment fraternity, that says simply, "follow the smart money." It means of course that one way to find a shrewd investment is to observe the actions of the wealthy, the sophisticated, those who have demonstrated beyond question their acquisitive abilities. And the "smart money" throughout history has seldom deviated from the course set by the ancient kings of the East. If anything, 3,000 years of experience with monetary systems have only intensified the faith of the astute in the security provided by the actual possession of rare and beautiful objects.

The smart-money investors in recent years continue with renewed intensity to seek out the traditional havens afforded by precious metals and rare objects. The big-money men showed a definite tendency to shun bank deposits, insurance policies, and bonds and to limit their stock market activities to purely speculative ventures such as puts and calls or straddles. But they invested heavily in paintings, antiques, art objects, rare books and manuscripts, stamps and coins.[1]

Of all these traditional store-of-value objects, I believe the gold coin is best suited to survive and succeed as an investment during

the period of great monetary uncertainty we are about to enter—
indeed, that we have already entered. Because they combine the
merits of rare and beautiful objects and the virtues of the most
precious of metals, gold coins, when prudently purchased, provide
the ultimate in safety: protection against both inflation and depression. It is an important consideration. If we remember our brief
review of monetary history, we will recall that after every inflationary "blow-off" there followed a painful return to reality. Most of
the excess credit and purchasing media had to be wiped out in order
to bring back economic efficiency and sanity. Whether it was done
with the bonfires of eighteenth-century France or through the bankruptcy courts of the 1930s, the results were the same: a so-called
reorganization crisis followed by a long period of economic
stagnation.

This, however, is certain: during the reorganization period, the
currency is always devalued in terms of gold. The new "noninflationary" currency will be refixed to gold at a substantially higher
price than was the old money before the inflation became uncon-
trollable. The holder of gold coins, providing he has allowed for
significant intrinsic value in his collection, will come through with
his investment intact, if not actually appreciated in value. Although
he might lose part of his gain in numismatic value, because of the
economic stagnation and depression, it will be offset by the gains
in intrinsic value from devaluation. (I must add that any slowdown
or retreat in numismatic values will be temporary. If the past is any
guide, the very long-term trend for coins of proven numismatic
value is definitely up, even in a stable economy.)

But the holders of speculative real estate, stocks (except for gold-
mining stocks), and other typical inflation hedges face, it seems to
me, a most impossible dilemma. If they sell out too soon, they will
simply be stuck with a lot of inflated paper, which may eventually
lose most of its value anyway. On the other hand, if they wait until
after the collapse and reorganization, they may find their property
falling disastrously in value and unsalable due to depression or
general stagnation of business.

I have predicted previously that inflation would continue *until our economy reaches the point of complete disorganization and collapse.* At what point that will come, unfortunately I cannot tell you. I can only deal in probabilities. It is my opinion that the present inflation cycle still has some distance to go before economic life becomes impossible. We have not yet begun the whole wretched business of wage and price controls, exchange restrictions, travel bans, and similar idiocies of totalitarian economics. The dollar will be devalued shortly, but that may not necessarily be the end of it. Unless devaluation is accompanied by complete monetary reform aimed at creating a sound banking and money system, the inflation will simply be resumed and continue to the point where still another devaluation is forced upon us (such has been the history of England, for example).

Furthermore, the United States just might succeed in turning the International Monetary Fund into a worldwide engine of inflation. Obviously our paper-gold schemes are really intended eventually to convert the IMF into a kind of international version of our own Federal Reserve System[2]—a system that has proven a most pliable tool in the hands of our New Economics money managers. We may yet go the way of South America, with its endless succession of devaluations.

Other possibilities must also be faced. The coming devaluation of the dollar may just be enough *in itself* to bring about serious world economic disorder. International trade may be drastically reduced as a result of the initial shock and monetary uncertainty, and, just as in the 1930s, rampant protectionism and the imposition of severe exchange controls would be sure to follow. Then to be considered are the present perilous overextensions in consumer installment debt, personal and corporate mortgages, and municipal, state and federal borrowing (not to mention the stock market).

A Few Basic Rules

If we are going to follow the smart money into gold coins, we would be well advised to acquaint ourselves with the basic rules of numismatic investment. The great collections of recent years, like the Willis du Pont and Josiah K. Lilly aggregations, were assembled with great care and under the most competent numismatic supervision. Since most of us will not be able to afford the services of professional numismatic advisers, or will not, like some millionaires, be able simply to turn an amount of money over to a professional numismatist or dealer and let him build a collection for us,[3] we will have to study and learn for ourselves. It is not difficult, and most entertaining.

Let us take first the matter of grading. In numismatics, the condition and appearance of a coin are of great importance. Collectors understandably want their coins to be as near perfect as possible; esthetics is an important factor in coin collecting. Therefore, the highest prices are paid for the most perfectly appearing coins of each specific type or date.

Unfortunately, there is no recognized uniform system of grading. But there is a generally accepted and workable vocabulary, in spite of minor variations. For example, the terminology preferred by R. S. Yeoman's famous and authoritative *Guide Book of United States Coins*, or Redbook, is as follows:

Redbook Grading System

PF.	*Proof*	Coin with a mirrorlike surface, specially struck for coin collectors.
UNC.	*Uncirculated*	New. Regular mint striking, but never placed in circulation.
EX. FINE	*Extremely Fine* ...	Slightly circulated, with some luster, but faint evidence of wear.
V. FINE	*Very Fine*	Shows enough wear on high spots to be noticeable. Still retains enough luster to be desirable.
F.	*Fine*	Obviously a circulated coin, but little wear. Mint luster gone. All letters and mottoes clear.
V.G.	*Very Good*	Features clear and bold. Better than good, but not quite fine.
G.	*Good*	All of design, every feature and legend must be plain and date clear.
FAIR	*Fair*	Coin has sufficient design and letters to be easily identified. Excessive wear.

However, Yeoman's practice is not consistently followed by most dealers and advertisers. They usually prefer a more complex table of description, a table that may seem downright hairsplitting compared with the Redbook. But this is the descriptive table we will most often see in general use, and consequently most often have to deal with:

General Grading Table[4]

PR.	*Proof*	Coin with an extremely sharp and vivid impression and a mirrorlike background, specially struck for collectors.
P.L.	*Prooflike*	An uncirculated coin so perfect and sharply struck that it resembles a proof.
Ch. B.U.	*Choice Brilliant Uncirculated*	A brilliant uncirculated coin in near perfect condition, perhaps with a very minimum of "bag marks" and minor abrasions.
B.U.	*Brilliant Uncirculated*	Just what the name implies: an uncirculated coin in brilliant mint condition. (A few minor abrasions or "bag marks" are permitted on BU coins.)
A.U.	*Almost Uncirculated*	A coin showing only very little wear, perhaps the minimum discernible.
X.F.	*Extremely Fine* . .	Only slightly circulated. Very fine hairlines partly obliterated.
V.F.	*Very Fine*	Noticeable wear on high spots.
F.	*Fine*	Obviously circulated but letters and mottoes still clear.
V.G.	*Very Good*	Features clear and still bold. Between good and fine.
G.	*Good*	Design features and legends and date clear, but not sharp.
FAIR	*Fair*	Worn but enough of design and lettering left to be identified.

Some numismatists insist that no such descriptions as "Choice BU" or "Strict BU" are possible; to them, a coin is either BU or it isn't. They contend that BU implies a nearly perfect condition; anything less must be AU. Perhaps a case can be made for terms such as "Choice" or "Strict" BU, but I contend that *any coin offered as BU must be absolutely uncirculated*, with full mint luster or "frosty" appearance. If you insist on absolutely no "bag marks" or minor abrasions on your coins, then go ahead and pay the premiums (and they will be premiums!) for choice or prooflike coins.

As for coins that are less than BU, obviously it may sometimes be difficult to draw the line, say, between AU and XF, or between XF and VF. Some cynics have suggested that the AU coin is AU when you buy it from a dealer, but XF when you try to sell it. Such difficulties can most easily be avoided by always purchasing your coins from dealers of established reputation. Most nationally known dealers, including those who do a sizable mail-order business, are scrupulously careful in maintaining their reputations. They want not only to gain your business, but to keep it, and the only way they can accomplish this is to be fair and honest at all times. You will seldom if ever have trouble of any kind if you do business with a reputable dealer, national or local. If you have any doubt, investigate before you buy.

As a basic rule I would say, *buy BU coins whenever you can.* However, coins in BU or even AU condition are not always available in certain dates and types. In some cases, XF or even F is the highest grade for a particular coin that is generally available. But if you have a choice, that is, if you can buy a BU coin for only a few dollars more than the same coin in AU or XF, by all means take the BU. Understandably, collectors always prefer the most perfect coin they can get, and your BU coins will always have prime numismatic value.

Of course, if you are interested only in bullion, you will buy the lowest grade coins you can get, but this is not as easy as it sounds. Common–date gold coins are seldom available in grades lower than XF, or perhaps VF; most of the lower grades, having little or no numismatic value, were melted down long ago. In any case, I do not recommend buying coins only for bullion; there is not enough price advantage in buying inferior coins, or coins without any numismatic value, to make it worthwhile. Numismatic values are always too important to overlook, and will be of even greater significance in any future wave of hyperinflation.

Having briefly reviewed grading, one of the key factors of numismatic value, let us now consider the question of intrinsic value. The weight of pure or "fine" gold is always determined in terms of troy ounces and pounds, rather than the more familiar "avoirdupois" system that is used for nearly all other commodities. There are only 12 troy ounces to the troy pound compared with 16 ounces to the avoirdupois pound, but the troy pound is slightly heavier than the avoirdupois. Then there is the matter of grains and grams. Modern gold coins are frequently identified by weight in terms of grams, which are units of the metric system, as well as the older grains, typical of troy measure. The term "pennyweight" (abbreviated, dwt.) is also used in the troy system, although usually in reference only to minor coins. The overall relationship between the units of troy measure, the metric system, and the avoirdupois weights can best be illustrated by the chart, Figure 6. The troy system itself is defined as follows:

Troy Weight

24 grains — 1 pennyweight (dwt.)
20 dwt. — (480 grains)—1 ounce (oz.)
12 oz. — 1 pound

The percentage of gold to other metal in a coin, or its "fineness," is usually expressed as a decimal (normally carried to a minimum of three places). U.S. standard gold coins, for example, are 90 percent gold and 10 percent alloy—or .900 fine.

The addition of silver to gold lightens its yellow color, but a copper content gives gold a deeper, more reddish hue than is typical of pure gold. A small amount of copper (usually 10 percent or less) is nearly always added to gold used for coinage in order to increase its hardness. Pure gold is too soft for efficient coinage use, although some ancient coins were made of pure or almost pure gold.[5] The chemical symbols for the metals most common to coinage are:

Au — Gold
Ag — Silver
Cu — Copper

Fig. 6

COMPARISON OF WEIGHTS

Kilograms	Grams	Grains	Avoirdupois Pounds	Avoirdupois Ounce	Troy Pound	Troy Ounce
1.	1,000.	15,432.36	2.20462225	35.27396	2.679229	32.15075
.001	1.	15.43236	.002204622	.03527396	.002679229	.03215072
.00006479	.064798	1.	.000142857	.002285	.000173611	.002083
.45359237	453.59237	7,000.	1.	16.	1.215	14.58333
.02834952	28.3495	437.5	.0625	1.	.07595486	.911458
.3732417	373.242	5,760.	.82285716	13.16568	1.	12.
.03110348	31.1035	480.	.06857143	1.097	.08333	1.

Notes:

1. Both the avoirdupois and troy weights developed from traditional English usage.
2. The metric system was originated in France at the end of the eighteenth century.
3. The metric system was legalized in the United States in 1866, and can be used in addition to or as a substitute for the English-derived U.S. standard weights that are in regular use.

Chemically "pure" gold is 1.000 fine (it is very difficult to obtain and seldom exists outside the laboratory). Most commercial and monetary gold is "three–nine" gold or .999 fine, pure enough for most practical uses. Fineness can also be expressed in terms of karats (abbreviated, k.).* This ancient but less precise terminology is generally preferred by jewelers and goldsmiths. The relationship between fineness and karat is:

Fineness	Karat	Percent of Gold
1.000	24.	100
.900	21.6	90
.800	19.2	80
.700	16.8	70
.600	14.4	60
.500	12.	50
.400	9.6	40
.300	7.2	30
.200	4.8	20
.100	2.4	10

British standard gold coinage (modern) is 22 k., or 91.67 percent Au, 8.33 percent Cu, or .9167 fine.

The standard gold coinage of the United States, France, Germany, Italy, Mexico (after 1905), Switzerland, and the majority of other nations that adhered to the international gold standard after 1830 was .900 fine or 21.6 k.

American gold coins are made from an alloy of 90 percent gold, 7.5 percent copper, and 2.5 percent silver. It was found that the addition of a small percentage of silver was necessary to preserve the true color of natural gold. The use of an all-copper alloy gives gold coins better wearing qualities, but it is also inclined to give them a distinctly reddish cast. Our coinage laws originally provided that the alloy part of U.S. gold coins should consist of not more than one-half silver, but in actual practice it was determined that one-quarter silver was the ideal mixture.

Early Spanish American and Mexican gold coins (*escudos*) were

---

* The word *carat* is equally appropriate, but the abbreviation remains the same.

usually made with an all-silver alloy, and consequently look quite pale. Some of the European and other foreign gold coins, particularly among the more modern issues, are made with an all-copper alloy, which gives them a noticeably red appearance.

U.S. gold coins come closest perhaps to preserving the natural color of pure gold, although most of the Mexican decimal series gold coins and the majority of European issues are very similar in appearance. But there are detectable variations in color and tone among various types of gold coins, even though these differences are often quite subtle.

A Few Basic Tools

The list of equipment and supplies required by the gold-coin collector is mercifully brief (excluding, of course, the numismatic library). A small magnifying glass of at least three power (3 ×) will be very useful. The 2″ × 2″ plastic coin holders are readily available at coin stores and can be obtained in sizes that will accommodate most gold coins (although not all of them will fit exactly, buy the size that most nearly fits).[6] Heavy cardboard or plastic file boxes are also available for the 2″ × 2″ holders, and being narrow they fit nicely into the standard document-type safe-deposit box.

A small scale, capable of weighing precisely in terms of grams and grains, although not necessary for the average collector, will prove helpful and entertaining, especially if you become interested in ancient or some of the older and less well known European coins. The kind of scale formerly used by druggists, chemists, and photographers will do.[7] It does not need to be a troy scale, as long as it can be used to determine weight in grams and decimals of a gram. (Note: The apothecaries' weights are similar to the troy system: 480 grains to the ounce; 12 ounces to the pound.)

A small steel rule, divided into millimeters and centimeters, will prove handy, especially for those equipped with a scale. Coins are always described by diameter and thickness in terms of millimeters.

As the writer has his thesaurus and the banker his interest tables, the collector of gold coins requires a few basic reference catalogues. For those intending to concentrate solely on the coins of the United States, the aforementioned Redbook will probably be adequate to begin with. But if you decide to include foreign coins among your interests (and I think you will eventually find it profitable to do so), the basic reference is Robert Friedberg's *Gold Coins of the World*, 2nd ed. (New York: Coin and Currency Institute, 1965). It took Mr. Friedberg, author and internationally known numismatist, five years of the most painstaking effort to research and compile this catalogue, which illustrates and gives an approximate valuation for *every* known gold coin minted from A.D. 600 to 1965. It is a beautiful book; by all means add it to your library.

Another excellent and beautifully done catalogue, this one specializing in European gold coins struck since 1800 (which are probably the only European coins most gold collectors will need a reference to), is Hans Schlumberger's *Gold Coins of Europe since 1800* (New York: Sterling Publishing Co., 1968). This recent volume contains mintage figures and approximate valuations (as of 1967–68) for all European gold coins minted from 1800 to 1968. All coin types and the principal variations are illustrated. This book also makes an attractive and valuable addition to any numismatic library, and I highly recommend it. I think it would be essential for any collector–investor planning to include European gold coins among his interests.

The coin valuations shown in the catalogues just cited will of course be helpful in a general way, but we will obviously not be able to rely on them to guide our day-to-day collecting program. Coin prices, to be meaningful, must be as current as possible, and immediacy is hardly possible in a hard-cover book, even in an annual such as the Redbook. The best source for current price data (as well as a mine of general numismatic information) is our weekly contact with the numismatic press. Both the comparison of dealers' ads and the news reports of current auction results are enough to keep the average collector sufficiently informed of price trends.[8]

But there is still another excellent source of price trend information available to the serious collector–investor. Stack's, Inc., the noted New York dealer and coin auction house (123 West 57 Street, New York, N.Y. 10019), provides a unique service: it will mail you the catalogue for every auction it conducts, and will follow it up with a list of prices realized. The fee for this program is only $5.00 annually, and Stack's includes with it a copy of all other items of numismatic literature it publishes during the year, including six issues of a very interesting numismatic journal. In addition, you will have the opportunity to submit bids by mail on the items in the auction catalogues.

Many other auction houses and dealers who conduct auctions frequently will no doubt be happy to send you catalogues, bid sheets, and lists of prices realized. Usually there is a small charge for this service, or for the individual catalogues, but it is worth it, even if you don't bid very often. The catalogues themselves are often so beautifully done that you may find yourself keeping many of them as permanent reference material in your library.

Having touched the bases at least of grading,[9] intrinsic weight, and price information, the reader is hopefully ready to direct his interests to specific coins. The best place to start is with the gold coins of the United States. For a variety of reasons, as we shall see, the gold coins of the United States should be well represented in, if not the basic part of, every gold-coin collection.

Notes

CHAPTER VI

1. *Wall Street Journal*, Jan. 1, 1968.
2. See Francis Cassell, *Gold or Credit?* (New York: Praeger, 1965), for a survey of various proposals for a world central bank.
3. Such as Stack's "Executive Collection Plan." (Stack's built the Josiah K. Lilly collection.)
4. Compiled from various issues of *Coin World* and various dealers' catalogues.

5. The *bezant* was .975 fine; the florin was 100 percent gold, as were the gold coins of France before 1400. Most of the U.S. Pioneer pieces were virgin gold (natural purity).

6. Plastic holders are available at present in exact sizes to fit all regular U.S. gold coinage. Always keep your coins in protective holders to guard against accidental injury.

7. I found a small scale in a secondhand shop for $2.50 (some time ago!). However, professional quality troy scales can also be purchased new from most dealers in scientific instruments or from specialists in mining and prospecting supplies. A wide selection of models is generally available at reasonable prices.

8. Understanding any market is mainly mastering its price structure and trends. Suggestion: keep a weekly record of price changes in coins you are interested in.

9. For a comprehensive, illustrated, and detailed review of numismatic grading standards for U.S. coins, see Brown and Dunn, *A Guide to the Grading of United States Coins* (Racine, Wis.: Whitman Division, 1968).

VII

Gold Coins of the United States

"Money is, in its effects and laws, as beautiful as roses."
—RALPH WALDO EMERSON

THE MONETARY SYSTEM OF THE UNITED STATES HAS BEEN, throughout its history, constructed more by expedient and accident than by calculation and foresight. In this characteristic it parallels the monetary history of the world. The earliest settlers of British North America had little immediate use for coined money. Their modest commerce could be carried out quite satisfactorily by the barter of agricultural products, beaver skins, tobacco, musket balls, Indian wampum, etc.[1] But as soon as the population grew larger and stable enough to support the rudiments of urban civilization, the need for a more effective money mechanism became acutely apparent.

Traders arriving from Europe began demanding coined money for the manufactured goods they brought. In turn, the colonists readily accepted and used nearly all foreign coins that came to them in the course of their own expanding commerce. The French *louis*, English *guineas*, German *thalers*, Dutch *ducats*, Portuguese *moidores* and, most predominant of all, Spanish milled silver dollars, or "pieces of eight,"[2] eventually became integral parts of the colonial money system. The colonists had to make do with this haphazard accumulation; the inept British governments of the time did little or nothing to establish an efficient monetary system for their American possessions.[3]

During the American Revolution, the Second Continental Congress tried to finance the costs of the war with issues of paper money. The government itself was too poor in coin and bullion to permit the issuance of any substantial amount of specie, and it hesitated to impose high taxes in support of a cause that hardly enjoyed universal popularity at the time. On May 10, 1775, the first issue of paper "continentals" was authorized in an amount equal to two million Spanish silver dollars.[4] As usual, the process had to be repeated many times during the course of the war. Over $240 million (face value) were eventually issued. The depreciation of the continental was rapid, and all coins were quickly driven out of circulation in the usual response to Gresham's Law.

Historically anticipating the French *assignat* debacle that was to come only a decade later, the continental paper currency at once set off a most profligate and destructive inflation. By 1780, coffee was $12 a pound and flour $150 a barrel.[5] To make matters worse, additional fiat paper notes were issued by individual states. People who accepted and held large quantities of continentals were ruined. "Not worth a continental" became a popular expression (an expression that survived for decades as part of the colorful American idiom) for describing objects and ideas totally without value or merit. By 1781 paper currency had ceased entirely to be accepted as money. The Continental Government and the fate of the United States itself were saved only by timely loans of hard money from France.

During the early post-Revolutionary period, however, an isolated attempt was made to originate a true American gold coinage, and this attempt resulted in the most unique and valuable specimens in American numismatics known today. In 1787 Ephraim Brasher, a well known goldsmith and jeweler, and nextdoor neighbor of George Washington in New York, produced a trial gold piece weighing 408 grains, approximately equal to the Spanish gold doubloon of the period. It is not known how many of these so-called "Brasher doubloons" were struck (there is only one known date: 1787), but only a very few have survived. They are now the most highly prized American coins in existence, and values as high as $100,000 have been placed on a single Brasher doubloon. Brasher also struck a half-doubloon by using his doubloon die with a planchet (metal blank) of reduced size. A specimen of the Brasher half-doubloon is now in the Smithsonian Institution's massive numismatic collection. The Brasher gold pieces were never recognized or authorized by any government body, but from their appearance it is evident that they might well have influenced the subsequent excellent design of America's first official gold coinage.

After the United States made good her independence, much debate and study were expended on the problem of establishing an efficient monetary system for the new nation, but it was not until 1792 that an act was passed establishing the first U.S. mint at Philadelphia. A further act of 1792 made the dollar the monetary unit of the U.S. and authorized the minting of the following coinage:

Fig. 7
ORIGINAL U.S. COINAGE AS ESTABLISHED IN 1792

Coin	Value	Grains Pure	Grains Standard
Gold Eagle	$10.00	247.50	270.
Gold Half Eagle	5.00	123.75	135.
Gold Quarter Eagle	2.50	61.875	67.5
Silver Dollar	1.00	371.25	416.
Silver Half Dollar	.50	185.625	208.
Silver Quarter Dollar	.25	92.8125	104.
Silver Disme (Dime)	.10	37.125	41.6
Silver Half Disme	.05	18.5625	20.8
Copper Cent	.01	11 dwt.	
Copper Half Cent	.005	5.5 dwt.	

Notes:
1. Pure means the unalloyed metal.
2. Standard is the total weight of coin.

The fineness of our first gold coins was established at 22 karat or .9166 fine. The law also provided for the "free coinage" of bullion, that is, anyone depositing gold or silver bullion with the mint was entitled to receive in exchange coins of equal weight in grains pure of the metal deposited.[6]

From its beginning, the monetary system of the United States encountered major difficulties. The new American silver dollars could too easily be exchanged for worn Spanish dollars and other European silver and exported or melted at a profit. Our gold coins were also undervalued and subject to attacks by speculators, who turned a fast profit exporting them to Europe as bullion. After 1804, the minting of the $10 Eagle had to be suspended entirely. Coinage of silver dollars had to be stopped that year also. Most of the lesser denominations were frequently hoarded. Altogether, American coinage from 1792 to 1834 achieved only negligible circulation. Underweight foreign gold coins, miscellaneous foreign silver, and a great variety of private bank notes became the *de facto* currency of the United States during this period. The so-called wildcat private bank notes especially flooded the country and were far more common than coin.[7]

A law of 1834 partly relieved the situation by reducing the fineness of U.S. gold coins to .8955 and slightly altering their standard weights. But it was the general revision of the coinage laws, completed in 1837, that finally stabilized both gold and silver coins at .900 fine (where they remained until their respective ends in 1933 and 1965). Other desirable changes were also made in the U.S. monetary system at this time, including the establishment of branch mints at Dahlonega, Georgia, and Charlotte, North Carolina, to handle the coinage of gold close to its principal sources. The mintage of the $10 Eagle was resumed in 1838, and a branch mint at New Orleans was opened in that year.

The discovery of gold in California in 1848 gave great impetus to the minting of U.S. gold coins. It was responsible for some of our most interesting and historic gold pieces, the so-called Pioneer or Territorial gold coinage. These private issues, intended for local, state, and territorial use, were originally designed to meet emergency needs for coinage in booming frontier areas. They are today among the most highly valued of American numismatic items. The following table (Fig. 8) includes the best known of these "private" issues.[8]

Fig. 8

U.S. PIONEER GOLD COINAGE

Minting Agency	Denominations	Dates
Baldwin & Co., San Francisco, Calif.	$5, $10, $20	1850–51
Christopher & August Bechtler, Rutherford, N. Carolina	$1, $2½, $5	1830–52
Clark & Gruber, Denver, Colorado	$2½, $5, $10, $20	1860–61
Augustus Humbert, U.S. Assayer of Gold, San Francisco, Calif.	$10, $20, $50	1851–52
Kellogg & Co., San Francisco, Calif.	$20, $50	1854–55
Moffatt & Co., San Francisco, Calif.	$5, $10, $20	1849–53
Mormon Territory Gov't., Salt Lake City, Utah	$2½, $5, $10, $20	1849–60
United States Assay Office of Gold, San Francisco, Calif.	$10, $20, $50	1852–53
Wass, Molitor & Co., San Francisco, Calif.	$5, $10, $20, $50	1852–55

Notes:

1. Augustus Humbert was official U.S. assayer at San Francisco. He also placed his name and stamp on the coins of Moffat & Co.
2. United States Assay Office of Gold was a private company, actually a successor to Moffat & Co.
3. Small stamped ingots of Pioneer gold are also extant, but they are very rare and highly valued (see Redbook).
4. This list is by no means complete; there are still other items of Territorial and Pioneer gold that are even more rare and unique than the above and consequently they are even more expensive and difficult to obtain (see Redbook).

California Small Denomination Gold.   Gold quarters, halves, and dollars were also privately struck in California during the gold rush to relieve the chronic shortage of "small change" that resulted from the relative isolation of the West. Various private mints turned out these diminutive coins from 1852 until 1882, when the U.S. government passed a law forbidding all private coinage. Both round and octagonal coins are known in each of the 25-cent, 50-cent, and $1.00 denominations (see Redbook).

The Gold Dollar and the Double Eagle. In 1849, two new gold coins became part of the U.S. currency: the gold dollar and the $20 double Eagle. The gold dollar was minted through 1889, but the double Eagle continued to be struck in quantity until its end in 1933, and it perhaps became America's best-known (certainly our best-preserved) gold coin.

A branch mint was established in San Francisco in 1854, and this act ended the need for most of the Pioneer issues.

Three-Dollar Gold. A $3 gold coin was authorized in 1853. It was hardly a necessary or popular coin but it was, like the gold dollar, issued regularly through 1889. But although issued on a regular basis during these years, it was never minted in large quantities. Consequently, the $3 coins are quite rare today and all dates have a high numismatic value.

The Civil War and the Greenbacks. At the outbreak of the Civil War, coins became scarce. During this emergency, the United States in effect went off the gold standard,[9] when Congress authorized the issue of $450 million in United States notes—the so-called greenbacks. These notes were issued with the understanding that they would be redeemed and retired as soon as the emergency was ended. Nevertheless, the greenbacks depreciated to such an extent that by July 1864, $100 in greenbacks was worth only $35 in gold.[10] In gold-rich California, people refused entirely to accept greenbacks. The greenbacks eventually were made fully convertible, but not until 1879 and then only over the vociferous objections of the inflationist Greenback party, which was organized in 1876 to advocate further issues of government fiat paper. But the greenbacks never were actually retired; under provisions included in the redemption law of 1879, they were reissued as fast as they were redeemed and therefore allowed to circulate indefinitely.[11]

The South of course was on a pure fiat money basis from the beginning, and the Confederate paper currency suffered a ruinous depreciation, eventually becoming worthless. But all coin, North as well as South, virtually disappeared during the war years. Fractional paper notes (shinplasters) and postage stamps had to substitute for small change.

The Carson City and Denver Mints.   In 1870, a branch mint was opened at Carson City, Nevada, to facilitate the coinage of the great new silver and gold deposits of Nevada and the Central West. The Carson City mint remained in operation until 1893, and provided numismatists with the rarest and generally the most valued mint mark on U.S. coins. In 1906, coinage functions in the West were renewed by the opening of a new branch mint in Denver, Colorado.

The Four-Dollar Gold "Stella."   The most unusual and certainly one of the rarest of the gold–coin types of the U.S. was the $4 Stella of 1879 and 1880. There may be some question whether these coins can be regarded as a legitimate issue, as they were only minted as trial pieces and existed solely in proof condition. They were never minted for circulation. But collectors have apparently no doubt about their numismatic value; the going rate for Stellas starts at $6,000 and goes to $17,000. There were two distinct types struck in both years of minting. One was the design by Barber in which the young lady (Miss Liberty) on the obverse wore her hair in flowing style, and the other was a design by Morgan showing her with coiled hair. Of the latter, there were only 20 struck, so don't worry too much about not having one. Incidentally, the title "Stella" comes not from the young lady's name, but from the star design on the reverse, which bears the inscription: "One Stella $4.00" (Stella, from Latin meaning star).

The Golden Age: 1900–1932.   During the remainder of the nineteenth century, the U.S. Treasury experienced recurring difficulties trying to maintain full convertibility for the various issues of government paper that had come into existence. In addition to the greenbacks, there were then silver certificates and Treasury notes of 1890.[12] The Gold Standard Act of 1900 finally made it official that all forms of United States currency were to be maintained at full parity with gold and to be fully convertible into gold coin or bullion.

But the golden age did not last long; just a little over 32 years later, in the midst of another national crisis, the worst since 1860, President Franklin Roosevelt issued, on March 5, 1933, a "Proclamation of National Emergency," which temporarily suspended all banking operations, ended the minting of gold coins, prohibited all further transactions in gold coin or gold certificates, and forced the surrender of most privately held gold coin and bullion to the Federal Reserve System by threatening prison for the holders on the grounds of "hoarding."*

An Emergency Banking Act passed on March 9, 1933, gave Congressional sanction to the measures taken by the President, and under this act, on April 5, 1933, regulations were issued permitting the limited use of refined gold for certain industrial and technical purposes and allowing the private possession of "rare and unusual gold coins of special value to collectors." There were further technical changes and orders regarding gold issued during the remainder of 1933, and in January 1934 the passage of the Gold Reserve Act formally ended the era of gold coinage in the United States, an era that had lasted (with occasional interruptions) for 96 years. Gold coins were demonetized, gold was nationalized and made a government monopoly and the "defined" dollar was devalued from $20.67 to $35.00 per ounce troy of gold.

That very briefly is the monetary history of the United States as it concerns our regular gold coinage. But there are further matters concerning U.S. gold coins that deserve our attention.

U.S. Gold Commemorative Coins. Outside of its regular issues, the U.S. government produced a brief series of gold commemorative coins celebrating certain historical and topical events. They consisted of nine gold–dollar types, two quarter Eagles, and two types of the only $50 coin ever struck by the U.S. mint. All U.S. commemorative gold pieces were minted in quite limited quantities, and they are now, understandably, of very high numismatic value.

---

* The authority for these orders was derived from an old wartime law of October 6, 1917, which had never been repealed, and which gave the President complete control over all banking and currency transactions during periods of national emergency.

Fig. 9

U.S. COMMEMORATIVE GOLD

Date	Commemoration	Quantity Minted
*1903	Louisiana Purchase Jefferson Dollar	17,500
*1903	Louisiana Purchase McKinley Dollar	17,500
1904	Lewis and Clark Exposition Dollar	10,025
1905	Lewis and Clark Exposition Dollar	10,041
1915s	Panama-Pacific $50 Round	483
1915s	Panama-Pacific $50 Octagonal	645
1915s	Panama-Pacific Exposition $2.50	6,749
1915s	Panama-Pacific Exposition Dollar	15,000
1916	McKinley Memorial Dollar	9,977
1917	McKinley Memorial Dollar	10,000
1922	Grant Memorial Dollar (with star)	5,016
1922	Grant Memorial Dollar (without star)	5,000
1926	Philadelphia Sesquicentennial $2.50	46,019

*Proofs were also struck

Mint Marks.   U.S. coins struck at any of the branch mints bear a small identifying initial, usually on the reverse. This mint mark is found *only* on coins struck at branch mints; the coins of the main Philadelphia mint are unmarked.[13] (However, some dealers describe Philadelphia coins by adding the letter *P* after the date—why this redundancy I don't know.) The letters identifying the various mints are as follows:

C—Charlotte, North Carolina	(1838–1861)
CC—Carson City, Nevada	(1870–1893)
D—Dahlonega, Georgia	(1838–1861)
D—Denver, Colorado	(after 1906)
O—New Orleans, Louisiana	(1838–1909)
S—San Francisco, California	(after 1854)

Note:
    See Redbook for exact location of mint mark on specific coins.

Mint marks are very important to some collectors of U.S. coins, because coinage at branch mints has nearly always been smaller than at Philadelphia. Many branch mint coins are consequently quite rare. Nevertheless, my advice concerning mint marks is this:

do not pay high premiums for coins *only because of rare mint marks*. The value placed on a rare mint mark is, in my opinion, a type of numismatic value that is most vulnerable to reconsideration (and downward adjustment) at any time, especially if there is a deflationary period, a recession, or even a temporary slackening in the inflationary outlook. The risk in paying high prices for rare mint marks on otherwise common coins is just too great; it is much safer and wiser to seek out rare *dates* in coins before rare mint marks, and rare *types* ahead of rare dates. If you can get a rare mint mark for a reasonable premium over what you would pay for the same date plain—fine. But don't pay a great price for it. To take a specific example, one would be wiser to spend $250 or so on a U.S. $3 gold piece than an equivalent sum on a $20 double Eagle whose premium value depended solely on a rare mint mark.

The U.S. gold coins the typical collector–investor will most commonly encounter, and therefore should become the most familiar with, are those series and types shown in Figure 10.

Fig. 10

REGULAR U.S. GOLD COINAGE, 1838–1933

$20	Double Eagle	Liberty Head	1849–1907
$20	Double Eagle	St. Gaudens Type	1907–1932
$10	Eagle	Liberty Head	1838–1907
$10	Eagle	Indian Head	1907–1933
$ 5	Half Eagle	Liberty Head	1839–1908
$ 5	Half Eagle	Indian Head	1908–1929
$ 2½	Quarter Eagle	Liberty Head	1840–1907
$ 2½	Quarter Eagle	Indian Head	1908–1929
*$ 1	Gold Dollar	Liberty Head	1849–1854
*$ 1	Gold Dollar	Indian Head	1854–1889

* I hesitated before including gold dollars as part of the *regular* coinage, as they are now quite scarce, but their mintage was fairly large (at least for a gold coin) in some years. But there was no hesitation regarding the $3 gold; nearly all were of very small mintage and are definitely *rare*.

There are a number of minor design variations in each of these regular-series coins, and of course a variety of mint marks as well as a wide range of dates and mintages. All of these things understandably contribute to large differences in numismatic value. A

quick perusal of the Redbook will adequately illustrate these variations and the resulting wide range of prices for different coins in the
same series. Numismatic values are not specific; they are a compound of many intangibles. Consequently it is difficult to describe
exactly what constitutes numismatic value. In chapter one we
touched on the psychology of collecting—the mysterious attraction
to objects that are rare and beautiful. Certainly, scarcity, historic
association, and artistic merit are essential factors in determining
numismatic values. But how are these things to be translated,
reasonably and consistently, into currency of account—into dollars,
francs, pounds or marks? The answer obviously is by observing the
action of the market itself.

The Market as a Guide to Value .

In a free auction market (and we must include what we have
previously described as the coin market as a free and open auction
market) buyers and sellers meet and determine prices strictly according to the ancient laws of supply and demand; this is the
essence and virtue of a free market. Values are established and then
tested again and again in the cauldron of the market place. It is
this lengthy seasoning, the constant testing and reappraisal, that
eventually determines true value. It takes time.

An old saw in the stock market says: "A stock is worth exactly
what it is selling for." Whether a stock is being underestimated or
overestimated, undervalued or overvalued, makes no difference; the
only thing that has validity is the most recent selling price, or the
most recent bid; all else is mere conjecture. The same is true of
the price of a rare coin.

Another piece of Wall Street wisdom states: "Once a trend has
been established it tends to continue." In other words, once prices
begin to move consistently in one direction, the odds are that they
will continue to move in that direction, until this trend is opposed
by some very strong (and usually unexpected) counterforce. It is
also recognized that the longer a specific trend has existed, the more
validity it has; that is, the greater the odds that it will continue. It

is also said that "prices [like nearly everything else in life] move in the direction of the least resistance." This principle applies as aptly to a rare coin as to a stock. I might add here, don't be anxious to buy anything that is "easy" to buy, that is being offered frequently, and at price concessions, by a number of dealers simultaneously. On the other hand, items that are "hard to buy," coins that dealers have a difficult time finding or keeping in stock, items that are sold out quickly whenever they are advertised, coins you must query several major dealers to find offered, almost always are sound investments.[14]

A further axiom of investment that applies to the coin market is this: always invest in things of *proven value*. Buy items that have demonstrated their worth over and over again in the market place. Don't buy anything of promised numismatic value unless it has been thoroughly tested and retested by actual sales (including auctions) over a period of months, and preferably years. Don't accept merely the advertising of a single dealer or even several dealers, or the results of a single auction. Before buying a high-priced coin of supposedly great numismatic or historical value, make sure it has a market history—preferably a long market history. When you are urged to buy rare coins of supposedly great numismatic value, remember that *value*, in the words of Justice Brandeis, "is a word of many meanings." Monetary value can be established only in the open market; and it takes time.

There is little more one can say definitely about the intangibles that are embodied in numismatic value. Perhaps the following five points best sum up the certainties to be remembered:

1. A rare coin is worth exactly what it can be sold for, or what is currently being bid for it—no more, no less.
2. Once a definite price trend is established, it tends to continue; the longer the trend has existed, the more reliable it is.
3. Prices tend to move in the direction of the least resistance; past market history indicates what this direction *has been*.
4. The best and safest investments in rare coins are those that have proven their monetary value by repeated tests in the market over a long period of time.

5. When a particular coin consistently is hard to buy, it indicates that demand is greater than the supply and that its price will probably rise.

What I have said in this chapter concerning judgment of the numismatic value of U.S. gold coins goes double for European and other foreign coins, and triple for ancient golds.

Of the principal factors that contribute to numismatic value—scarcity, historic association, sentimental remembrance, and artistic merit—the number-one factor is scarcity; but don't jump to a conclusion. There are far more subtle things involved in the value of a truly rare coin than just scarcity. There are, for example, many foreign and ancient coins that are very scarce and even unique, but they do not sell for a fraction of the price of a Stella or an 1875 proof $3 gold. The late Jim Kelly[15] once told a story about a noted American dealer who possessed a great rarity, a huge gold coin of India, struck to commemorate the wedding of a prince. Two specimens were struck, one for the maharaja and one for the maharani; then the die was broken in their presence. When asked how much the coin was worth, the dealer replied, "Slightly over bullion." "You see," he continued, "only one person known to me collects this type of material, and he already owns the other coin."

The lesson here is elementary. It is not only how scarce an item is, but how many people want to possess it that counts. In short, we are driven back to our original thesis that only the action of the market itself—the inexorable operation of the law of supply and demand—is a reliable guide to value.

The combination of conscious and subconscious, sentimental, historic, and economic associations that gives rise to demand will never be adequately rationalized, but that in itself is of no great consequence to the numismatic investor; it is only the effects of such demand as they are recorded in market history and are available for analysis that need concern us.

The most obvious place for an American to look for numismatic values is in the gold coins of the United States. A great many Americans can afford to collect and invest; they have surplus capital. They also have strong sentimental and emotional ties to their own

1. *A GOLD COIN OF THE ANCIENT WORLD.*—Bactria; 20 staters, struck about 160 B.C. Alexander the Great conquered the ancient province of Bactria (present-day Afghanistan) during his march to India. Although Greek art was generally in decline by the time of Alexander, the coinage of the short-lived Graeco-Bactrian kingdom was outstanding, as this portrait coin of a warrior attests. Alexander introduced both Greek art and Macedonian gold coinage to the Middle East, and while his military conquests proved ephemeral, these cultural achievements left a permanent mark.

Courtesy of *Historical Pictures Service,* Chicago

2.   *BYZANTINE GOLD.*—Noumisma of Romanus III (1028-34), showing
the Emperor being crowned by the Virgin Mary (modesty was apparently
not one of his notable virtues). Gold coins of this type, popularly known as
bezants, gave the Byzantine Empire hundreds of years of prosperity and
commercial superiority.

Courtesy of *Smithsonian Institution*

country and its history. American gold coins are very attractive and well struck. Some of them are very rare; a great many others are quite scarce.

In the author's opinion, all U.S. gold coins have numismatic potential, and this numismatic potential has not yet begun to be fully realized. The mintage figures for gold coins are meaningless, for no one really knows how many of each date or series still exist. The gold surrender order of 1933 may have inadvertently caused the near destruction of some dates with a large mintage and spared nearly all of some dates with very small mintages. There could actually be extant more coins of certain small mintage dates than of others with a much larger mintage. We will find that as interest in gold coins increases (and I am sure, because of the many factors cited in this book, that it will), many so-called common U.S. gold coins will be found far more scarce than presently realized, and prices will be adjusted accordingly. It was not too many years ago that a silver dollar was just a silver dollar. Now it is realized that many dates and mint marks are very scarce, causing the silver dollar to make some spectacular advances in price. I believe that many U.S. gold coins, especially among the Eagles and half Eagles, are due for the same sort of realization.

What evidence can be mustered to support this conclusion? Let's take a look first at the example of the silver dollar (both the well-known Liberty Head or "Morgan" type and the "Peace" type minted after 1920). The selected examples presented in Figure 11 show what can happen when numismatic values are fully appreciated.[16] The period illustrated is from 1950 to 1969.

In Figure 11, the selection of silver dollars shows some of the more spectacular rates of appreciation. Not all silver dollars did this well; a few even declined slightly. The group presented is not all-inclusive or completely representative; it is designed to prove this point: many silver dollars have enjoyed a fantastic increase in numismatic value. Nevertheless, I have tried to be objective by including coins from the more recent decades, and not necessarily the biggest movers of those decades either. The very rare and prohibitively expensive coins have been left out altogether. The mintage figures for silver dollars should not be accepted as a totally reliable gauge of present availability, because many of these coins were never released for circulation but were retained by the Treasury as backing for silver certificates and later melted. Records of the particular dates and the quantities that were routinely melted are not available. Still others were melted under the provisions of the Pittman Act of 1918 and exported to India as bullion. Nevertheless, the fact remains that most silver dollars minted after 1865 still exist in considerable numbers, even if they are no longer readily available for sale, and the majority of them have had excellent increases in value over the last 18 years, often exceeding 100 percent per year.

Fig. 11

SILVER-DOLLAR APPRECIATION 1950–1969

Liberty-Head Type

Date & Mint Mark of Coin	Mintage	Price 1950	Price 1969	% Increase in Price
1879 CC	756,000	$ 17.50	$ 195.00	1,014%
1886 S	750,000	2.75	40.00	1,354
1889 CC	350,000	12.50	900.00	7,100
1892 S	1,200,000	25.00	1,200.00	4,700
1893 O	300,000	17.50	195.00	1,014
1893 S	100,000	200.00	5,100.00	2,450
1895 S	400,000	15.00	500.00	3,233
1899 S	2,562,000	3.50	40.00	1,043
1901	6,962,813	6.00	75.00	1,150
1902 S	1,530,000	5.00	75.00	1,400
1904	2,788,650	4.00	20.00	400
1904 S	2,304,000	5.00	185.00	3,600
Peace Type				
1921	1,006,473	4.00	35.00	775
1924 S	1,728,000	3.00	40.00	1,233
1926	1,939,000	2.00	10.00	400
1927	848,000	3.00	30.00	900
1927 D	1,268,900	2.50	35.00	1,300
1928	360,649	4.00	110.00	2,650
1934	954,057	2.50	25.00	900
1934 D	1,569,500	3.00	35.00	1,067
1934 S	1,011,000	15.00	250.00	1,570

Source of data: Redbooks, dealers' ads, auction records.
Fractions omitted in percentages.

Fig. 12
$5 HALF-EAGLE APPRECIATION 1950–1969
Liberty-Head Type

Date & Mint Mark of Coin	Mintage	Price 1950	Price 1969	% Increase in Price
1856	197,990	$30.00	$ 80.00	167%
1861 S	18,000	40.00	175.00	337
1865 S	27,612	40.00	150.00	275
1871 S	25,000	32.50	195.00	500
1878	131,740	25.00	55.00	120
1883 S	83,200	17.50	55.00	214
1891	61,413	16.50	55.00	233
1896	59,063	16.50	50.00	203
1902	172,562	15.00	47.50	217
1906	348,820	15.00	47.50	217
Indian-Head Type				
1908 D	148,000	15.00	65.00	333
1910 D	193,600	15.00	90.00	500
1912 S	392,000	20.00	85.00	325
1914 D	247,000	17.50	67.50	286
1915 S	164,000	22.50	95.00	322

Source of data: Redbooks, various dealers' ads and past auction records.
Fractions omitted in percentages.

Now let's see what happened to our regular gold coins during the same period. Figure 12 shows a selection of $5 half Eagles; Figure 13, $10 Eagles; and Figure 14, the redoubtable $20 double Eagle. These tables were constructed with the same caveats that were applied to the silver dollar (Fig. 11): the very high-priced items were omitted, and an attempt was made to be typical rather than inclusive. Mintage figures are of course unreliable because of the gold surrender order, but on the whole, mintage figures for gold are obviously very much smaller than for silver dollars.

But what has happened? Why the very modest increase in the numismatic value of the majority of our regular gold coins? The answer, it seems to me, is that collectors and investors have habitually regarded our higher denomination regular-series gold coins, except for the very lowest mintages, not as numismatic treasures, but as mere bullion; they are at present still being valued at 80 percent to 90 percent in terms of devaluation-hedge intrinsic value. But don't depend on this situation continuing for very much longer; increasing inflationary pressures and growing numismatic interest and investor sophistication rule against it. I can but conclude that among our regular-issue gold coins are to be found some of the numismatic bargains of the century—bargains comparable to those available in silver dollars in 1950.

One more gold crisis may be all that is needed to drive enough additional gold coins into permanent hiding, thus causing an explosive scarcity situation to develop in the market. An almost identical situation did take place with the silver dollars during the great Treasury silver fiasco of 1964–65.

The numismatic values of the early gold issues, the Pioneers, gold proofs, and the real rarities have long been recognized (see Fig. 15 for examples), but the majority of our regular issues are still selling

Fig. 13

$10 EAGLE APPRECIATION 1950–1969

Liberty-Head Type

Date & Mint Mark of Coin	Mintage	Price 1950	Price 1969	% Increase in Price
1851	176,328	$55.00	$ 90.00	64%
1854	54,250	47.50	95.00	100
1861	113,233	55.00	88.00	60
1868	10,655	60.00	225.00	275
1874	53,160	45.00	100.00	122
1878	73,800	45.00	75.00	66
1884	76,905	50.00	70.00	40
1895 S	49,000	35.00	65.00	86
1896	76,348	35.00	60.00	71
1906 O	86,895	35.00	60.00	71
Indian-Head Type				
1909	184,863	35.00	85.00	143
1910	318,704	35.00	85.00	143
1912 S	300,000	32.50	87.50	169
1914	151,050	35.00	88.00	151
1916 S	138,000	37.50	165.00	340

Source of data: Redbooks, various dealers' ads and past auction records.
Fractions omitted in percentages.

Fig. 14

$20 DOUBLE-EAGLE APPRECIATION 1950–1969

Liberty-Head Type

Date & Mint Mark of Coin	Mintage	Price 1950	Price 1969	% Increase in Price
1855	364,666	$ 90.00	$200.00	122%
1860	577,670	75.00	180.00	140
1871	80,150	75.00	250.00	233
1880	51,456	75.00	170.00	127
1885 S	683,500	70.00	110.00	57
1890	75,995	85.00	140.00	65
1898	170,470	75.00	135.00	80
1901	111,526	75.00	125.00	67
1905	59,011	75.00	180.00	140
1906	69,690	75.00	170.00	127
St. Gaudens Type				
1909 D	52,500	85.00	270.00	218
1911	197,350	65.00	127.00	95
1915	152,050	67.50	120.00	78
1920	228,250	100.00	110.00	10
1927	2,946,750	85.00	75.00	−12

Source of data: Redbooks, dealers' ads, auction records.
Fractions omitted in percentages.

at prices reflecting little more than devaluation–hedge bullion buying. Therefore, in this light we will consider them next.

First, the question is obviously dependent on the gold content and weight of the coin, and this information is presented in the accompanying table (Fig. 16).

Fig. 15

RARE U.S. GOLD-COIN APPRECIATION 1940–1969

	Rare Gold Coin		1940– 1942	Price 1950	Price 1955	Price 1960	Price 1965	Price 1969
$20	1854 O	BU	$65.00	$200	$250	$350	$1,225	$3,350
$20	1870 CC	BU	91.00	250	350	900	6,000	10,000
$20	1883	PF	465.00	1,000	1,000	1,950	5,500	8,000
$20	1884	PF	385.00	750	1,000	2,100	5,000	6,500
$20	1900	PF	61.00	200	250	600	1,600	2,300
$20	1901	PF	62.50	200	250	600	1,500	2,400
$20	1903	PF	72.50	210	250	600	1,600	2,100

RARE U.S. GOLD-COIN APPRECIATION 1940–1969 *(Continued)*

	Rare *Gold Coin*		*1940–* *1942*	*Price* *1950*	*Price* *1955*	*Price* *1960*	*Price* *1965*	*Price* *1969*
$20	1904	PF	62.50	200	250	600	1,600	2,400
$20	1906	PF	61.00	200	250	600	1,800	2,500
$20	1932	BU	76.00	300	350	400	1,400	2,250
$10	1801	VF	27.00	75	90	150	460	750
$10	1855	PF	87.00	250	300	1,100	4,000	5,000
$10	1875	PF	375.00	750	825	925	3,200	4,000
$10	1907	PF	22.00	80	100	190	625	850
$10	1907	BU						
With	Periods		24.50	125	135	600	1,200	8,250
$10	1920 S	BU	81.00	225	250	500	3,000	4,250
$10	1930 S	BU	83.50	250	275	900	3,500	4,000
$10	1933	BU	110.00	500	600	800	3,500	5,000
$ 5	1795	VF	51.00	150	160	300	975	2,000
$ 5	1821	BU	372.50	750	750	850	3,500	4,500
$ 5	1856	PF	65.00	200	200	585	2,200	3,000
$ 5	1875	BU	78.00	300	300	380	3,000	3,250
$ 5	1887	PF	122.00	350	350	575	1,700	2,500
$ 5	1915	PF	16.50	30	35	145	700	1,000
$ 4	1879	PF						
Flowing	Hair		170.00	500	800	2,000	6,000	6,000
$ 4	1879	PF						
Coiled	Hair		485.00	1,000	1,300	4,500	14,500	16,500
$ 4	1880	PF						
Flowing	Hair		377.50	800	1,000	3,500	12,250	14,500
$ 4	1880	PF						
Coiled	Hair		497.00	1,100	1,500	4,750	15,000	16,500
$ 3	1854 D	BU	43.00	135	150	475	2,100	2,850
$ 3	1874	PF	34.00	85	100	400	1,200	2,200
$ 3	1876	PF	185.00	550	550	950	8,100	7,250
$ 3	1877	BU	26.00	125	165	275	825	1,200
$ 3	1881	BU	22.00	65	75	350	750	950
$ 3	1885	PF	28.00	75	80	190	1,200	2,000
$ 2½	1848	BU						
"Cal."	stamp		100.00	250	300	600	5,000	6,000
$ 2½	1854 S	BU	725.00	1,500	1,500	2,000	5,000	7,600

RARE U.S. GOLD-COIN APPRECIATION 1940–1969 *(Continued)*

Rare Gold Coin			1940–1942	Price 1950	Price 1955	Price 1960	Price 1965	Price 1969
$ 2½	1881	BU	16.00	50	90	140	500	650
$ 2½	1894	PF	7.00	27	28	95	450	625
$ 2½	1900	PF	6.00	25	26	70	250	385
$ 2½	1914	PF	7.00	20	20	75	700	750
$ 1	1849	XF	3.50	11	12	29	58	60
$ 1	1849 D	XF	6.25	25	32	65	280	315
$ 1	1854 Type II	XF	2.85	10	12	32	150	200
$ 1	1855	XF	2.25	9	12	35	165	200
$ 1	1860 S	BU	18.50	38	40	70	170	200
$ 1	1870 S	AU	82.50	175	200	250	700	800
$ 1	1886	PF	8.00	23	20	53	150	275
$50	1855 Wass Molitor	BU	485.00	1,250	1,600	5,500	8,500	9,000
$50	1915 S Panama Pacific (Round)	BU	150.00	625	900	2,250	4,200	6,000
$10	1861 Clark & Gruber	BU	38.50	100	100	225	500	750
$ 5	1849 Norris Grieg and Norris	BU	53.50	150	190	400	1,275	1,000
1903–1926 Complete set $1–$2½ Commemoratives (11 coins)			75.00	283	495	937	2,610	2,200

Notes:
1. Selection of coins is random, guided only by author's possession of auction and catalogue data.
2. Initial base prices, 1940–1942, from prices realized at various auctions during this period.
3. Subsequent price data from auction catalogues, news reports of prices realized, and Redbooks.

Fig. 16

WEIGHTS OF U.S. GOLD COINS 1838–1933

Coin	Grains Standard	Grams Standard	Grains Pure	Troy oz. Pure	Troy oz. (Nominal)
$20	516	33.4370	464.4	.9675	1.00
$10	258	16.7185	232.2	.48375	.50
$ 5	129	8.3592	116.1	.241875	.25
$ 2½	64.5	4.1796	58.05	.1209375	.125
$ 1	25.8	1.6718	23.22	.04837	.05

Notes:
1. All coins .900 fine.
2. Pure means unalloyed gold.
3. Standard is total weight of coin.
4. Difference between nominal value of gold dollar and actual gold content by weight is due to the original seigniorage granted the Treasury by the law of 1837, under which the statutory troy ounce worth $20.67 in bullion was exchanged for $20 in coin. This small "profit" was allowed to offset minting expenses.

The next step is to translate these intrinsic values into monetary terms based on both the present and possible future prices for gold. This is shown in Figure 17.

Fig. 17

INTRINSIC VALUE OF U.S. GOLD COINS BASED
ON INCREASED MARKET PRICE OF GOLD

U.S. Gold Coin	Gold Price $35 oz.	Gold Price $50 oz.	Gold Price $70 oz.	Gold Price $100 oz.	Gold Price $150 oz.
$20	$35.00	$50.00	$70.00	$100.00	$150.00
$10	17.50	25.00	35.00	50.00	75.00
$ 5	8.75	12.50	17.50	25.00	37.50
$ 2½	4.37	6.25	8.75	12.50	18.75
$ 1	1.75	2.50	3.50	5.00	7.50

Note:
Gold prices based on nominal values for convenience. (These coins will never be turned in for melting regardless of the official gold price, so there is no point in going to the refinement of stating pure values, less melting charge, etc.)

Now you can readily see that anyone presently paying $70 for a BU double Eagle of any date, and anticipating a devaluation to $70 (in the opinion of many prominent economists, including Jacques Rueff, $70 an ounce would be the minimum devaluation that would do the U.S. any good, that is, allow us to pay off a substantial amount of our international debt), is paying absolutely nothing for its possible numismatic value. If he pays even $85 or $90 for this coin, he is investing only $15 to $20 of it in numismatic potential. If the market value of gold goes higher (there is literally no limit, once inflation gets out of hand), the numismatic value becomes again "free."

The $10 Eagle, with incredibly low mintages (and who knows how many melted), can still be had in some dates and in BU condition for less than $50. If you are willing to pay up to $70 for an Eagle, you can still get some really choice dates and mint marks, and actually be investing only one-half or less of the total amount in numismatic potential; the rest is simply a very favorable bet on further inflation and devaluation.

It is evident that the current selling prices of half Eagles, quarter Eagles, and gold dollars are based primarily on numismatic values, and I would avoid chasing them at high prices. However, I would not think that anyone paying $35 to $40 for a BU half Eagle would be taking any great financial risk.

The collector-investor should constantly review *Coin World*, *Numismatic News*, etc., and check the local dealers in his area for the latest advertised prices, but I will illustrate here some typical dealer prices as of July 1969 for purposes of comparison within this essay:

$20 BU Libertys (July 1969)

1876	$85.00
1882	88.00
1884S	84.00
1891S	76.00
1894	72.00
1900	72.50
1904	72.50
1907	72.50

$20 BU St. Gaudens (July 1969)

1909S	$86.00
1910S	82.50
1913	85.00
1920	85.00
1922	75.00
1927	72.50

$10 Eagles (July 1969)

Ten-dollar Libertys and $10 Indians were being offered in at least 100 different dates from 1842 to 1932, mainly in XF to AU condition (although quite a few BUs were included) at prices in the $45-to-$75 range. (We are not considering here any of the really high–priced items.)

BU $10 Libertys—dealer's choice of date—were offered at $45 to $50.

BU $10 Indians—dealer's choice of date—$70.

$5 Half Eagles (July 1969)

Five-dollar Libertys and $5 Indians were offered in at least 100 different dates from 1834 to 1916, mainly in XF to AU condition (although some BUs were included in dealers' lists) at prices from $45 to $60 (again, high-priced items are not considered).

BU $5 Libertys—dealer's choice of date—$45.

BU $5 Indians—dealer's choice of date—$70.

It is hoped that the reader will have seen enough evidence by now to make a sound judgment about the investment merits of the regular–issue gold coins of the United States. I would only add that the purchase of very expensive pieces, whose prices are based entirely on numismatic attributes, be restricted to those who have a considerable amount of investment capital to spare. For the investor of modest means—one who has funds not exceeding $5,000 available for this kind of investment—I would suggest that the collection be concentrated rather heavily in the $20 and $10 pieces, with only about one-third of the total capital being allowed for pieces whose value is very largely or entirely determined by numismatic considerations.

Get as many different dates and mint marks as you can, without paying excessive prices for them. Don't buy ten or twenty all of one date, just because you can get them a dollar or two cheaper that way. It is much better to spend a few more dollars per coin and thus greatly increase your numismatic potential. (Remember what happened to British collectors; we too may one day have to register with the Treasury Department, and if we have too many duplicates —Big Brother may think we are not bona fide collectors.) And don't be alarmed by variations in price between various dealers or at different times of the year—it's all part of the functioning of a free market. Just keep your eye on the long term, and when you see a bargain—act!

Most books giving investment advice, as you may have observed, are inclined to hedge by letting the reader make all the final judgments (so the burden of error does not fall too heavily upon the author). I hope the information in this book will be sufficient for the reader to make successful investment decisions in the field of gold coins. But so there is no doubt concerning the point of view and responsibility of this author, let me say this: I believe that any U.S. gold coin in BU condition that can be bought for twice its present intrinsic value, or less, is reasonably priced. (Don't forget, the free market price of gold has already been $45 per ounce.)

1. Any BU double Eagle (Liberty or St. Gaudens) at $70 or less appears to be reasonably priced at this time even though it has risen about 20 to 25 percent in the last few months (and about 50 percent in the last 2 to 3 years). I would avoid chasing this type at higher prices, however, unless there is a bargain to be had in an unusual or rare date. Those not having *any* gold-coin position could well begin careful buying at the $65-to-$80 level, but I would recommend deferring more aggressive accumulation until a significant reaction occurs—say, to the $50–$60 area. When buying dealer's-choice dates, one sometimes gets one of the more scarce dates or mint marks. It really can happen; on two different occasions in the last two years, the author ordered dealer's-choice double Eagles by mail and received coins with both a recently recorded auction price and a Redbook value more than 50 percent higher

than the price actually paid. In such cases, the $70 price is more than reasonable—it is a real bargain.

2. Any BU Liberty-head $10 Eagle under $40 is an excellent buy. In the last year, however, it has enjoyed a rather sharp advance, moving from the $35–$40 level to the $45–$50 range. Apparently it is becoming more generally recognized that the $10 Liberty is a far more scarce coin than it was formerly thought to be. Beginning investors, and collectors who have previously concentrated too heavily on the $20 coins, may commence cautious buying at the $40–$50 level, but active buying should await periods of reaction. Most large gold dealers offer extensive lists of Eagles in grades from XF to AU and at prices ranging from $40 to $75, and among them are often many older or definitely scarce low mintage dates. BU Eagles in any but the most common dates are becoming very hard to find. The Liberty Eagle is rapidly becoming one of our really scarce coins, and buying a few of the low mintage dates, even at present prices, would probably be a minimum risk.

The $10 Indian has always been considered scarce, and sells primarily on numismatic value. But it is an *excellent* numismatic value, and its price should hold up well even in the most adverse circumstances. With present prices for dealer's-choice dates in the $70-to-$75 range, this coin, like nearly all gold coins, has had a sharp rise in the last year alone. Again I would recommend cautious buying. One or two at this price would offer only a limited risk, but aggressive investors could suffer a temporary setback.

3. The $5 Liberty half Eagle has also enjoyed a sharp rise in the past year, moving up from the $30 to the $45 level for BU common-date coins. As in the case of the Liberty Eagle, this coin is finally being recognized as a real numismatic rarity. It is one of the coins I would watch carefully for buying opportunities. Every U.S. gold collection of significant value should include specimens of this fine series, in choice AU or BU condition.

The $5 Indian, like its $10 counterpart, is a recognized numismatic rarity, and in 1969 it reached the $65–$70 area for BU dealer's-choice coins. My recommendations on the $10 Indian would also be appropriate here.

4. Gold dollars, quarter Eagles, $3 golds, and the really rare numismatic pieces among U.S. golds are a definite risk at this point, because many of these items have already had huge increases in price, and their growth trends may have flattened somewhat (see Fig. 15). However, some rare coins still appear to be in basic long-term uptrends, and may have considerable growth yet ahead of them. A small portion of one's funds in a few very rare items may yet be a good risk, if one can afford to take risks. Remember, numismatic values (but not intrinsic values) can be subject to substantial downward readjustments during any prolonged business recession.

I should advise the reader that my recommendation to begin cautious buying, even at current high levels, particularly of U.S. $5 and $10 gold pieces, is based partly on events that took place at the last Metropolitan Coin Convention in New York. The Metropolitan show is traditionally one of the foremost numismatic events of the year. The intense interest in gold at this show was unprecedented. Strength in the half Eagles and Eagles was particularly noticeable. Buying at the new higher price levels for U.S. gold coins was extremely active, but confined mainly to dealers. It was said that most of these purchases were destined for Europe, where prices for U.S. gold coins are still substantially higher than in the United States.

Discussions with dealers doing most of the buying brought out the opinion that the U.S. $5 and $10 pieces would not only maintain their present high price level, but move considerably higher over the long term. These same dealers admitted that U.S. gold collectors, for the most part, had not yet come to accept the higher 1969 prices, but they were confident that higher price levels for all U.S. gold coins would have to be accepted eventually; these coins are scarce now, and sure to become even more scarce with their continuing export. The dealers are stocking up now. The European collectors also appear to know what they are doing; the final collapse of the pound sterling and another devaluation of the franc appear imminent. Many Europeans are getting something of real value while there is still time.

Nevertheless, I am not suggesting that hasty or uncritical buying is in order (now or at any other time). Establish a basic position, and continue to add to it, carefully and methodically, but do not plunge. A wise investor plans to do the bulk of his buying in quiet markets after reactions, not during the most volatile upthrusts. Furthermore, a business recession of significant dimensions is now enough of a possibility to warrant being prepared for some near-term reaction in numismatic values. (The long-term outlook is distinctly inflationary, however, as I have outlined in the final chapter of this book.) If the investor will keep in mind the long-term point of view towards gold-coin collecting, as outlined in earlier chapters, short-term uncertainties and fluctuations in prices will not be unsettling, but welcomed.

In line with my advice to concentrate on investments of proven value, I recommend that the typical American collector-investor begin with and keep most of his collection of the gold coins of the United States. But there are other areas that, with proper reservations, can also be of great interest and potential profit to us. One of the principal areas is the gold coins of our southern neighbor, *Los Estados Unidos Mexicanos*—The United States of Mexico.

Notes

CHAPTER VII

1. All these things were at various times used as money. Indian wampum, or strings of beads made from mussel shells, remained legal tender in Massachusetts until 1661.
2. So–called because the unit was divided into eight fractional parts or "bits." The quarter–dollar coin is still popularly known as two bits.
3. A great variety of local copper pieces were coined, however, and used in the colonies. The surviving specimens are very valuable today (see Redbook).
4. The Spanish milled silver dollar, the so–called pillar dollar, was by far the most popular coin in the Americas, and it was the model

for our own monetary unit. Spanish dollars remained legal tender in the U.S. until 1857.

5. Charles L. Prather, *Money and Banking* (Chicago: Irwin, 1941), p. 203.

6. The first gold coins returned by the U.S. mint were 744 half Eagles, delivered July 31, 1795.

7. In addition to the "wildcat" label, the private bank notes also enjoyed such colorful names as "red dogs," "stump tails," and "shinplasters"; such names give some idea of the general level of confidence they achieved. Many were greatly overissued and suffered deep discounts. Others eventually became worthless.

8. All United States coins struck outside the U.S. mint system are considered to be "private"; no state or territorial government or U.S. assayer has legal authority to coin money.

9. Even though it was only a *de facto* gold standard that operated after 1837. The U.S. was legally on a bimetallic standard in 1860.

10. Prather, *op. cit.*, p. 205.

11. There were still $346 million in greenbacks in existence in 1940, and through the Thomas Inflation Act of 1934 the government gained the authority to issue some $3 billion more (Prather, *op. cit.*).

12. The fathers of the Constitution thought they had effectively prevented the government from ever issuing fiat paper money; it was assumed that all federal powers were delegated, and since no specific power was granted to issue paper money, it could not be done (Prather, *op. cit.*, p. 205). They didn't realize that the argument would one day be turned around and the federal government would claim the right to all powers not specifically forbidden.

13. The rare exceptions are the coins minted in 1942 and the wartime silver 5¢ pieces. No other Philadelphia coins are marked.

14. All types of gold coins have become increasingly hard to buy. Many U.S. and foreign golds that seemed common in 1965 and 1966 all but disappeared from dealers' offerings in 1968.

15. Mr. James F. Kelly, author, numismatist, auctioneer, and columnist for *Coin World*, died suddenly in December 1968. He was a very knowledgeable and entertaining gentleman, a redoubtable writer of directness and objectivity. His passing leaves a void in the numismatic world.

16. Perhaps overappreciated: prices for scarce silver dollars have softened somewhat in recent months. The prices shown in Figure 11 are for 1969, and do not always show the extreme point of advance.

VIII

The Gold of Mexico

"It is a common observation that any fool can get money, but they are not wise that think so."

—C. C. COLTON

THE MONETARY HISTORY OF MEXICO IS IN MANY WAYS CLOSELY related to that of the United States. Our currencies share a common beginning in the Spanish silver dollar. Our famous "Trade Dollar" of 1873–1885 was coined primarily to compete with the Mexican 8–*real* silver crown for the trade of the Orient. The Mexican economy suffered from the instabilities of bimetallism throughout the nineteenth century. However, the numismatic development of Mexico has been exceptionally rich. Mexican coinage has had an historic and economic importance that extends far beyond Mexico's legal jurisdiction; Mexican silver pesos still form a significant part of the circulating media in many areas of the Orient. Although a few notable collections of Mexican coins have been built up in Europe and the Americas, even a moderate general interest in Mexican coins is almost a contemporary development.

In past years, Mexican gold and silver coins, often far more scarce than comparable U.S. coins, usually sold for considerably less than their U.S. counterparts. The modern Mexican gold series, begun after the monetary reform of 1905, are of high esthetic merit and relatively small mintage, yet prior to the gold crises of the

1960s they could be bought for little more than their bullion value. The price trends of Mexican gold coins have recently begun to move up to levels that put them at or near parity with similar U.S. gold coins, at least in terms of price versus intrinsic value. However, there still appears to be considerably more investment potential remaining in Mexican gold, both in intrinsic values and in numismatic appreciation. Next to the gold coins of the United States, I believe Mexican gold coins are most favorably situated for profitable investment.

There are several reasons, besides the growing awareness of the advantages of gold-related investments in a world paper economy, why interest in Mexican numismatics may show a dramatic rise in the future. The first of these reasons is the growing affluence of the Mexicans themselves. There is no question, for example, that the tremendous rise in the price of choice U.S. numismatic items during the postwar years (as illustrated by the brief samplings in Figure 15 in the previous chapter) was the result of a sudden surge of interest in numismatics, not merely by the affluent in our supposedly affluent society, but by the very wealthy. The same sequence of events is taking place in Mexico today. A monied class has also developed in Mexico, which class is not only wealthy, but educated and possessed of a new patriotic pride in the history and civilization of its country. The impact of a wealthy Mexican elite upon Mexico's numismatic market will one day send the price of many genuinely rare Mexican coins soaring. The development of a larger and growing middle class, also a phenomenon of the "new" Mexico, will undoubtedly also have a very positive effect on the numismatic values of even moderately scarce coins. At present (1970), interest in numismatics in Mexico is nowhere near as broad or intense as it is in the United States, but there is little doubt that it is growing fast. Already there are reports of Mexican coin dealers buying Mexican coins from U.S. dealers at premium prices to supply the needs of their own Mexican clients.

Another important factor in the potential increase in Mexican numismatic values comes from the United States. U.S. collectors and investors with higher than average numismatic sophistication recognize that certain Mexican gold coins of extremely low mintage can still be obtained for one-fifth to one-tenth of the price commanded by a U.S. gold coin of comparable scarcity. As the really rare U.S. golds now appear so infrequently on the market, and bring such intense competition in demand when they do, the astute American collector of ample means, who desires to build a collection of highly significant numismatic rarities, may well turn to Mexico to find them. Even for the investor of modest capital, the gold coins of Mexico offer some above-average numismatic opportunities, some of which will be indicated in this chapter. For the sake of investment safety, however, we will consider the modern Mexican gold coins primarily in the light of intrinsic value—as a devaluation hedge—and will regard potential numismatic values as a possible bonus (and they could turn out to be very fat bonuses indeed).

Many Americans have an instinctive affinity with Mexico and the Mexican people. Those who visit Mexico or who have lived there are invariably charmed. Throughout its development, the United States has probably been more directly involved with Mexico than with any other nation, except perhaps Great Britain. At many points our histories are inextricably woven into a common tapestry. Nowhere is this more true than in our economic histories; it was so from the very beginning.

Many American collectors of U.S. gold coins, with their obvious feeling for Americana, will probably find it easier and more natural to branch out into Mexican gold than to develop any great passion for European pieces, unless of course they have strong ethnic ties to some European nation. The opportunity to acquire complete type- and date-series collections is also an advantage found more readily in Mexican gold than among the coins of other nations. Building significant or complete type or series collections in European areas is generally far more difficult and expensive, because of the much more extensive mintings, the many more varieties, and the relative inaccessibility of European gold coins for most Americans.[1] Therefore let us take a close look at Mexican gold, and the best place to start is at the beginning.

Historical-Economic Background of Mexican Coinage

Hernán Cortés captured the Aztec city of Tenochtitlán in 1521; it was immediately made the capital of New Spain and renamed México, or Mexico City. The Spaniards wasted little time in exploiting the fabulous wealth of gold and silver they found in Mexico, wealth possessed by the unfortunate Indians in the form of ornament and that remaining to be mined and smelted. The founders of New Spain determined that the treasure could best be exported, as well as utilized locally, in the form of coin, and petitioned their king to establish a mint in Mexico. After many delays and difficulties, the Mexico City mint was opened in 1536, and is today the oldest operating mint in the Western Hemisphere.

The monetary unit introduced into Mexico was the Spanish *real*, defined in 1536 as being 52.8 grains of silver .9305 fine. Silver coins were struck in ½, 1, 2, 4, and 8 *reales*, the last–named being the famous "piece of eight" or Spanish dollar, which was the model for the U.S. monetary unit. The Spanish–Mexican silver *eight reales* dollar not only became the standard coin of the New World, but was eventually exported in great quantities to the East to finance the China trade, and consequently became the standard coin of most of the Orient as well.

The gold unit of colonial Mexico was the *escudo*. Gold coins of ½, 1, 2, 4, and 8 *escudos* were struck, the ½ *escudo* being equal in value to the 8 *reales*. The Spanish colonial coinage system was by far the most efficient and best-known coinage system operating in the world at that time. Spain owed as much of her world eminence to the mint at Mexico City as to the treasure of Mexico itself.

The Mexican War of Independence began in 1810; like the Revolutionary War of the United States, it was neither a brief nor an easy struggle. Final independence was not achieved until 1821. Under the nineteenth-century Mexican Republic, the *eight reales* silver coin continued to be struck in great quantities. Significant numismatic events of the republican period were the opening of 13 branch mints, both as a convenience to the mining areas and as a device whereby the several Mexican states could assert their authority,[2] and the abortive empire of Maximilian, which, whatever else its imperfections, left Mexico with a modern decimal system of coinage.

In 1869 an attempt was made to complete the decimal system by replacing the 8–*reales* coin with a new decimal coin of similar value, the silver peso. However, the new peso, although of the same intrinsic values as the 8 *reales*, was inadvertently made slightly smaller in size, and as a result suffered a discount at the hands of the Chinese.[3] Since the export of silver coins was so important an item in Mexico's economy, Mexico reluctantly returned to the old 8 *reales* design in 1873, although henceforth the 8 *reales* was divided into 100 *centavos* rather than the traditional eight "bits." The Mexicans were not able to return to the preferred silver peso until 1898. But as far as minor coin and the gold coinage were concerned, the decimal system was instituted in 1870, as these coins were not exported.

Republican Decimal Gold Coinage, 1870–1905

The number-one economic problem of Mexico during the second half of the nineteenth century was the overproduction of silver. Mexico was on a free-coinage silver standard, and when most other nations began turning to the full gold standard, Mexican exports of silver declined drastically; the world price of silver fell in relation to gold as demand receded. As a result, more and more silver was brought to the mints to be coined for internal use; nothing else could be done with it. The net effects of this excessive circulation of silver coin were:

1. A decline in the foreign exchange value of the silver-based peso.
2. Domestic price inflation.
3. Gold coinage was driven entirely out of circulation.

The gold that Mexico produced was either exported to gold–standard countries as bullion or, if minted into coin, immediately put into hiding. At any rate, gold did not circulate. A variety of gold coins was produced and most dates were represented with one or more types, but as they were not intended to circulate, mintages were uniformly small. It is in this area, the nineteenth-century decimal gold coinage of Mexico, that there could be great promise for further numismatic advance. (Already these coins are somewhat expensive and therefore suitable only for those with ample investment capital.)

The varieties of *escudos* produced before the decimal reform are also of very low mintage, but I would not recommend them to any except advanced numismatic specialists, with particular interest in early Latin American coinage. They do have considerable numismatic value, but I do not think they offer anywhere near the opportunities available in the decimal gold. There are just too many problems involved with the *escudo* (the difficulty of building series or type sets, problems of identification, and the possibility of forgeries, to name a few) that discourage all but the most sophisticated collectors. Furthermore, the *escudo* is a hangover from the colonial days, and for this reason it will not be as desired as the decimal coinage in the future.

Gold Twenty Pesos, Emperor Maximilian, 1866. The gold Twenty Pesos coin of Emperor Maximilian, the sole gold coin of his brief reign and the first decimal gold coin struck in Mexico, was limited to a mintage of 8,247. This coin is obviously a unique historical curiosity, but what its numismatic potential is would be hard to say. Friedberg estimates its value at $250 (uncirculated). At that price, it might be a worthwhile numismatic investment.

Regular Decimal Gold Coinage, 1870–1905. The first regular gold coin of the decimal series was the One Peso, supposedly equal in value to the silver peso and the 8 *reales*. The coin was never minted in great quantity (only in the last years did minting consistently exceed 5,000 pieces) but it was struck in every year from 1870 to 1905, with several different mint marks. The Two and One-Half Pesos gold piece was initiated in 1870, but minted very sparingly for the next twenty-three years. The Five Pesos gold coin was struck through 1905, but in extremely limited quantities; the largest minting, 1900 Q (Culiacán), amounts to only 1,536 pieces. The gold Ten Pesos was struck consistently by the majority of mints but mintage was again low; for more than half of the mint types and years, the quantity issued was less than one thousand.

The best-known coin of the 1870 series was the gold Twenty Pesos, and although this coin was struck in significantly greater quantities than the lesser values, mintage was still not large; quite a few years and mint marks were also below one thousand. The largest Twenty Pesos striking was 1904 M (México), and that amounted to only 51,513. Bank transfers probably accounted for the larger quantities minted in the Twenty Pesos series. In the lesser denominations, demand for gold coins to be used as gifts, keepsakes, jewelry ornaments, and personal commemoratives for birth dates, weddings, etc., was probably responsible for what little production there was.

The Five, Ten, and Twenty Pesos bear the balanced-scale design on the reverse. The One and Two and One-Half Pesos bear only a numerical designation surrounded by a wreath. The obverse of all coins bears the Mexican Eagle-and-Snake coat of arms.[4] These are very attractive and impressive coins. They are slightly larger than their U.S. counterparts, that is, the Twenty Pesos balanced-scale type is about the same diameter as the U.S. $20 gold piece, and slightly heavier. The Ten Pesos is about the size of a $10 U.S. gold, but slightly heavier. The fineness of the Mexican series was slightly less, however, and this made the intrinsic values for the two countries comparable. The following table (Fig. 18) includes all of the old decimal series:

Fig. 18

MEXICAN DECIMAL GOLD COINAGE 1870–1905

Coin Type	Standard Weight (grams)	Dates Minted
1 Peso	1.692	1870–1905
2½ Peso	4.23	1870–1893
5 Peso	8.46	1870–1905
10 Peso	16.92	1870–1905
20 Peso	33.841	1870–1905

Note:
    All coins .875 fine.

As was indicated earlier in this chapter, these very low mintage coins could be real opportunities as far as numismatic values are concerned; they are very scarce, but demand is not yet strong. However, prices have advanced sufficiently so that intrinsic values, even with a 100 percent devaluation, would cover only one-quarter to one-third of the present cost; but compared with prices paid for U.S. coins of equal scarcity, the old Mexican decimal series has not even begun to reflect appropriate numismatic valuation. For examples, see Figure 19 for a few comparisons between some of the rarest of the old decimal gold series of Mexico and some equally rare U.S. gold coins.

Of course, it must be remembered that the mintages shown in Figure 19 do not represent the present available supplies of these coins. Nobody really knows how many coins are left; there can't be extant more than the original mintage, and in all probability there are fewer. A glance at the Redbook and at current catalogues of Mexican coins will reveal many more comparisons similar to those illustrated in Figure 19.

For those with capital to spare, and who want a unique and very interesting numismatic holding, the old decimal series of Mexican gold coins, if it can be bought under the proper circumstances, may be a great opportunity. But that series is not easy to find; it appears very rarely at auctions. A dealer specialist in Mexican material may be the only ready source of assistance. Furthermore, in an emergency these coins would probably be a little more difficult to sell quickly, without price concession, than would rare U.S. coins of comparable value. For these reasons, most of us with modest investment capital will find more practical opportunities in the modern decimal gold coinage of Mexico.

Modern Mexican Gold Coinage

By 1905 the Mexican coinage system was in dire need of reform. A complete currency and coinage reform was undertaken in 1905, designed to eliminate silver as the *de facto* standard of value[5] and to place the country on the international gold standard. To do this,

Fig. 19

COMPARATIVE COSTS—RARE U.S. & MEXICAN GOLD COINS

Type of Coin	Date & Mint Mark of Coin	Known Mintage	Recent Price (Uncirc.)
U.S. $ 1	1856 D	1,460	$3,000.
U.S. $ 1	1860 D	1,566	4,250.
U.S. $ 1	1875	420	1,650.
Mex. $ 1	1889 M	500	65.
Mex. $ 1	1891 M	746	60.
Mex. $ 1	1894 R	180	130.
U.S. $ 2½	1854 S	246	7,000.
U.S. $ 2½	1856 D	874	4,500.
U.S. $ 2½	1875	420	1,300.
Mex. $ 2½	1886 M	400	95.
Mex. $ 2½	1889 M	240	140.
Mex. $ 2½	1891 M	188	150.
U.S. $ 5	1875	220	3,000.
U.S. $ 5	1878 CC	9,054	800.
U.S. $ 5	1892 O	10,000	900.
Mex. $ 5	1887 R	140	210.
Mex. $ 5	1890 M	149	200.
Mex. $ 5	1897 M	370	185.
U.S. $10	1877	817	1,250.
U.S. $10	1879 O	1,500	1,050.
U.S. $10	1883 O	800	1,650.
Mex. $10	1875 E	312	220.
Mex. $10	1885 E	370	340.
Mex. $10	1891 M	133	310.
U.S. $20	1870 CC	3,789	7,500.
U.S. $20	1882	630	1,750.
U.S. $20	1886	1,106	1,750.
Mex. $20	1888 M	351	310.
Mex. $20	1891 M	237	315.
Mex. $20	1897	959	210.

Notes:
1. Dollar sign with Mexican coin indicates pesos.
2. Prices given in U.S. dollars.
3. Cost data: 1967–1969 base.

the standard gold coins were reduced in size by 50 percent and the composition changed to .900 fine, to conform to international gold-standard practice. The reform was a great success, due in part to a fortunate rise in the world price for silver that began in 1904–05. Some 70 million silver pesos were exported in exchange for gold bullion. By the end of 1906, about 45 percent of the nation's monetary medium was made up of the new $5 and $10 gold coins. A final item in the reform program was the closing of all remaining branch mints; henceforth all Mexican coins were produced by the Mexico City mint.

Mexico remained on the gold standard until the world economic crisis of 1931. After the devaluations of the 1930s, gold coins were still sold freely by the Mexican central bank, but at prices averaging 10 percent above the world (London) quotation for gold bullion. Despite paying this seigniorage, Mexican citizens who elected to keep their wealth in gold coins certainly did not suffer any loss— the peso was devalued three more times after 1934. All sales of gold coins through the banking system were suspended by the Bank of Mexico during the world gold crisis of March 1968, and the bank's remaining stocks of gold coins were transferred to the country's central currency reserve.

Looking back, we can see that the Mexican peso in 1870 was equal, if not actually superior, to the U.S. dollar in foreign exchange value (we coined our famous Trade Dollar in self-defense). By the reform of 1905, the peso, after a long slide, was stabilized at about one-half the value of the U.S. dollar, where it remained until 1930. From then on, economic mismanagement and paper currency took their toll. In the last 40 years, the peso has lost 90 percent of its gold value. The once proud silver peso, the former rival of the U.S. silver dollar, is now a base coin only .100 fine. Any Mexican who stored his retirement funds in paper pesos would not have much to retire on today. This is why Mexicans of moderate means, as well as those who are wealthy, do not use paper pesos as a store of value, but instead accumulate gold and silver coins. Not many bonds are sold in Mexico, and life insurance is hardly a popular investment either. The following inflation chart (Fig. 20), which shows the destiny of the peso since 1923, provides the reason for these things (and provides still another object lesson on the virtues of gold-related investments).

Figure 20 gives rather dramatic evidence of the impact of this age of inflation upon the Mexican economy, but it does not tell the full story. Not only has the peso lost 90 percent of its value in terms of gold and foreign exchange, but living costs in Mexico, during the same 40-year period, have advanced more than 1,500 percent. Furthermore, although the foreign exchange (gold) value of the

Fig. 20

MEXICAN INFLATION CHART 1923–1969

Year	Value of Peso in U.S. Cents	Gold Value of 1,000 Pesos
1923	48.55	23.45
1924	48.51	23.43
1925	49.39	23.85
1926	48.31	23.35
1927	47.21	22.80
1928	48.11	23.25
1929	48.18	23.28
1930	47.13	22.80
1931	35.49	17.15
	Peso Devalued Officially	
1932	31.85	15.40
1933	28.10	8.04
1934	27.74	7.92
	U.S. Dollar Devalued	
1935	27.78	7.93
1936	27.76	7.93
1937	27.75	7.92
1938	22.12	6.32
1939	19.30	5.47
	Peso Devalued Officially	
1940	18.55	5.30
1941	20.54	5.87
1942	20.57	5.88
1943	20.58	5.88
1944	20.58	5.88
1945	20.58	5.88
1946	20.58	5.88
1947	20.70	5.92
1948	20.70	5.92

MEXICAN INFLATION CHART 1923–1969 *(Continued)*

Year	Value of Peso in U.S. Cents	Gold Value of 1,000 Pesos
	Peso Devalued Officially	
1949	11.58	3.31
1950	11.60	3.32
1951	11.60	3.32
1952	11.61	3.32
1953	11.63	3.33
	Peso Devalued Officially	
1954	8.00	2.28
1955	8.00	2.28
1956	8.00	2.28
1957	8.00	2.28
1958	8.00	2.28
1959	8.00	2.28
1960	8.01	2.29
1961	8.01	2.29
1962	8.01	2.29
1963	8.02	2.29
1964	8.02	2.29
1965	8.02	2.29
1966	8.01	2.29
1967	8.01	2.29
1968	8.01	2.29
1969	8.01	2.29

Notes:

1. Gold price used is $20.67 per ounce for years prior to 1934 and $35.00 for 1934 and after.
2. Gold values for 1,000 pesos are given in terms of troy ounces.
3. Data from *World Almanac* and *Wall Street Journal*.
4. 1969 price as of July 31.

peso has been held steady since 1954, living costs have continued to climb sharply. Consequently the peso was under real pressure during the 1968 gold crisis, so much so that the Mexican government was forced to suspend gold sales. The peso at present appears relatively strong, as world currencies go, but it could never survive a dollar devaluation, and possibly not even a severe recession. How long it can survive the continuing inflationary pressure is anyone's guess, but Mexican citizens would be wise to continue their traditional trust in gold and gold coins.

Regular-Issue Gold Coins, 1905–1959.   The first two gold coins issued as a result of the 1905 currency reform were the Ten Pesos "Hidalgo" and the Five Pesos "Medio ['half'] Hidalgo." Each of these coins bears on its reverse a portrait of Mexico's great patriot, Miguel Hidalgo y Costilla. Father Hidalgo, a parish priest in the little town of Dolores, helped organize the first resistance movement against Spanish rule. A powerful patriotic sermon he delivered in 1810 is considered to have been the spark that ignited the Mexican War of Independence. He was captured and executed by the Spanish in 1811. The obverse of the coins bears the traditional Eagle-and-Snake coat of arms. These coins were struck intermittently until 1920, and then mintage lapsed until 1955, when another issue of the Five Pesos was made, and 1959, when a brief issue of the Ten Pesos piece was also struck.

Gold Two and One-Half Pesos, 1918–1948.   A gold Two and One-Half Pesos coin was added to the new gold series in 1918. The design was identical to that initiated by the $5 and $10 gold coins, featuring the bust of Hidalgo and the coat of arms. The popular name for this coin is the Quarto Hidalgo, or one-quarter of a Ten Pesos Hidalgo.

Gold Two Pesos, 1919–1948.   A Two Pesos denomination was introduced in 1919, and it is the smallest denomination of the new gold series. It was released in two substantial issues, 1919 and 1920, and then not struck again until 1944. The coin is popularly known as the Quinto Hidalgo or one-fifth Hidalgo, even though it does not bear the likeness of the patriot, but only the inscription "Dos Pesos" surrounded by a wreath, on the reverse.

Gold Twenty Pesos "Azteca", 1917–1959.   The largest coin of the new regular series is the Twenty Pesos Azteca, so called because the reverse bears a finely detailed miniature of the famous Aztec calendar stone now preserved in the Mexican National Museum. The obverse shows an attractively redesigned coat of arms, with the eagle displayed in three-quarter profile. The Azteca Twenty Pesos coin contains 14.999 grams of fine gold, and is therefore very similar to the U.S. $10 gold coin containing 15.047 grams pure. The Azteca, the third Twenty Pesos gold type in Mexican numismatics, was introduced in 1917 and minted regularly through 1921. Mintage was then suspended until 1959, when a small issue of 12,500 was released. The 1959 coin is a "legal date" (by ruling of ODGSO) for U.S. citizens, and with such a small mintage it could have substantial numismatic potential. In 1969 it was selling for less than twice its bullion value in BU condition, and at that price it appears to be an excellent buy, both for numismatic potential and for intrinsic-value safety.

The reader will notice several low mintage dates in the $2, $2.50, $5, and $10 tables (Figs. 21–24) in the back of this chapter. Some of them have prices that reflect numismatic potential; some do not. However, prices for all dates have risen quite sharply in the last two years, and this price rise appears to have discounted a substantial increase in the price of gold. This is especially true of the smaller denominations. It may be that the $2, $2½, and $5 coins, because of their tendency to circulate more widely, suffered considerable attrition due to wear and remelting, whereas the higher denominations were held by banks or as personal bullion holdings and did not circulate very much. It is possible, therefore, that the small denominations are far more scarce than their mintages would indicate.

However, I would still be inclined to buy only the small mintage dates (25,000 and under) for numismatic potential, and then only if they could be found at prices that would guarantee about 50 percent protection in terms of intrinsic value, assuming a maximum future price of gold at $70 per ounce. The remainder of these coins should be regarded primarily in the light of their intrinsic value and be judged only by their potential for profit in the event of devaluation, or as a store of value against inflationary extremes. Do not hesitate to write to dealers, especially those advertising Mexican material, if you would like quotations on the prices of specific coins by date. Dealers are invariably happy to oblige. (A stamped self-addressed envelope will help speed their answers, however.) The larger retailers may also get some Mexican stock in from time to time—watch for those low mintage dates.

It should be noted that the relatively small number of mintage years and the general availability of modern Mexican gold coins offer unusual opportunities to complete date-series collections, that is, collections of all the dates of one type or denomination. In addition to the personal satisfactions involved, there is an investment benefit; complete date-series collections generally command a higher price than that which can be obtained by selling the coins individually.[6]

Gold Fifty Pesos, Centenary of Independence, 1921–1947. In 1921, the largest gold coin of Mexico was introduced as a commemorative piece to celebrate the centennial of Mexican independence. The coin proved so popular that it was minted on a regular basis through the next ten years. In 1943, "Centenarios," as they were popularly called, were reissued with the denomination "Fifty Pesos" omitted. From 1944 through 1947, Centenarios were struck with the denomination resumed, although it had not been relevant since 1931 (as was true of other Mexican gold coins; Centenarios were sold by the banks at about 10 percent over bullion value). After 1947, additional quantities were struck from existing dies.

The Centenario is a beautiful and impressively large gold coin, now very much in demand. In 1969 they were definitely in the hard-to-buy category. A very few years ago, the Fifty Pesos coins were readily offered in the U.S. at $50 each; now they are difficult to find at $75 as, apparently, many of them have disappeared into safe-deposit boxes for good.

The first year of issue, 1921, undoubtedly has the greatest numismatic potential. The 1931 piece is next in demand. The 1943 version may also be scarce. The quantities of restrikes issued after 1947 were very likely made from the 1944–47 dies. The obverse of this coin carries the typical Mexican coat of arms, identical to the Hidalgo design, but the reverse bears a symbolic winged Victory, with the mountains Iztaccihuatl and Popocatepetl in the background;[7] it is a very attractive coin.

The Centenario is a very popular coin with American collectors and investors, and a complete set of the Fifty Pesos, 1921–1931, in AU or BU condition would be a most secure holding, even if not

Fig. 21

GOLD TWO PESOS "QUINTO HIDALGO"

Gold Two Pesos—Regular Issue, 1919–1948

Year	Quantity Minted	Recent Price
1919	1,670,000	$5.00
1920	4,282,418	5.00
1944	10,000	7.50
1945*	140,000	5.00
1946	167,500	4.50
1947	25,000	6.00
1948	45,000	5.00

* During the period from 1951 through 1959, 725,000 pieces were restruck, dated 1945.

Notes:

1. Diameter, 13 millimeters; weight, 1.666 grams.
2. Composition: .900 gold, .100 copper alloy.
3. Cost data: 1968–1969 base, uncirculated coins.

Fig. 22

GOLD TWO AND ONE-HALF PESOS "QUARTO HIDALGO"

Gold Two and One-Half Pesos—Regular Issue, 1918–1948

Year	Quantity Minted	Recent Price
1918	1,704,000	$5.50
1919	984,000	5.50
1920	607,060	5.50
1944	20,000	10.00
1945*	180,000	5.50
1946	163,000	5.50
1947	24,000	7.00
1948	63,000	6.00

* During the period from 1951 through 1959, 920,000 pieces were restruck, dated 1945.

Notes:

1. Diameter, 15.5 millimeters; weight, 2.083 grams.
2. Composition: .900 gold, .100 copper alloy.
3. Cost data: 1968–1969 base, uncirculated coins.

a particularly exciting investment from a numismatic point of view. (The same can be said for a complete series of Aztecas.)

Most of the Centenarios, as well as the regular gold series (except those with very low mintage) will probably continue to be valued primarily for their intrinsic gold content. The relatively strong demand at present for Mexican gold coins is in all probability just an extension of the traditional devaluation-hedge buying, from both Mexican and U.S. sources. The best way these values can be represented is by charts showing the weights of modern Mexican gold coins (Fig. 27) and their potential future intrinsic value under various devaluation conditions (Fig. 28). Comparing the current prices for these coins (as given in the individual mintage tables in this book, or secured by the most recent dealer quotes) with the prices given in the intrinsic-value chart (Fig. 28) should provide an adequate basis for judgment as to the invesment- and capital-protection merits of these gold coins. As a rough guideline, I would say that, at present, any price 15 percent or more under the $70-per-ounce level would be a very safe purchase for all but the very low mintage dates; for these you should go a little higher, as previously described. The long-range outlook depends primarily on the progress of inflation; let the chart be your guide.

In any case, putting money into Mexican gold coins at the present rate guarantees the buyer a safety "floor" under his investment, at the maximum of no more than 30 percent below the purchase price (and the odds against any retreat in prices of that magnitude are substantial). At the same time, such an investment provides unlimited devaluation and inflation protection. That is a lot better, in my opinion, than what you can get from the stock market at this point.

The "recent price" shown for the Centenario (Fig. 26), and for all the other modern Mexican gold coins listed in this chapter as well, is the *average* dealer price for the period from July 1968 to July 1969. Prices for such relatively common gold coins gyrated quite a bit during the past year; at times they were considerably higher, and at other times they were even a bit lower. The prices shown in these tables will probably turn out to be the average levels for the 1969–70 year (barring devaluation).

Fig. 23

GOLD FIVE PESOS "HALF HIDALGO"

Gold Five Pesos—Regular Issue, 1905–1955

Year	Quantity Minted	Recent Price
1905	18,076	$40.00
1906	4,638,000	9.50
1907	1,088,000	9.50
1910	100,000	16.00
1918	609,000	9.50
1919	506,000	10.00
1920	2,384,598	9.00
1955*	48,000	9.00

* Additional pieces were restruck, all dated 1955: 55,240 in 1956; 20,000 in 1957; 231,202 in 1959.

Notes:
1. Diameter, 19 millimeters; weight, 4.166 grams.
2. Four million pieces were struck at the Philadelphia mint in 1906. These are identical to those struck at the México mint.
3. Cost data: 1968–1969 base, uncirculated coins.
4. Composition: .900 gold, .100 copper alloy.

Fig. 24

GOLD TEN PESOS "HIDALGO"

Gold Ten Pesos—Regular Issue, 1905–1959

Year	Quantity Minted	Recent Price
1905	38,612	$60.00
1906	2,949,000	17.00
1907	1,589,000	17.00
1908	890,000	17.00
1910	451,000	17.00
1916	26,000	50.00
1917	1,966,500	17.00
1919	266,000	17.00
1920	11,603	50.00
1959	50,000	17.00

Notes:
1. Diameter, 22.5 millimeters; weight, 8.333 grams.
2. One million pieces were coined at the Philadelphia mint in 1906. These are identical to México-mint issues.
3. Cost data: 1968–1969 base, uncirculated coins.
4. Composition: .900 gold, .100 copper alloy.

Fig. 25

GOLD TWENTY PESOS "AZTECA"

Gold Twenty Pesos—Regular Issue, 1917–1959

Year	Quantity Minted	Recent Price
1917	852,000	$30.00
1918	2,830,500	30.00
1919	1,093,500	30.00
1920	462,198	30.00
1921	921,500	30.00
1959	12,500	30.00

Notes:
1. Diameter, 27.5 millimeters; weigh, 16.666 grams.
2. Composition: .900 gold, .100 copper alloy.
3. Cost data: 1968–1969 base, uncirculated coins.
4. Reverse of coin includes the inscription: "15 Gr. ORO PURO" (15 grams pure gold).

Fig. 26

GOLD FIFTY PESOS "CENTENARIO"

Gold Fifty Pesos—Centenary of Independence, 1921–1947

Year	Quantity Minted	Recent Price
1921	180,400	$85.00
1922	462,600	70.00
1923	431,800	70.00
1924	439,400	70.00
1925	716,000	70.00
1926	600,000	70.00
1927	606,000	70.00
1928	538,000	70.00
1929	458,000	70.00
1930	371,600	70.00
1931	136,860	85.00
1943 (No Denomination)	89,400	95.00
1944	592,900	70.00
1945	1,012,299	65.00
1946	1,587,600	65.00
1947	309,200	65.00

After 1947, additional quantities of Centenarios were struck from earlier dies, in the following amounts: 386,000 in 1949; 326,200 in 1952; 173,300 in 1954; 523,100 in 1958; 296,900 in 1959.

Notes:

1. Diameter, 37 millimeters; weight, 41.666 grams.
2. Composition: .900 gold, .100 copper alloy.
3. Cost data: 1968–1969 base, uncirculated coins.
4. Reverse of coin includes the inscription: "37.5 Gr. ORO PURO" (37.5 grams pure gold).

Fig. 27

WEIGHTS OF MEXICAN GOLD COINS, 1905–1959

Gold Coin	Grams Standard	Grams Pure	Grains Standard	Grains Pure	Troy oz. Pure
$50	41.6666	37.4999	643	578.7	1.2056
$20	16.6666	14.9999	257.2	231.5	.4823
$10	8.3333	7.500	128.6	115.75	.24115
$ 5	4.1666	3.750	64.3	57.875	.12057
$ 2½	2.0833	1.875	32.15	28.94	.06029
$ 2	1.6666	1.4999	25.72	23.15	.04822

Notes:

1. All coins .900 fine.
2. *Pure* means unalloyed gold.
3. *Standard* means total weight of coin.
4. Dollar sign indicates value in pesos.

Fig. 28

INTRINSIC VALUE OF MEXICAN GOLD COINS, 1905–1959
BASED ON INCREASED MARKET PRICE OF GOLD

Gold Coin (Pesos)	Gold Price $35 oz.	Gold Price $50 oz.	Gold Price $70 oz.	Gold Price $100 oz.	Gold Price $150 oz.
50	$42.20	$60.28	$84.40	$120.56	$180.84
20	16.88	24.12	33.76	48.24	72.36
10	8.44	12.06	16.88	24.12	36.18
5	4.22	6.03	8.44	12.06	18.09
2½	2.11	3.01	4.22	6.03	9.04
2	1.69	2.41	3.38	4.82	7.23

Notes:

1. Prices based on troy oz. pure gold in each coin.
2. All prices given in U.S. dollars.

Notes

CHAPTER VIII

1. In terms of intrinsic value received, modern European gold coins are also generally more expensive than Mexican pieces, particularly when sold in the United States (see chapter 10).

2. Mexican mint marks are somewhat complex, and as all branch mints were closed in 1905, a discussion of Mexican mint marks is not necessary to this work. For further details see Theodore V. Buttrey, *A Guide Book of Mexican Coins* (Racine, Wis.: Whitman Division, 1969).

3. The Mexicans were not alone; the U.S. silver dollar was also discounted by suspicious Orientals; hence the Trade Dollar. For a full and illuminating discussion of the Mexican and U.S. silver money used in the China trade during the eighteenth and nineteenth centuries, see Barbara C. Walrafen, *Influencia de Plata Gruesa* (Topeka, Kan., 1968).

4. The Mexican coat of arms is taken directly from an Aztec legend. According to this legend, handed down through many generations, the first Aztecs were instructed by their gods that "when you . . . find an eagle, sitting on a cactus on a stone in the water, tearing with his beak and claws a snake asunder, there you shall settle." Later, Aztecs were supposed to have seen this very sight on the shores of Lake Texcoco, and as a result established their capital city of Tenochtitlán (now Mexico City) at this location. The Mexican eagle has been shown in a variety of positions and types on their coinage, but it is always perched on a cactus and grasping a snake in its beak. For most Mexican coins, the national emblem is considered the main obverse device, rather than the "head" side, as is traditional with most other countries.

5. Like the U.S., Mexico was officially on a bimetallic standard in the nineteenth century, but like the U.S., it could not be made to operate.

6. All coins in the series should be of the same (highest) quality, i.e., all BU, or all AU-BU, or at the minimum all EF-AU. Consistently try to achieve the highest possible quality throughout the series. (Modern Mexican gold coins grading less than XF are worth little more than bullion, unless they are the scarcest dates.)

7. The twin mountains are symbolic of an Aztec legend. According to this tale, an Indian prince, Popocatepetl, fell in love with a princess, Iztaccihuatl, from another tribe, and they eloped. For this violation

of tribal laws they were permanently exiled. They are said now to be eternally asleep, personified by the mountains that bear their names. (Another legend has it that they will one day awaken and drive the invaders from Mexico.)

IX

Canadian Gold Coins

IN THE ONE HUNDRED YEARS SINCE ITS CONFEDERATION, CANADA has issued only six varieties of gold coins. A single gold type was struck by the government of Newfoundland, prior to the time it joined the Canadian union, but whether or not this type can be included under Canadian coinage is open to question. If it can be included, that still makes a total of only seven gold-coin types for a nation whose history and economy have been and still are very much involved with gold and gold production. It may seem curious that this country, now the second largest producer of gold in the world, and by far the largest producer in the Western Hemisphere, should have such a limited numismatic history concerning gold, but that is the case.

The explanation lies partly in the special relationship Canada has had as part of the British Empire, a relationship that lasted until 1926, when Canada finally completed its evolution to full equality and self-government. Prior to that time, the ready convertibility of Canadian currency into sterling and the availability of British gold sovereigns satisfied most Canadian requirements. Furthermore, the Royal Canadian mint at Ottawa was not opened until 1908; before that time all Canadian coinage was struck at the Tower mint in

London or at private British mints under contract. Another consideration is that the major development of the Canadian gold-mining industry is largely a twentieth-century phenomenon; throughout most of the nineteenth century, it was the U.S. that dominated world gold production.

The first gold coin to be struck for use in British North America after Canadian confederation was the $2 piece of Newfoundland, minted intermittently from 1865 through 1888. This attractive little coin bears the head of Queen Victoria and was struck to British standard fineness, but intrinsically its value was adjusted to equal two U.S. gold dollars. Since Newfoundland did not join the Dominion of Canada until 1949, it may be disputed, as we have said, whether or not this coin is really a Canadian issue, but I think anyone attracted to Canadian numismatics, and particularly to Canadian gold, will feel that this coin belongs to their area.[1]

In keeping with their British ties, the first recognized Canadian gold coins were sovereigns—one-pound pieces bearing the likeness of the king. These coins were in every way identical to British gold sovereigns of the same date, except for the Ottawa mint mark.[2] The first Canadian sovereign was the Edward VII design, struck in only three years, 1908, 1909, and 1910. The second and final Canadian sovereign variety bears the image of Edward's successor, George V, and was minted for most of the years from 1911 through 1919. Both coins were struck to British standard fineness (.91667) and can be identified only by the mint mark C found on the ground below the horse. (A mounted figure of St. George slaying the dragon is on the reverse of each coin.)

Possibly revealing something of Canada's political ambiguity at the time, a dollar series of gold coins, corresponding to U.S. standards and values, was introduced in the years 1912, 1913 and 1914, even though the George V sovereign continued to be minted through 1919. There were only two coins in the series: a $5 and a $10 piece, both corresponding exactly in weight, value, and fineness to their U.S. counterparts. Both coins bear the bust of George V on the obverse, but have the Canadian coat of arms and the denomination on the reverse.

It will be noted from the charts in this chapter that, with the possible exception of the George V sovereign, all Canadian gold coins are selling at prices that indicate considerable scarcity. Original mintages were not large and obviously there has been considerable attrition since then; most of them were probably melted for bullion to take advantage of the higher gold price after 1934. (The intrinsic values as shown by the tables are, in most cases, no longer a significant factor in their price.) The market price of these coins had shown a sharp rise prior to 1965, but since then the price appears to have levelled or risen more slowly. In view of the dynamic and growing Canadian interest in numismatics, as well as an expanding interest in Canada by U.S. collectors, Canadian gold coins seem to be an attractive long-term holding from a strictly numismatic point of view. However, as with any coins that are primarily dependent on numismatic considerations, they should not be "chased," but bought only during periods of price concession.

Although these few Canadian gold coins have enjoyed a substantial increase in price levels, they appear to have reached a temporary peak and may even be easing off somewhat from their highs. A close check on their past price history might help in locating bargain levels. Remember, in purely numismatic investing, patience is a great virtue. Wait until you can get a real bargain, then act. There always exists the possibility of catching a "sleeper" at an auction or mail auction—it has been done.

As far as Canadian coins are concerned, an old market aphorism well applies: "Buy right: sit tight." As with all coins of high numismatic value, this means buy only when you see a bargain, or at least a fair price, and hold for the long term. To help put the whole matter in better perspective, I have included a chart showing intrinsic values at possible future gold prices. By referring to this chart (Fig. 31) one can accurately judge the amount of capital actually being risked on numismatic potential alone, at various prices and under different economic conditions. For example, by paying $85 for a $10 piece while anticipating a $70 future gold price, one is assuming a risk of about $50 on numismatic potential, or by paying $25 for a George V sovereign under the same assumption, one limits the numismatic risk to a mere $8, etc.

Obviously, at present price levels, Canadian gold coins are not the ideal devaluation hedge, but they could very well be considered for the numismatic part of the portfolio. They probably will respond well with time or any further intensification of the present inflationary cycle.

For a concluding summary of the specific details concerning the regular-issue Canadian gold coinage of the period 1865–1919, the reader is referred to Figures 29, 30, and 31, which follow in this chapter.

Fig. 29

CANADIAN GOLD COINAGE

Canada and Newfoundland—Regular Issues, 1865–1919

Gold Coin	Dates	Quantity Minted	Recent Price
$2 (Victoria)	1865	10,000	$60.00
Newfoundland	1870	10,000	60.00
	1872	6,050	75.00
	1880	2,500	600.00
	1881	10,000	60.00
	1882 H	25,000	45.00
	1885	10,000	55.00
	1888	25,000	40.00
One Pound	1908 C	636*	350.00
(Edward VII)	1909 C	16,273	125.00
	1910 C	28,012	110.00
One Pound	1911 C	256,946	24.00
(George V)	1913 C	3,715	550.00
	1914 C	14,891	140.00
	1916 C	6,111	Rare
	1917 C	58,845	28.00
	1918 C	106,516	28.00
	1919 C	135,889	30.00
$5 (George V)	1912	165,680	65.00
	1913	98,832	85.00
	1914	31,122	350.00
$10 (George V)	1912	74,759	130.00
	1913	149,232	110.00
	1914	140,068	120.00

* May be proofs only; it is not known whether or not they were actually put into circulation.

The prices shown in the first table (Fig. 29) are *average* retail prices for AU-BU coins based on the period from July 1968 to July 1969. Any price reaction to levels significantly below these values would undoubtedly present an excellent long-term buying opportunity. For a detailed, illustrated review of the criteria for grading Canadian gold coins, see J. E. Charlton and R. C. Willey, *A Guide to the Grading of Canadian Decimal Coins* (Racine, Wis.: Whitman Division, 1965).

Fig. 30

WEIGHTS OF CANADIAN GOLD COINS

Gold Coin	Grams Standard	Fineness	Grams Pure	Troy oz. Pure
$ 2*	3.2828	.9167	3.0093	.09675
£ 1	7.9881	.9167	7.3227	.2354
$ 5	8.3592	.900	7.5233	.2419
$ 10	16.7185	.900	15.0466	.4838

* Newfoundland

Fig. 31

INTRINSIC VALUE OF CANADIAN GOLD COINS
BASED ON INCREASED MARKET PRICE OF GOLD

Can. Gold Coin	Gold Price $35 oz.	Gold Price $50 oz.	Gold Price $70 oz.	Gold Price $100 oz.	Gold Price $150 oz.
$ 2*	$3.39	$4.84	$6.78	$9.68	$14.52
£ 1	8.24	11.77	16.48	23.54	35.31
$ 5	8.46	12.10	16.93	24.19	36.29
$ 10	16.93	24.19	33.86	48.38	72.57

* Newfoundland

Notes:
  1. All prices given in U.S. dollars.
  2. Values based on troy oz. pure gold in coin.

Twenty-Dollar Gold Centennial, 1967. The first and only gold commemorative coin in Canada's numismatic history, and the first gold coin minted after a lapse of 48 years, is the $20 commemorative honoring the 100th anniversary of Canadian federation. The $20 gold was issued in 1967 in proof condition as part of a seven-coin proof presentation set. The history of this coin, brief as it is, should be of considerable interest to Americans. In the first place, we were forbidden by our government to acquire this historic and unique piece; ODGSO has ruled against its importation. A once-in-a-lifetime opportunity to obtain this beautiful numismatic memento of perhaps the most significant event in modern Canadian history was lost to Americans, because our government and its bureaucrats, by following the demented logic of neo-Keynesian fiat money economics, are committed to this and other absurd suppressions of liberty.

Throughout history, fiat money and tyranny have gone hand in hand. For a recent example, that master of oppression, Adolf Hitler, waged a relentless war on gold to the very end of his brutal and despicable empire. Intrinsic-value money allows the individual to fashion, to a great extent, his own economic destiny; fiat money puts him at the mercy of the state; if the state is the sole arbiter of value, then the state can change the value of its money or inflate the supply at will—and the citizen can go whistle for his lost savings. This rather obvious lesson of history was not lost on Hitler, who recognized immediately that gold was an enemy of the authoritarian state and consequently did his best to banish it from the Reich.[3] Fiat money, in the final analysis, can circulate only by fiat, that is, by force, and it inevitably changes any republic into a despotism. People who allow their money to lose its intrinsic value, can expect eventually to lose their freedom as well.

Canada is a great country. Although not without its share of Keynesian spendthrift politicians, Canada at least recognizes and respects the right of its citizens to protect themselves financially. Canadians are free to buy all the gold they want. For many years Canada's coin dealers were able to offer a tremendous variety of world gold coins at prices 20 percent to 25 percent below American prices for our limited number of comparable (legal) coins. Formerly, when an American gold collector looked at a Canadian dealer's list, the feeling of frustration he was likely to develop could only be described as acute. Fortunately this situation was partially rectified by the 1969 amendments to the U.S. Gold Regulations. These amendments have removed the long-standing prohibition against importing pre-1933 gold coins. Americans are now free to purchase at least some of the coins offered by Canadian dealers. However, many desirable numismatic items, including most Israeli gold coins and the 1967 Canadian centennial $20 gold piece, are still barred.

The $20 gold centennial coin in a leather presentation case, with six other proof silver and copper coins, was originally sold by the Canadian mint for $42. This gold coin was also available separately, if so desired, and the proof sets could also be obtained with the silver centennial medal in lieu of the gold coin. Counting those included with the presentation proof sets and those sold separately, the total mintage of the 1967 gold centennial proof coin was reported at 337,512. The 1969 dealer's price for the proof set with gold was $100, and for the $20 gold coin separately, the asking price was $75. See what you missed, Yankee? Remember that, next time you hear your political candidates trying to explain their economic views.

Notes

CHAPTER IX

1. Canadian coin catalogues uniformly include a section covering the coins of Newfoundland. See J. E. Charlton, *Standard Catalogue of Canadian Coins, Tokens and Paper Money*, 17th ed. (Racine, Wis.: Whitman Division, 1969).
2. Again, it is arguable whether or not sovereigns are actually Canadian coins. The sovereign was not a unit of Canadian currency; further-

more, the Ottawa mint was, at that time, technically just a branch of the Royal mint in London. Most British catalogues consider all sovereigns to be British coins. But the Canadians view them as Canadian coins and Canadian catalogues list them as Canadian coins, and as far as I am concerned, the Canadians are the final authorities on Canadian coins.

3. Charles Rist, *The Triumph of Gold*, trans. Philip Cortney (New York: Philosophical Library, 1961), p. 5.

X

European and Other Foreign Gold

"The only freedom which deserves the name is that of pursuing our own good in our own way, so long as we do not attempt to deprive others of theirs, or impede their efforts to obtain it."

—JOHN STUART MILL

THE FIELD OF EUROPEAN AND WORLD GOLD COINAGE IS, UNDERstandably, rather extensive, so extensive that a substantial library of numismatic, economic, and historical works would be needed to give it adequate coverage. Any thorough numismatic-historical survey of European and world gold coinage would have to begin about A.D. 600 and include comment and background information on virtually all the gold coins listed in Friedberg. Such a monumental task obviously could not be accomplished in a single volume, however huge, and certainly not in a single chapter. But as this book is concerned primarily with gold and numismatic investment for the investor of moderate means, we need be concerned here only with the obvious—the European and world gold coins that are now most widely offered for sale. Those readers who might wish to invest in the much more expensive and numismatically sophisticated European rarities and pre-nineteenth-century world gold should do so only after thorough study of the subject or competent and trustworthy professional numismatic advice.

Buying and selling gold coins in Europe and in some countries of the Middle East, Asia and Latin America is big business. The citizens of the Continental countries (and lately those of Great Britain), as well as most Asians and Latin Americans, have a deep distrust of paper money; as modern history has so forcefully demonstrated, their suspicions are hardly without justification. Gold bars and gold coins are sold by many banks and retail dealers throughout Western Europe, and they are traded at special exchanges designed specifically for that purpose, notably those at Paris, Zurich, and Frankfurt. In all, fourteen nations and colonies permit free and unrestricted gold trading. They are:

Belgium	Laos	Saudi Arabia
Canada	Lebanon	Switzerland
France	Macao	Uruguay
Jordan	Paraguay	West Germany
Kuwait	Peru	

In several other nations, limited gold trading is permitted to the extent that internal dealings are relatively unrestricted, but import and export controls are imposed. In still other countries, gold-trading laws and restrictions are on the books, but the authorities are inclined to wink and look the other way. Altogether, gold and gold-coin trading are well represented around the world, but the area with the most intensive activity is Western Europe.

Although most Western Europeans are free to buy gold bullion, gold coins are still highly favored by the small investor and the person of moderate means. One reason is that the smallest ingot sold on the official markets costs about $1,400 (smaller bars are available from private sources, but their cost per ounce is generally much higher). Another reason is that Europeans really like their gold coins; they are pretty to look at and interesting to collect. A velvet-lined collector's box of napoleons or sovereigns or guilders is much more desirable to the average European investor than a mere store of bullion. Furthermore, gold coins make inexpensive and always acceptable presents. They are not only handsome trinkets, but indestructible, safe from the ravages of fashion, immune to taxes and death duties, and virtually secure from depreciation. Finally, history has shown that gold coins have always been a safe and satisfactory *long-term* investment (and at the same time, have always remained readily negotiable).

European buyers, as well as Latin Americans, Arabs, Indians, and Orientals, willingly pay from 50 percent to 100 percent premium over the current intrinsic value of most gold coins, and Americans who want to acquire them will also have to pay these premiums, if not more. Furthermore, the European gold-coin markets are flooded with restrikes, official and unofficial—not to mention counterfeits. But the European and other buyers are not in the least deterred; their faith in gold and gold coins easily overcomes these seemingly formidable obstacles to productive investment.

Even the most articulate and persuasive Keynesian economist would have a hard time convincing Europeans that their passion for sovereigns, ducats, napoleons, and the like is just an ignorant delusion or fetish. The laughter that would greet such a suggestion would be derisive indeed; imagine the reaction of any German, Austrian, or East European over 40, to whom the total destruction of a nation's fiat currency is not a remote fact of history, but a personal experience. Nor would any Frenchman, Italian, Arab, or Oriental be swayed by sophistries from Harvard, the U.S. Treasury, or the London School of Economics, knowing as he does that his currency is now worth only one two-hundredth or less of its former value under the full gold standard in 1914.

Nor, apparently, do the people of Great Britain, at least those fortunate enough to have earned a little surplus under the most difficult conditions, seem to be moved by the oratory of their socialist government; imports of gold coins soared from an annual rate of $1.7 million in 1960 to $23.8 million in 1965. In 1966 the socialist Labour government finally plugged that escape hatch by instituting strict import and exchange controls, registering all coin collectors, and forbidding even the manufacture of, among other things, small religious medals from gold. Needless to say, all this has hardly enhanced the world's respect for pound notes or the Labour government.

Paris is the world's busiest retail market for gold. The London market is larger, but it is a wholesale market, limited to central banks of other nations and to certain licensed dealers and agents. For the center of gold-coin trading in Europe we must go to the basement of the Palais de Bourse. There, every business day between 12:30 and 1:00, immediately after the close of the foreign exchange market, 30 to 40 agents and couriers gather to watch the latest bid and asked prices for gold bars and gold coins flash by on an electronic board. Typical of the commodities traded, besides the one-kilogram ingots, are the 20-franc coins of France and Switzerland, U.S. $5, $10 and $20 pieces, British sovereigns, German 10 and 20 marks, Dutch guilders, and Mexican 50-peso coins. Buyers, whether French or foreign, place their orders through stockbrokers, banks, or coin dealers, and orders are relayed by phone to the trading floor.

Most of the coins traded are the demonetized pieces of the old gold-standard nations, but more and more, restrikes are being fed into the system. With coins generally selling for 50 percent to 85 percent above their intrinsic value, several governments have been turning a nice profit by quietly restriking their old gold coins. Other countries, as we shall observe in the next chapter, have been openly reissuing gold coins for this trade. Still other nations, such as Great Britain, occasionally have minted sovereigns and other gold coins specifically to facilitate trade with the Middle East and the Orient. And of course private schemers can hardly be expected to ignore such a lucrative business; counterfeit coiners in the Middle East, principally Lebanon, turn out quite a respectable product; not perfect perhaps, but the better ones deliver full gold content.

While the standard one-kilogram bar generally sells for barely 2 percent over its market value in fine gold, prices for coins at the end of January 1967, a relatively calm period, commanded the following premiums over intrinsic value: French 20 Francs, 49 percent; Swiss 20 Francs, 58 percent; U.S. $20, 29 percent; German 20 Marks, 85 percent; and Dutch 10 Florins, 50 percent.[1] During the "gold rush" of March and April 1968, the premiums were in most cases 50 percent higher than those quoted. At first glance, it would seem that European gold-coin buyers, having paid 50 percent to 100 percent over parity for gold in the form of coins with little or no real numismatic potential, have only the slenderest chance of making their investment pay off. But the Europeans are not inexperienced in such matters; perhaps they know what they are doing. After all, they can buy bullion if they wish; but they still buy a lot of gold coins.

The French alone are believed to have some 4,000 tons of gold stashed away in mattresses, old socks, and safe-deposit boxes, much of it in the form of coin. That little nest egg is worth somewhere between $4 billion and $6 billion, depending on the division between coin and bullion. Either way it is a lot of gold, in fact a lot more than the Bank of France has at the moment. Considering the recent "revolution" in Paris, the present uncertainty of the franc, and what might ultimately result from the passing of de Gaulle, one would be rash indeed to conclude that it is a bad investment.[2]

All in all, despite the massive private holdings, despite the restrikes and counterfeits, and despite the ready availability of bullion, the demand for gold coins in Europe and in the rest of the world remains unsated; prices continue strong, and are apparently growing stronger. But should North American investors consider the modern European and other world gold coins? The only answer I can give is: in some cases maybe. To understand this will require a brief review of world gold coins, other than those of North America, most commonly available to collectors and investors.

In most cases, perhaps the best that can be said for common world gold coins, except for those we have already discussed in previous chapters, is that they offer an interesting and entertaining way of preserving capital. I don't mean to imply that the protection and preservation of wealth isn't a worthwhile or necessary objective in itself, but I remind the reader that our ideal of gold-coin investing is to combine intrinsic values with numismatic potential, whenever possible. We want not only to preserve wealth, but to make a profit if we can. With that consideration in mind, we can now survey the remaining common gold coins of the world, or at least the best known, in terms of their intrinsic value, and comment only on those that have, in addition, numismatic values and possibilities.

WELL-KNOWN GOLD COINS OF THE WORLD

Note:

Weights are given only in troy ounces of pure gold in each coin. Therefore, to determine intrinsic value of a specific coin at any given market price for gold, one has only to multiply the weight in troy ounces pure by the prevailing market price for gold.

ALL EUROPE

THE DUCAT: 1280–1969 (All Ducat denomination coins are .986 fine.)	*Troy Oz.* *Pure Gold*
100 Ducats	11.0952
50 Ducats	5.5476
20 Ducats	2.2190
10 Ducats	1.1095
5 Ducats	.55475
4 Ducats	.4436
3 Ducats	.3327
2 Ducats	.2218
1 Ducat	.1109

Note: Certain historic and modern European gold coins, commemorative coins, restrikes and gold art medals have been issued in denominations, weights, and fineness corresponding to the ancient *ducat* system originated in the Venetian Republic (Venice) about 1280. Ducats are always gold coins; the ducat is never denominated in any other metal or form.

AUSTRALIA

Sydney Mint Sovereigns:		*Mint Dates*	*Troy Oz.* *Pure Gold*
1 Sovereign	Rev. "Australia" (Sydney mint)	1855–1870	.2354
½ Sovereign	Rev. "Australia" (Sydney mint)	1855–1866	.1177

British-Type Sovereigns:

Mint Marks
M—Melbourne
P—Perth
S—Sydney

Note: Australian one-pound and half-pound sovereigns are identical to the British, except for the Australian mint mark.

| 1 Pound | (Rev. St. George, mm) | 1871–1931 | .2354 |
| ½ Pound | (Rev. St. George, mm) | 1871–1918 | .1177 |

Typical Obverse Designs:

Victoria	(1837–1901)
Edward VII	(1901–1911)
George V	(1910–1936)

Comment: the "Australia–Sydney mint" sovereigns have considerable numismatic value, and no doubt further potential, but they are already selling at prices that reflect this. It might be a safe holding if acquired at a reasonable price—say, 25 percent to 40 percent below highest sale price.

AUSTRIA (Empire 1806–1918)		Mint Dates	Troy Oz. Pure Gold
4 Ducats		all dates	.4438
1 Ducat		all dates	.1109
8 Florins—20 Francs		1870–1892	.1867
4 Florins—10 Francs		1870–1892	.0933
20 Corona	Franz Joseph (Laureate Head)	1892–1909	.1960
10 Corona	Franz Joseph (Laureate Head)	1894–1909	.0980
100 Corona	Franz Joseph (Plain Head)	1909–1915	.9802
20 Corona	Franz Joseph (Plain Head)	1909–1916	.1960
10 Corona	Franz Joseph (Plain Head)	1909–1912	.0980
100 Corona	Commemorative 60th Year of Reign	1908	.9802
20 Corona	Commemorative 60th Year of Reign	1908	.1960
10 Corona	Commemorative 60th Year of Reign	1908	.0980
(Republic 1918–1938)			
100 Kronen	Large Eagle	1923–1924	.9802
20 Kronen	Large Eagle	1923–1924	.1961
100 Schillings		1926–1938	.6807
25 Schillings		1926–1938	.1702

Comment: the 1908 commemorative series definitely has considerable numismatic potential and current value. The 100 Corona commemorative is a very handsome and impressive piece, much favored by European collectors. The reverse shows a female figure reclining on a cloud, instead of the usual Austrian coat of arms. Schlumberger gives the following prices:

BU	100 Corona	1908	(S—646)	$225.00
BU	20 Corona	1908	(S—647)	50.00
BU	10 Corona	1908	(S—648)	50.00

Any substantial concession from these prices would offer an opportunity, particularly to those who already have a good portfolio of U.S. and other gold. I particularly like the 100 Corona piece, but all three make a nice series. The 100 Kronen republic pieces (S—675, S—676) are also recommended, if one can be found at $250 or less in BU condition. One caution, however: the Austrian government is rather notorious for issuing restrikes (see chapter 11). They have not as yet reissued any of the coins recommended, and in my opinion they are not likely to do so. However, one cannot entirely rule out the possibility. I like these coins, but they do have that small extra risk.

BELGIUM		Mint Dates	Troy Oz. Pure Gold
20 Francs	Leopold I	1865	.1867
20 Francs	Leopold II	1866–1882	.1867
20 Francs	Albert I	1914	.1867

BRAZIL		Mint Dates	Troy Oz. Pure Gold
20,000 Reis	Peter II	1853–1889	.5284
10,000 Reis	Peter II	1853–1889	.2642
5,000 Reis	Peter II	1854–1859	.1321

Comment: Brazilian gold coins have been rather extensively, and in some cases expertly, forged and counterfeited (see chapter 12).

BULGARIA		Mint Dates	Troy Oz. Pure Gold
20 Leva	Ferdinand I	1894	.1867
20 Leva	Ferdinand I	1912	.1867
10 Leva	Ferdinand I	1894	.0933

COLOMBIA 1856–1885	Mint Dates	Troy Oz. Pure Gold
20 Pesos	1859–1877	.9335
10 Pesos	1856–1877	.4667
5 Pesos	1856–1885	.23335
2 Pesos	1856–1876	.09335
1 Peso	1856–1878	.04667

1913–1930		
10 Pesos	1919–1924	.4708
5 Pesos	1913–1930	.2354
2½ Pesos	1913–1928	.1177

Comment: the gold coinage of Colombia (sometimes known as *Nueva Granada* or "New Granada" in the nineteenth century) was extensive, but most of the early issues are now quite scarce, if not rare. The modern series coins of 1913–1930, however, are generally available.

CUBA		Mint Dates	Troy Oz. Pure Gold
20 Pesos	José Martí	1915	.9675
10 Pesos	José Martí	1915–1916	.48375
5 Pesos	José Martí	1915–1916	.2419
4 Pesos	José Martí	1915–1916	.1935
2 Pesos	José Martí	1915–1916	.0967
1 Peso	José Martí	1915–1916	.04837

Comment: the entire gold coinage of Cuba is presented here. It was issued for only the two years, 1915 and 1916. These coins were struck at the U.S. Philadelphia mint and were based on the U.S. gold standard, that is, the Cuban peso was identical in gold value to the U.S. dollar. Therefore, the Twenty Pesos coin is the same size and weight as the U.S. $20 double Eagle, etc. The coins bear the head of Cuban patriot-hero José Martí (1853–1895), a gallant leader of the war of independence against Spain. The reverse bears a Cuban heraldic shield. Mintage was low for all denominations and the Cuban government melted unknown amounts. Cuban gold is apparently quite scarce, although in recent years significant amounts have been brought into the U.S. by refugees from the Castro government. Only the Ten Pesos and Five Pesos coins seem to be around in any quantity, but the whole series is available through dealers at good-to-high prices; demand appears strong. I am inclined to recommend them as a good series collection, which would fit nicely with any basic collection of U.S. and Mexican gold. I believe these coins have further numismatic potential, but at the moment prices may have run ahead too fast; $225 is the current asking price for the 20-pesos coin.

DENMARK	Mint Dates	Troy Oz. Pure Gold
20 Kroner	1871–1931	.2593
10 Kroner	1873–1917	.1297

EGYPT

(Kingdom, 1803–1952) Administration:	*All coins .875 fine.*	
Turkish Sultans	1803–1915	
Independent Sultan	1915–1917	
Egyptian Kings	1917–1952	

1803–1960	Mint Dates	Troy Oz. Pure Gold
500 Piastres	1861–1960	1.1956
100 Piastres	1839–1960	.23912
50 Piastres	1839–1958	.11956
20 Piastres	1923–1938	.04782
10 Piastres	1839–1909	.02391
5 Piastres	1839–1909	.01195

(Republic 1953–1958)	*Coins .9167 fine.*	
5 Pounds	1955, 1957	1.1770
1 Pound	1955, 1957	.2354

Note: Piastre coins produced 1953–1960, same standard as for kingdom.

Comment: all 500-piastre gold coins of Egypt are quite expensive, as far as intrinsic value is concerned, but they should make sound numismatic investments if they can be bought at some concession below the high prices established in recent years. All nineteenth-century-piastre coins are handsome pieces and attractive from a numismatic point of view. But as with all such coins, prudence dictates that they should be accumulated during corrective periods in the coin market, when a good price advantage can be obtained.

FRANCE 1803–1914	*Mint Dates*	*Troy Oz.* *Pure Gold*
100 Francs	1855–1913	.9335
50 Francs	1855–1904	.4667
40 Francs	1803–1839	.3734
20 Francs	1803–1914	.1867
10 Francs	1854–1914	.09335
5 Francs	1854–1889	.04667
1929–1936		
100 Francs	1929–1936	.1895

Principal Obverse Designs:

Napoleon Bonaparte (Napoleon I)	1801–1815
Louis XVIII	1814–1824
Charles X	1824–1830
Louis Philippe I	1830–1848
Louis Napoleon (President)	1848–1852
Napoleon III (Emperor)	1852–1870
Second and Third Republics:	1848–1852
	1870–1940

Angel Writing
Head of Ceres
Head of Republic (Reverse Rooster)
Winged Head (100 francs 1929–36 only)

Comment: the first French gold franc coins were issued by Napoleon in 1803. Only two denominations were struck, the 20 Francs and the 40 Francs. The gold franc was defined as being .32258 grams, .900 fine, and France was able to maintain that standard unchanged until 1914, despite two monarchies, another empire, two republics, two revolutions, several wars, and one more massive defeat in the century after Waterloo. The franc, based solidly on gold, gave the French people at least economic stability to carry them through these trials. But when France was forced off the gold standard in 1914, the franc was doomed: it soon became a millstone rather than an anchor for the French economy.

Many of the later republican coins have probably been restruck; they are, with few exceptions, readily available. The 20-franc coins of Napoleon III are also in plentiful supply. The 100- and 50-franc coins, however, are not easy to find. These and the 20- and 40-franc coins of Napoleon I probably have considerable numismatic value. I recommend them, particularly the

40-franc coins of Napoleon I, in XF or AU condition, especially at significant concessions below their 1967–69 average.

GERMANY (Empire 1871–1918)	Mint Dates	Troy Oz. Pure Gold
20 Marks	1871–1915	.23046
10 Marks	1872–1914	.11523
5 Marks	1877–1878	.05761

Note: Various German states (Prussia, Bavaria, Baden, etc.) continued to issue their own coinage after 1871, but to a uniform standard. Strictly speaking there are no German gold coins. The above coins are typical and bear the heads of several different state monarchs, but the reverses are identical and bear the German eagle and the inscription "Deutches Reich." A truly national German coinage did not begin until the formation of the German republic after 1918, but this government did not issue any gold coins.

Anyone looking for outstanding German numismatic rarities should consider the only three gold coins of Germany's former colonial empire; they should prove a sound long–term investment.

	Coin	Date	Mintage	Price*
GERMAN NEW GUINEA	20 Marks	1895	1,500	$1,250
GERMAN NEW GUINEA	10 Marks	1895	1,000	1,500
GERMAN EAST AFRICA	15 Rupees	1916	16,198	200

* Price from Schlumberger

GREAT BRITAIN Sovereigns: 1817–1964	Mint Dates	Troy Oz. Pure Gold
5 Pounds	1820–1953	1.1770
2 Pounds	1820–1953	.4708
1 Pound	1817–1964	.2354
½ Pound	1817–1953	.1177

Principal Obverse Designs:

Queen Victoria	1837–1901
King Edward VII	1901–1910
King George V	1910–1936
King George VI	1936–1952
Queen Elizabeth II	1952–

Note: The 5-pound and 2-pound gold sovereigns are generally quite scarce, and in some cases rare.

HUNGARY (Dual Monarchy with Austria, 1867–1918)	Mint Dates	Troy Oz. Pure Gold
8 Florins—20 Francs	1870–1892	.1867
4 Florins—10 Francs	1870–1892	.0933
100 Korona	1907–1908	.9802

20 Korona			1892–1916	.1961
10 Korona			1892–1915	.0980

ICELAND

(Republic 1944–)		Date	Mintage	Troy Oz. Pure Gold
500 Kronur	(Legal Date)	1961	10,000	.2593

Comment: Iceland's only gold coin commemorates Jon Sigurdsson (1811–1879), perhaps the most outstanding figure in modern Icelandic history. A renowned scholar and writer (Icelandic history, law, and literature), he was even greater as a statesman. After many years of effort, in 1874 Sigurdsson succeeded in obtaining home rule from Denmark. This limited-issue coin currently sells for about $65; it may be a worthwhile numismatic holding, although future demand is uncertain. If the price comes down somewhat, or if you can afford it now, take a chance.

ISRAEL

(Republic 1948–)		Date	Mintage	Troy Oz. Pure Gold
20 Pounds	Herzl	1960	10,500	.2354
100 Pounds	Weizmann	1962	6,203	.7863
50 Pounds	Weizmann	1962	6,202	.39315
50 Pounds	Bank of Israel	1964	6,014	.39315
100 Pounds	Victory	1967	9,004	.7863
100 Pounds	Jerusalem	1968	12,500	.7863

Comment: nearly all numismatic and philatelic items issued by the government of Israel since its inception in 1948 have had an outstanding record of value appreciation. The gold coins of Israel have all been limited-issue commemoratives struck in proof condition. I recommend them, even at present high prices. The long-term future of Israel numismatics appears extremely bright. Most Jewish people in the U.S. and Europe have at least a strong sentimental if not a personal attachment to Israel, and consequently Israel's coins will continue in strong demand. I advise buying any new issues whenever you have the opportunity; the original-issue price of any Israeli commemorative coin is invariably a bargain. Unfortunately, however, the citizens of the United States presently face a severe problem in the area of Israeli gold; ODGSO has ruled against the importation of all of Israel's gold coins except the 20-pound Herzl. For U.S. collectors I can only advise that you write to your elected representatives and protest these and other rulings (such as that on the $20 Canadian centennial) of ODGSO.

ITALY

(Kingdom 1861–1945)		Mint Dates	Troy Oz. Pure Gold
100 Lire	All Types	1861–1927	.9335
50 Lire	All Types	1861–1927	.4667
40 Lire	Napoleon I	1804–1814	.3734
20 Lire	Napoleon I	1804–1814	.1867
10 Lire	Napoleon I	1804–1814	.09335

		Mint Dates	Troy Oz. Pure Gold
Lira Devalued after 1927		*Mint Dates*	*Pure Gold*
100 Lire	Victor Emanuel III	1931–1933	.2546
50 Lire	Victor Emanuel III	1931–1933	.1273

Comment: I still like the coins of Napoleon I for numismatic values, based on historical association. I believe interest and demand will last indefinitely and grow stronger.

LIECHTENSTEIN
All coins .900 fine.

		Troy Oz.
1898–1900	*Mint Dates*	*Pure Gold*
20 Kronen	1898, 1900	.1960
10 Kronen	1898, 1900	.0980
1930–1952		
100 Franken	1952	.9335
20 Franken	1930, 1946	.1867
10 Franken	1930, 1946	.09335
1956–1961		
50 Franken	1956, 1961	.3267
25 Franken	1956, 1961	.16335

NETHERLANDS

(Monarchy 1814–)		*Mint Dates*	Troy Oz. *Pure Gold*
10 Guilders	William III	1875–1889	.1947
10 Guilders	Wilhelmina	1890–1933	.1947
5 Guilders	Wilhelmina	1912	.09735
1 Ducat	Netherland's East Indies Trade Coin (Standing Knight Obverse):		
		1814–1938	.1109

NORWAY

(Swedish King 1872–1905)		*Mint Dates*	Troy Oz. *Pure Gold*
20 Kronor	Oskar II	1874–1902	.2593
10 Kronor	Oskar II	1874, 1877, 1902	.1297
(Norwegian King 1905–1957)			
20 Kronor	Haakon VII	1910	.2593
10 Kronor	Haakon VII	1910	.1297

POLAND

(1st Republic 1919–1939)		*Mint Dates*	*Mintage*	Troy Oz. *Pure Gold*
20 Zloty	Boleslaus	1925	27,240	.1867
10 Zloty	Boleslaus	1925	50,350	.0933

Comment: these two gold coins were struck to commemorate the 900th anniversary of the Polish nation, and are the only two gold coins of the modern Polish state. They are low in intrinsic value, but demand for them is strong and prices have gone up considerably in recent years. Persons of Polish ancestry represent one of the larger ethnic groups in the United States and Canada, and it has been my experience that many of them are avid coin collectors. With this strong present and potential demand, these coins appear to be an interesting and safe long–term numismatic holding. Profit potential, however, depends to a great extent on buying at a reasonable price.

ROUMANIA

		Mint Dates	Troy Oz. Pure Gold
20 Lei	Carol I	1870–1906	.1867
25 Lei	(Commemorative)	1906, 1922	.2333
50 Lei	(Commemorative)	1906, 1922	.4667
100 Lei	(Commemorative)	1906, 1922,	.9335
		1939, 1940	.9335

RUSSIA

(Empire before 1917)

		Mint Dates	Troy Oz. Pure Gold
15 Roubles	Nicholas II	1897	.3734
7½ Roubles	Nicholas II	1897	.1867
10 Roubles	Nicholas II	1898–1911	.2489
5 Roubles	Nicholas II	1897–1911	.12446

SOUTH AFRICA

British Sovereigns: 1923–1960

St. George Reverse, Mint Mark "SA"

		Mint Dates	Troy Oz. Pure Gold
1 Pound	George V	1923–1932	.2354
½ Pound	George V	1923–1926	.1177

Springbok Reverse:

1 Pound	George VI	1952 (Proof)	.2354
½ Pound	George VI	1952 (Proof)	.1177
1 Pound	Elizabeth II	1953–1960 (Proof)	.2354
½ Pound	Elizabeth II	1953–1960 (Proof)	.1177

Republic: 1961–

2 Rand	(All Types)	1961–1967	.2354
1 Rand	(All Types)	1961–1967	.1177

SPAIN

	Mint Dates	Troy Oz. Pure Gold
100 Pesetas	1870–1897	.9335
25 Pesetas	1871–1885	.23335
20 Pesetas	1889–1904	.1867
10 Pesetas	1878	.09335

Principal Obverse Designs:

Alfonso XII	**1875–1886**
Alfonso XIII	**1886–1931**

SWEDEN

		Mint Dates	Troy Oz. Pure Gold
20 Kronor		1873–1925	.2593
10 Kronor		1873–1901	.1297
5 Kronor		1881–1920	.0649

Principal Obverse Designs:
Oscar II   1872–1907
Gustave V   1907–1950

SWITZERLAND

		Mint Dates	Troy Oz. Pure Gold
20 Francs	Girl's Head	1871–1947	.1867
10 Francs	Girl's Head	1911–1922	.09335

TUNISIA

	Mint Dates	Troy Oz. Pure Gold
20 Francs	1891–1928	.1867
10 Francs	1891–1928	.09335
100 Francs	1930–1937	.1895

TURKEY

	Mint Dates	Troy Oz. Pure Gold
500 Piastres	1839–1960	1.0635
250 Piastres	1839–1960	.53175
100 Piastres	1839–1959	.2127
50 Piastres	1839–1961	.10635
25 Piastres	1839–1961	.05317

Note: Each denomination of Turkish gold coins was struck in two varieties, the standard size, and a deluxe size, which is larger, but much thinner. Both types, however, are of the same weight and fineness (.9167). Turkish gold coins are very handsome pieces. Before 1929, they featured a variety of designs composed of elaborate Arabic inscriptions and ornament. From 1943 onward, the obverse design features the portrait of a Turkish president, either Kemal Ataturk or Ismet Inonu.

Comment: if they could be bought for a price not too far from double intrinsic value (at $35 per ounce), the larger Turkish coins, both standard and deluxe, in BU or AU condition, would certainly add a nice exotic touch to any collection. The 500 Piastres is about 10 percent heavier than the U.S. double Eagle, and approximately the same size; the deluxe version is quite a bit larger. The 250 Piastres is also about 10 percent above the U.S. $10 gold in intrinsic value.

VATICAN		Troy Oz.
All coins .900 fine.	*Mint Dates*	*Pure Gold*
100 Lire	1866–1870	.9335
50 Lire	1868–1870	.4667
20 Lire	1866–1870	.1867
10 Lire	1866–1869	.09335
5 Lire	1866–1867	.04667
100 Lire	1929–1935	.2546
100 Lire	1936–1969	.15046

Comment: all Vatican coins to date have been of limited issue, and consequently are valued almost entirely on numismatic considerations. For all practical purposes they should be regarded as gold commemorative medals rather than coins.

VENEZUELA		Troy Oz.
	Mint Dates	*Pure Gold*
100 Bolivares	1875–1889	.9335
50 Bolivares	1875–1888	.4667
25 Bolivares	1875	.2334
20 Bolivares	1879–1912	.1867
10 Bolivares	1930	.09335
5 Bolivares	1875	.04667

Comment: except for the 20 and 10 Bolivares, all Venezuelan gold coinage is in the "very rare" category. The 100, 25, and 5 Bolivar pieces of 1875 exist as proofs only.

European Gold; Economic Considerations

Our very brief review of some of the better-known and most generally available European and world gold coins is now concluded. It will be obvious to the reader from earlier comments, and also from any review of current price lists of U.S. dealers, that as far as intrinsic values are concerned, few bargains are presently being offered—or are likely to be offered. However, one should not expect to buy gold coins at virtually bullion price. The mere fact that the gold has been processed into an attractive and symbolic object, so basic a part of civilized human experience as the coin, gives it a permanent added value. In that sense, all gold coins, no matter how common, have numismatic value. I would say, therefore, that as a general rule: any modern gold coin in BU condition has a minimum value of 25 percent to 30 percent over its intrinsic worth.

But the fact that we may be, at this writing, close to a major devaluation of the dollar and other world currencies, perhaps justifies paying considerably more than 30 percent over intrinsic value for common gold coins. After all, many of them are most attractive to look at and certainly offer other satisfactions to anyone with the collector's instinct.

The Queen Elizabeth sovereign,[3] for example, is a very pretty little coin. However, it is safe to assume that few if any of these most recent and extensively minted gold pieces will ever have significant numismatic appreciation. But let us see if a case can be made for buying such coins purely on economic considerations. The sovereign contains .2354 of an ounce of fine gold; therefore, even at the minimum world "support price" of $35 per ounce for gold,[4] the sovereign contains $8.24 worth of the yellow metal. If we add the 30 percent premium that has just been cited as being typical for gold coins, simply because they are coins (a premium that certainly can be accepted as a valid minimum because it has maintained itself for many years, even through periods when there was no gold "problem"), we have an additional $2.47 in monetary value, which establishes the basic worth of the gold sovereign (1 pound) at $10.71 (U.S. currency).

During 1968 and 1969, U.S. coin dealers offered a variety of sovereigns in XF condition at prices ranging from $15 to $17; therefore, let us assume that a sovereign can be purchased by an American collector for $16. At that price the buyer is assuming a basic capital risk of only $5.29 ($16.00 less $10.71) not $16.00. But there remains one other factor to consider: the cost of selling. We cannot be completely candid about an economic appraisal and overlook the possibility that we may be forced by personal circumstances to sell at an inopportune time. In 1968–69, the difference between dealer's buying and selling prices for common-date U.S. gold coins, as typically advertised, amounted to only 5 or 6 percent. I think it is safe to conclude that the dealer's "spread" on foreign gold coins would be somewhat higher—say, 10 percent. Let us be very safe then and assume a selling cost of 10 percent of the *basic value* of the coin, though I really can't imagine any present or future turn of events that would reduce common gold coins to this basic value; nevertheless, for absolute safety let us assume such an occurrence. Therefore, we must deduct 10 percent or $1.07 from the basic value, for possible selling concession, leaving a net absolute *maximum* monetary risk of $6.36 or about 40 percent of the total investment.

If this seems like a substantial maximum risk, consider these two points: 1) The maximum risk condition in any investment situation is always a temporary phenomenon—after things get as bad as possible they can only improve. 2) The maximum risk condition in real estate, the stock market, and other securities (even including at times government bonds) can be 100 percent. There have been several periods when real estate was virtually unsalable, not that it had completely lost its value but because money conditions were so restricted that mortgage loans were refused all but entirely riskless applicants (who didn't need them). As for the stock market, who can forget that between 1929 and 1932 the Dow Jones Industrial Average lost nearly 90 percent of its monetary value and thousands of corporations disappeared into bankruptcy.

Sometimes bonds fare little better—even government bonds. Devaluations, inflation, and rising interest rates have wiped out as much as 80 percent of the original value of British war bonds. Older bonds of Brazil, Cuba, and several other Latin American countries are either worthless or nearly so. The same can be said of most of the prewar bonds of nearly all of Europe. And the holder of what is generally considered to be the safest and most conservative investment around—U.S. government bonds—hardly has cause to rejoice; he need only reflect on the 50 percent decline in the purchasing power of the postwar dollar and on the 200 percent rise in interest rates to realize the severity of the loss suffered by the owners of long-term U.S. Treasury issues.

From our example of the gold sovereign, one can see that while the absolute maximum possible loss on common gold coins would be held to 30 to 40 percent, the inflation protection offered would be absolutely unlimited. I chose the sovereign for this example, not because it has any specific merit, but because it is typical of common foreign gold coins. The reader can substitute any other coin in our list and arrive at the same realizations shown in Figure 32 for the sovereign.

Fig. 32

BASIC ECONOMICS OF THE GOLD SOVEREIGN (1 POUND)

When Market Price of Gold is:	$35	$40	$50	$70	$100
Intrinsic Value of Coin is:	8.24	9.42	11.77	16.48	23.54
Add 30% Numismatic Factor:	2.47	2.83	3.53	4.94	7.06
Basic Value of Coin is:	10.71	12.25	15.30	21.42	30.60
Subtract Selling Concession:	−1.07	−1.23	−1.53	−2.14	−3.06
Minimum Net Value of Coin:	9.64	11.02	13.77	19.28	27.54
Actual Maximum Monetary Risk or Gain at $16 Cost:	−6.36	−4.98	−2.23	+3.28	+11.54

Obviously, buying common foreign gold coins, except perhaps for those previously cited as having some additional numismatic potential, is not the road to large capital gains. But as the free market price for gold has already approached $45 per ounce, and as the maximum discount I have illustrated is largely theoretical, the monetary risk involved in buying foreign gold coins, even at 100 percent over their intrinsic value at $35 per ounce, appears very modest. Although I would hardly recommend buying such coins in large quantities as an investment, any collector who feels attracted to them need not have any qualms about adding such specimens to his collection, even at double their present intrinsic value (at $35 per ounce). I don't know where else you can get *cheaper* and *safer* inflation insurance, as well as a devaluation hedge, than you can by buying gold coins—even common ones—thereby entertaining and educating yourself at the same time.

Furthermore, if you time your purchases right and are a bit lucky, you may yet acquire gold coins at considerably less than 100 percent over intrinsic value. There may be one or more technical dips in the price of gold or in the prices of many gold coins, or both, before the next inflationary blow-off and devaluation occur (though I am writing in terms of months, not years). Any sizable dip in gold–coin prices in the near future should be looked upon not as a danger but as a grand opportunity.

The most recent reports from European and American gold–coin markets reveal a most interesting development, a development that provides a fitting conclusion for this chapter. Prices for BU and choice AU foreign gold coins have moved up sharply. For example, while a common-date sovereign in the usual XF-to-AU grade sells for about $16 to $17, choice BU specimens generally command more than twice that figure. The indication is that the numismatic aspects of European golds are now becoming an important consideration. This conclusion is reinforced by further reports that disclose that great numbers of European gold collectors are beginning to collect by date and type, instead of simply holding their coins as mere bullion. As a result, they are discovering that many dates, types, and mint marks are quite rare. Furthermore, this recent "numismatic" buying pressure exposed the fact that *nearly all European gold coins in choice AU or BU condition are far more scarce than was thought just a few months ago.*

Although I do not advise chasing them without any regard for intrinsic values, it does appear that the numismatic future of European golds is going to be most interesting. For the present, therefore, shopping for a few nice AU or better European gold coins, at prices not too far from twice their intrinsic value, would appear to be a prudent action. More extensive buying should be done after one of the periodic reactions that are inevitable in both the coin market and the world gold market.

Notes

CHAPTER X

1. *Barron's*, March 6, 1967.
2. It has been a most appropriate investment thus far; the August 8, 1969, devaluation of 12½ percent was the 18th legally admitted devaluation in 41 years, and the seventh since World War II.
3. Unfortunately, the gold coin of the second good Queen Bess is now illegal for Americans to hold. For the time being we will have to be satisfied with the sovereigns of Edward VII, George V, and Queen Victoria.
4. At the annual meeting of the International Monetary Fund in September 1968, the Republic of South Africa was given a virtual guarantee that the Fund would buy all private gold offered to it, should the free market price ever decline to $35 per ounce. South Africa in return would be obligated to sell all its gold on the free market, anytime the free market price was above $35 per ounce. So far, South Africa has not seen the necessity of accepting this offer, with its provisions, from the IMF. Instead, South Africa is negotiating directly (and secretly) with various central bankers for partial sales to their respective banks *now* at the $35 level, in return for a guaranteed $35 "support price," should it ever be needed. In any case, the $35-per-ounce "floor" is without a doubt absolutely firm.

XI

Restrikes, Medals, and Miscellaneous

"There is no altruism among nations."

—BISMARCK

THE PRODUCTION OF COIN RESTRIKES BY SOME GOVERNMENTS IS one of the less appealing facts of life with which coin investors and collectors must learn to live. A restrike is a coin, either struck from an original die, or produced from a new die identical to the original one, but at a later date—usually a considerable time after the mintage of the original coin was concluded. There are several motives for issuing restrikes. One is simply to take advantage of numismatic demand for certain rare coins (if restriking is done surreptitiously it amounts to little more than forgery—official or not). Another obvious reason is to satisfy the demand for gold coin merely as bullion. A gold restrike can be purchased for much less than the original coin, yet contains the same amount of gold.

A third motive concerns national pride. Small nations can call attention to themselves and relive their hours of past glory by re-issuing the coins of former empires and conquests. But regardless of the principal reason for doing so, it is clear that issuing restrikes can be and is a nice, quiet, profitable business. The opportunity to buy bullion at $35 per ounce and turn it into coins that sell at $40 to $50 per ounce has proven to be an irresistible temptation to several European nations. The sale of restrikes will no doubt be

with us for quite a while and I think we will even see some further
spreading of this practice, regardless of the wishes of the majority
of the numismatic fraternity. Nations, as Bismarck observed so
piquantly a century ago, are prone to act in their own self-interest.

The majority of collectors, dealers, and investors realize that
restriking will downgrade the original in collectors' eyes and will
reduce its price—sometimes drastically. Rarities can and do become
commonplace overnight, when quantities of restrikes are dumped
on the numismatic market. Some government restrikes are marked
in some way to identify them as such, but more often they are not.
If a coin is so marked and can be readily identified as a restrike,
then, of course, its impact on the outstanding original coins, in terms
of their numismatic value, is much less. But even when restrikes
are marked for recognition, the identifying mark is seldom obvious.
For example, Spain marks its restrikes with a virtually microscopic
true date of issue on the stars flanking the earlier date, and some
Hungarian restrikes bear a small rosette before the mint mark, or
the tiny letters *up* somewhere on the coin (most Hungarian restrikes,
though, are unmarked). However, at the risk of sounding as cynical
as Bismarck himself, I must observe that those very minute identification marks can be most easily removed by a skilled jeweler or
engraver.

The proponents of restrikes—and there are a few—insist that
restrikes are not all bad. They like to point out that restrikes make
available to collectors specimens of rare and desirable coins at
modest prices, when most collectors could never afford the originals.
With some justification it can be said that restrikes, which are always
offered in choice BU if not prooflike or proof condition, provide
collectors with coins in far better condition than they are likely to
find among the originals. Some restrikes are released in proof condition, even though proofs were not part of the original issue, which
may satisfy at least the esthetic feelings of some collectors.

Another favorable factor to some investors is that restrikes provide a way of obtaining gold at a very modest price and in a most
desirable form. For instance, the 100 Corona restrikes of Austria,
which contain nearly a full ounce of gold and were struck in

beautiful prooflike condition, were sold by some Canadian dealers in 1967 for as little as $38.75,[1] and although restrikes are generally illegal in the U.S., I strongly suspect that some of these coins were sold here, but for $47.50 each.

One of the major sources of restrikes (labeled and unlabeled) is the Communist government of Hungary. Despite the watchdogs of the Treasury and ODGSO, the Hungarian foreign trading agency, Artex, has managed to sell U.S. dealers substantial amounts of re-struck coins without bothering to mention that they were restrikes, and these coins have been unwittingly (in some cases, wittingly) sold to unsuspecting U.S. collectors.[2] The gold restrikes of Hungary are illegal to import into the U.S. (Perhaps it would be appropriate to mention here that any gold coin illegally imported into the U.S. is subject to seizure, even though the present owner may have pur-chased it in good faith within the U.S.) An 1870 date on a gold coin does not prove that it was struck in 1870 (on the other hand I don't know how anyone can prove that it wasn't).[3]

Fortunately, the news staffs of *Coin World* and other numismatic journals do an excellent job of gathering information about re-striking activities around the world, and they report them as news stories as soon as the facts become available (this is the kind of material that should go into the reference scrapbook). A con-scientious reading of the numismatic press should protect you from deception, as far as restrikes are concerned, and the list included in this chapter covers most if not all the known issues up to mid-1969. Personally, I think we can live with restrikes, but we certainly cannot abide deception.

I look upon these restrikes in about the same way that I regard the most common world gold—merely as an interesting way of pre-serving capital through holding intrinsic-value metal in a more desirable and more negotiable form than plain bullion. I would not attempt to deter anyone from buying restrikes, as long as the buyer is aware that they are restrikes and are priced accordingly. If nothing else, buying some of these restrikes may be an inexpensive way of building up the intrinsic-value balance of a gold collection that includes coins of high numismatic value, but low intrinsic value.

As I have said, some of these European gold restrikes are available in the U.S., although they are seldom if ever identified as such (their low price gives them away, however). The chances are very great that if you are offered any European gold coins in BU or prooflike condition, of a date that is known to have been restruck, you are being offered a restrike. If the price seems attractive to you (U.S. citizen) and you buy it, then your quarrel is with ODGSO, not with me—just don't delude yourself that you are buying a scarce original with great numismatic potential. However, if you ease your conscience by making it an article of faith that those beautiful prooflike European gold coins in your collection are indeed originals, you will certainly not be challenged by me; but I sincerely hope you did not (or will not) pay more than 50 percent over intrinsic value (at $35 per ounce) for them.

But I would never advise anyone to violate any of the laws of his country, no matter how arbitrary or oppressive those laws may be. So, all this is mere speculation. But as long as we are speculating, I shall add another opinion, which applies to modern gold as well as restrikes: ODGSO will not be around forever. Sooner or later the delusion of the U.S. monetary authorities that we can escape the discipline of gold and conquer the economic world with paper promises will be exposed for what it is. The dollar will be devalued, the price of gold will soar, the economy of the U.S. will be dealt a staggering blow, and ODGSO and the rest of the Treasury's gold prohibitionists will be numbered among the prominent casualties.

My final word on restrikes is similar to my conclusions regarding common world gold in general: these coins may not be the best road to significant capital gains, but on the other hand there is no great risk in buying them. If some types attract you, I don't see how you can lose anything by adding a few to your collection if the price is reasonable (unless you are a U.S. citizen who has the rare misfortune to get caught by some ODGSO gumshoe). And you just might gain; sometimes the mintage of certain restrikes is held to a strictly limited edition—and they are gold. But whether you intend to buy them or not, you should know what is around, so as not to be taken by some offer that purports to be for an original coin, or that maintains a discreet silence on the subject. Here are some of the principal items:

WELL-KNOWN GOLD RESTRIKES

AUSTRIA

Official Austrian Mint Restrikes:

Item	Type	Grade	Date	Troy Oz. Pure Gold
8 Florins/20 Francs		BU	1892	.1867
4 Florins/10 Francs		BU	1892	.0933
4 Ducats	986/1000 fine	Proof	1915	.4438
1 Ducat	986/1000 fine	Proof	1915	.1109
100 Corona	Franz Joseph	BU	1915	.9802
20 Corona	Franz Joseph	BU	1915	.1960
10 Corona	Franz Joseph	BU	1912	.0980
100 Schillings*	Maria Zell	BU	1936	.6807
3 Ducats**	Tyrol	Proof	1642	.3325

* Resembles the original coin but not exactly—can be recognized as a different coin.
** Has tiny date 1963 under horse's hooves. Issue limited to 1,000 pieces.

HUNGARY

Official Hungarian Mint Restrikes:

Item	Type	Grade	Date	Troy Oz. Pure Gold
8 Forint	Franz Joseph	BU	1887	.1867
4 Forint	Franz Joseph	BU	1870	.0933
1 Ducat	986/1000 fine	Proof	1870	.1109
100 Korona	Franz Joseph	BU	1907	.9802
20 Korona	Franz Joseph	BU	1895	.1961
10 Korona	Franz Joseph	BU	1898	.0980
100 Korona	Coronation	BU	1907	.9802
100 Pengo	St. Ladislaus*	Proof	1929	1.1343
100 Pengo	St. Stephen*	Proof	1938	1.1343
100 Pengo	St. Stephen*	Proof	1938	.7581
40 Pengo	Fr. Rakoczi*	Proof	1935	.3038

* Restrikes of pattern or *essai* pieces. Originals never issued. Restrikes reported to be limited to 1,000 pieces. (Note: Restrikes limited to 1,000 pieces are said to be marked with the tiny letters *up* (*Ungarische Pragung*) on the reverse to identify them.)

LIECHTENSTEIN
Official Restrikes—986/1000 gold:

Item	Type	Grade	Date	Troy Oz. Pure Gold
1 Ducat	Jos. Joh. Adam	Proof	1728	.1109
1 Ducat	Franz Joseph	Proof	1778	.1109
1 Ducat	Jos. Wenzel	Proof	1758	.1109
10 Ducats	Jos. Joh. Adam	Proof	1728	1.1095
10 Ducats	Carolus	Proof	1616	1.1095
Thaler		Proof	1862	.9352
Square Thaler		Proof	1619	.4755

SPAIN
Official Spanish Mint Restrikes:

Item	Type	Grade	Date	Troy Oz. Pure Gold
100 Reales		BU	1861	.2416
100 Pesetas	Alfonso XIII	BU	1897	.9335
25 Pesetas	Alfonso XII	BU	1876	.23335
20 Pesetas	Alfonso XIII	BU	1896	.1867
20 Pesetas	Alfonso XIII	BU	1887	.1867
10 Pesetas	Alfonso XII	BU	1878	.09335
4 Escudos	Isabella	BU	1868	.0966

Note:

Examine all Spanish coins by checking the stars on either side of the date. If the coin is a restrike, the true date will appear minutely engraved in the stars. As far as we know, all Spanish restrikes to date have been so marked.

Medals and Miscellaneous

In addition to the official restrikes, there are a few more legitimate items of numismatic gold, other than regular coinage, with which the gold collector or investor should be familiar.

Offstrikes are also among the lesser–known varieties of gold coinage. An offstrike is a gold coin struck from a die originally used for a silver or minor coin. In former times the practice of offstriking was used occasionally, probably to economize in the manufacture of dies. In this practice, a die that was to be used for striking both gold and silver coins would have the denomination omitted.

In modern times the custom is rare, although the government of

Monaco in recent years has struck souvenir gold pieces of double thickness from the dies used for their larger silver coins. Modern offstrikes are almost always intended for numismatic souvenirs. Regard an offstrike as you would any other gold coin; if it is an old one, check its price history; if it is a new one, check its mintage and intrinsic value before you buy.

Pattern coins or *essais* ("essays") are trial pieces—proof specimens of coins that never got to the point of official acceptance or production. They are usually very rare and often quite expensive.

Gold geologic specimens such as ore concentrates, gold flakes, dust, and nuggets are also offered, usually by the ounce, in various numismatic publications. Unrefined gold of this nature is legal for an American citizen to possess, but unless you have an unquenchable curiosity about it, or you want a jar of gold flakes or nuggets to set on your mantle as a conversation piece, I see no advantage in buying it. Unrefined gold is virtually non–negotiable, except to sell to a refiner or assayer—and then the profit potential will be nil. In the first place, the retail cost of unrefined gold is generally 30 percent or more above its intrinsic value, and second, the refiner's or assayer's fee on small lots will take another 20 to 30 percent. It takes a really smashing devaluation to come out ahead on an investment with handicaps like those. Furthermore, such an investment disregards one of the central points of this book; that numismatic potential, which is always present in gold investments in the form of coins, is too important to overlook.

Private coinage: gold coins or tokens minted by private firms under license from or with the permission of the government concerned, and intended not to deceive or defraud but to serve some useful monetary or commemorative purpose, is fortunately no great problem as yet, even though the practice is not uncommon in some parts of the world.

Some of the private gold issues of past eras, such as the Pioneer or Territorial coins of the U.S., and the various "gold rush" Territorial coinage and stamped ingots of Australia and Argentina, have attained great numismatic value. But as for modern private coinage, don't depend on anything more than the actual intrinsic value. I grant that it is possible for some obscure private coinage of today to become tomorrow's great numismatic rarity, but buying on that basis is pure speculation, unless you have offset the cost with significant intrinsic value.

Information on the subject of private gold coinage is regrettably scarce, although the practice is widespread in the Near and Far East. The "tola" coinage of India and other parts of the Orient is a good example. These pieces were and are still issued by several Indian and Asian banking houses in denominations of ¼ tola to 10 tolas, the tola being the equivalent of about 11.6 grams of gold .9167 fine. There are many varieties of tola pieces, some are round but they also may be square, rectangular, diamond-shaped, or scalloped. Larger denominations (up to 100 tolas) are in the form of stamped ingots.

Private issues of Centenario-type coins are said to be available in Mexico, but I have yet to see one illustrated or hear one accurately described.

My advice is to regard private coinage just as the issuers do—merely as a convenient form of bullion. If you ever run across any privately minted coins or ingots, pay only for the gold value, and make sure it really is gold.

Medals and medallions are still other numismatic forms that the gold collector and investor may have occasion to consider. A medal may be described as any small disc or piece of metal, cast, engraved or die impressed with symbols or images to commemorate a specific event or person. Excluding those medals struck to honor participation in military campaigns and similar events, which are designed to be worn by the recipient with a ribbon or other device,[4] most medals closely resemble large commemorative coins, except that a medal has no monetary function and bears no marks of monetary value. But like coins, most medals are struck on both sides, that is, having an obverse and a reverse. *Medallion* is merely the term used to describe a large medal, two inches or more in diameter. Medallions are often struck on one side only.

Many great eras of medallic art have passed since the Italian artist Vittore Pisano began it all in 1438 with his portrait medal of the Byzantine emperor John VII, but none has exceeded our own —at least in sheer volume. In the last few years, the world's numismatic markets have been offering collectors an extraordinary number of privately struck medals and medal series, commemorating a great variety of events, occasions, and famous or noted individuals.

The public reception given this rather sudden and perhaps unexpected reawakening of the medallic arts has been nothing less than enthusiastic. The majority of the several private mints in the U.S., most of them established in very recent years, have prospered greatly, and some have expanded their operations into major, nationally known enterprises. I am sure that the owners and stockholders of these private mints must still be pleasantly stunned by the rapidity as well as the extent of their success. But there can no longer be any question: privately struck commemorative medals, or "art medals," are now a recognized and significant part of the international numismatic scene.

An assessment of the investment potential of modern art medals, however, is difficult to present in specific terms, despite the obvious current interest of collectors and investors in this special area of numismatics. For one thing, art medals have not had the lengthy seasoning in the market place that is necessary to establish reliable numismatic values and trends. Also, there are so many varieties of medals and medal series now in the hands of collectors, investors, and dealers that it would take a substantial volume on art criticism to examine the majority of them and to identify those medals with the greatest potential for investment success.

A work on art criticism would be required to treat the subject properly, because *the esthetic qualities of an art medal are the primary attributes of its value.* That is, at any rate, the considered opinion of this writer. Based on the typical offering price of most private medals, intrinsic value is only a secondary consideration— and that is as it should be. The precious-metal content of a medal is used, when it is used properly, primarily to enhance appearance and desirability, rather than to establish a specific monetary value on an intrinsic basis. Modern art medals, particularly those of superior achievement from an esthetic and technical point of view, with their brilliant high relief strikings and mirror- or matte-proof backgrounds are most impressive to look at. Such medals, when designed by an artist or sculptor of uncommon ability and executed by skilled and conscientious craftsmen, can be enormously attractive, and it is obvious from the numismatic press that many collectors and investors have already succumbed to such attractions.

Scarcity, of course, is also a factor that contributes to the investment merits of an art medal, but scarcity alone, without some recognizable esthetic merit, would be of little or no value at all. It is therefore primarily on esthetic merit, or value as a work of art, that judgment must be made concerning the investment potential of modern art medals, with limited issue as the principal supporting consideration. Although it is not appropriate in this volume on gold coins to examine the subject of art medals in great detail, I shall offer a few general recommendations to the prospective purchaser of such medals. But first, let me point out that this discussion as it relates to *gold* art medals is more or less academic as far as Americans are concerned. The present policy of ODGSO completely prohibits the importation and possession of these (gold) medals. Nevertheless, I shall continue on the grounds that a) perhaps not all the readers of this work are U.S. residents, b) my comments can be applied to silver, copper, and bronze medals, as well as to those of gold, c) ODGSO may not be around forever.

It should be clear from our discussion thus far that one of the first things to look for when trying to estimate the current value, investment potential, and desirability of an art medal is the reputation and prior work of the artist who designed it, and the artistic merit of the particular work under consideration—its design, overall appearance, subject matter, and technique. The next thing to consider is the quality of the minting. The craftsmanship and fidelity of the die engraving and the general quality of the strike should be maintained at the highest possible level, so as to enhance rather than degrade the work of the artist. Second only to the reputation and achievement of the artist-designer should be the reputation and prior successes of the mint, and the recognizable technical quality of the medal being considered.

The edition should be strictly limited. At the maximum, perhaps 10,000 pieces would qualify as a limited edition, although I would say that smaller editions, say, 1,000 to 5,000 pieces, are preferable. An edition can't be too small, however, or it will become virtually noncollectable. The best numismatic values are often established by items that are very scarce in relation to the demand for them, yet available in sufficient quantities so that a number of collectors can participate in collecting them (or perhaps compete with each other for possession). Whatever the primary reason, there must be a sufficient number of pieces available for sale or trading so that a market can be established. Strangely enough, items that are unique or almost so, like the Indian prince's wedding coin, are seldom of interest to an appreciable number of collectors.

Man is a gregarious creature. We have some vital need to share our activities, our interests, and even our collecting triumphs with others of kindred spirit. Understandably we want our treasured objects to be rare, even unique, but at the same time we prefer those precious items that are still comfortably familiar in terms of our own cultural and historical experience and background. An 1858 Eagle is worth more than $6,000 at present, because it is a tremendously scarce numismatic treasure. But at the same time it is still an Eagle, one of the most widely known and most honored of U.S. coins. So perhaps we should reserve some consideration for the subject matter of an art medal, at least to the extent that its nature is compatible with the American cultural and historic experience (assuming that it is a medal being offered for sale in the U.S.).

The intrinsic-value metal content, weight, and fineness of an art medal are assets that add to its overall appearance and desirability. One should expect the medium (in the case of an art medal the medium is the metal itself) to be worthy of the artist. Great paintings are not made on the backs of orange crates (the antics of the present pop-art generation notwithstanding). Nor will any artist worthy of the name print etchings or engravings on wrapping paper. Precious metals are therefore most fitting for medals, though copper and bronze have their place.

Throughout history, gold, silver, copper, and bronze have been considered metals of the arts as well as monetary metals. Copper and bronze are not precious metals in the same sense as we regard gold, silver, and platinum, but the use of copper and bronze has traditionally been reserved for objects of more than common value. When art medals are struck in gold or platinum, and particularly in the latter, intrinsic value naturally contributes substantially to the retail price. Platinum is an extremely expensive metal; its bullion price ranges from $150 to $250 per ounce.

Considering all factors, there are, in my view, three basic criteria that can be used to estimate the value and investment potential of an art medal, particularly one that has not yet had sufficient market exposure to establish a definite numismatic trend. They are:

1. The design and conception as a work of art.
   a. Past recognition of the artist.
   b. Merit of the work under consideration: design, technique, subject, style.
2. The quality of the medal as a precious object.
   a. The perfection of the die engraving.
   b. The precision of the minting.
   c. Intrinsic value, weight and fineness.
3. The limits of the edition.
   a. Minimum: perhaps 250 pieces.
   b. Maximum: about 10,000 pieces.

The reader with some art background will probably recognize that the previous criteria are to a large extent identical with those standards of evaluation one should apply to fine graphics, that is, etchings, engravings, lithographs, woodcuts, etc. Such a comparison is indeed appropriate. I believe art medals of superior merit could have an investment potential similar to that of fine graphics. It should be noted that the graphics of well-known artists have been, until now at least, one of the most rewarding areas of art investment.

I have gone into the subject of private art medals in this much detail partly because of the recent and unprecedented introduction of such medals, in platinum, silver, copper, and bronze, into the American numismatic scene. It must be recognized that American collectors *are buying* these medals in considerable numbers; hence some guidance seemed essential. Admittedly, as an American citizen, my exposure to gold art medals has been somewhat limited, but I did manage to see some modern gold art medals displayed by dealers in Canada. They were magnificent.

One final word: art medals are frequently offered as a series, with anywhere from five to fifty medals on the same theme or subject, attractively boxed and sold on a subscription basis. If you start buying one of these series, be prepared to buy the entire set of medals. Owning just a few art medals out of a matched series is like having only a few volumes from a set of encyclopedias. They might be just a little difficult to sell.

Special-award gold medals are yet another area of the medallic arts, although probably one that the typical gold collector will seldom if ever have any occasion to consider. These medals are usually of extremely limited issue, because they are presented only to an individual or a very small group, usually by a government or social organization, in recognition of some special service or achievement. They seldom appear on the numismatic market; when they do they are primarily of interest to the collectors of military awards, orders, and decorations.

Official gold commemorative medals, issued by a government, are more numerous, but they too are seldom available in sufficient quantity or variety to attract an enthusiastic following among collectors and investors. The last one I saw offered for sale was at a numismatic auction; there a Graf Zeppelin gold medal, struck in 1929 to honor the round-the-world flight of that famous airship, went for only $58, although I had guessed it would bring considerably more. It only goes to prove that accurately judging the market value of a gold medal is a far more difficult proposition than determining the approximate worth and potential of a gold coin. Thin markets, that is, those with only a small number of potential buyers and sellers, tend to be erratic and trendless.

The criteria for estimating the value of an official commemorative medal are basically the same as those outlined for an art medal, except that in the case of an official commemorative medal the event or person honored can be of primary importance. In a privately struck art medal the event or person commemorated is generally of secondary consequence, for there is usually no direct historic association, at least not in an official sense.

ODGSO policy regarding official commemorative medals of gold again offers little encouragement to the American collector who might wish to proceed further in this area. The importation and possession of these (gold) medals are generally prohibited in the U.S. A clarification of policy announced by ODGSO on June 10, 1969, states that henceforth only antique gold medals, that is, those 100 years old or older, will be considered for license. Prior to the 1969 revisions of the Gold Regulations, a few modern gold medals had been licensed on an individual basis.

At present several foreign governments periodically issue gold commemorative medals, some for public sale, and others only for special internal distribution. Perhaps the most widely known official gold commemorative medals are those struck periodically by the Vatican and the State of Israel Mint; they are also about the only contemporary gold medals struck in any appreciable quantity. Both of these gold medal series should undoubtedly prove to be sound investments, particularly new issues that can be purchased at the mint price. But most older medals of these states by now should have had sufficient market seasoning to establish reliable price trends, although these medals are seldom encountered by the typical American coin dealer. The larger numismatic specialty houses, especially Canadian and Continental firms, should be the best sources of information on Vatican, Israeli, and other foreign official gold medals (and private gold art medals, also).

Notes

CHAPTER XI

1. How anyone made a profit on that one I don't know. In my opinion, this is one case where the buyers will be the real winners.

2. *Coin World*, October 10, 1966.
3. Full details on U.S. gold policy pertaining to restrikes and all other coins may be obtained from the Office of Domestic Gold and Silver Operations, Treasury Dept., Washington D.C. 20220.
4. We also exclude military orders and decorations, which are a completely separate branch of numismatics.

XII

Counterfeits, Fakes, and Forgeries

"The buyer needs one hundred eyes, the seller not one."

—GEORGE HERBERT

THIS IS ONE CHAPTER I WISH I DIDN'T HAVE TO WRITE, BUT UN-
fortunately it is one of the most necessary. Dishonesty is probably
no more of a problem in numismatic investing than it is in any
other area of commerce; you can get swindled on a stock, a bond,
or a lot just as easy as you can on a coin. But the possibility is there,
and it can only be reduced or eliminated through the proper application of knowledge by the buyer. The victims of con men or cheats
in any field are invariably the ignorant and the gullible; even a
very modest knowledge of your investment interest should give
you adequate protection. If you know just the obvious things to
look for, and follow a few basic rules, your chances of being cheated
are virtually nil.

Counterfeits are certainly nothing new in the field of numismatics. It is probably safe to assume that as long as man has been
coining money, some men have been making counterfeits. Most of
them were crude copies that wouldn't fool anyone who looked
closely, and most of these have long been eliminated. Counterfeiting
in the usual semantic sense refers to the illegal reproduction of legal
tender money with the intent to defraud by putting it in circulation.
Our particular hazard, however, is not the old-time counterfeits,

though it is possible some might appear at rare intervals, but modern numismatic forgeries.[1]

The great expansion of interest in numismatics and in the collecting of rare coins that has developed in recent years has, unfortunately, also attracted some unsavory characters who seek to take advantage of it by supplying the numismatic market with forgeries. Forgery has reached the point where all collectors and investors should be aware of its extent and be concerned with its elimination, but it should by no means be an occasion for fear and panic. I believe it should be regarded as a challenge, a challenge that can easily be met when we are forearmed with knowledge and know the basic rules of our business.

It has long been recognized that every counterfeit or forgery has one or several clues on it that even the average student of coins can spot immediately. Some forgeries and fakes are obviously crude and made to be palmed off on the uninitiated and the tourists, but others are produced by more modern methods and with considerable skill, and these require a bit of study. Since some forgeries are designed to defraud even experienced numismatists, they can at times be quite dangerous. However, certain characteristics appear repeatedly on forgeries, probably due to the limited technical facilities generally available to forgers.

The milling or reeding is seldom consistent, and it is never as deep or as sharp as the original. It does not go straight across the width of the coin, usually being shorter and shallower than it should be, and the lines and spaces between them are not uniform.

Beading, when it occurs around the circumference, is never consistent or uniform. The dots may vary in shape or spacing, or both. On genuine coins the beads are very crisp and uniform. On forgeries they appear uneven and tend to fade in places.

Weight is apt to be a little off, usually too light, but occasionally it is on the heavy side. (This is where that little scale I told you about may be of use—see Friedberg for correct weights of coins.)

The entire coin may appear flat, with none of the engraving or relief pronounced and vivid.

Cast forgeries have a dull, minutely pock-marked surface, rather than the hard crisp appearance of a geninue coin. Cast coins may appear slightly eroded, or have an overall unpleasant shimmering appearance.

Planchets may not be true; they may be a little thicker or thinner on one side than on the other.

The gold may be too yellow, indicating that it is not the correct karat or alloy, or it may have a slight reddish appearance indicating that it might be modern gold. Sometimes there is a blackish dirty appearance in the details.

Lettering is often poorly executed, being irregularly spaced, or having letters too thick or slightly crooked. Fine lettering and serifs tend to fade out.

The whole appearance of forged coins is likely to be quite soft; hence, some of them are deliberately worn to VF condition in an effort to disguise this characteristic. Even a worn coin will have a certain crispness, but a forgery, particularly a cast one, will have a roundness and overall fuzziness in design.

Some minute parts may be missing altogether, such as the engraver's initials, small rosettes, stars, etc. Such defects are found by comparing the suspected coin with a photograph of a genuine one, or with the genuine coin itself.

All of the preceding defects can be easily detected with a little patience and a good magnifying glass. A 3-to-5-power glass is usually strong enough, although the advanced collector or specialist in ancient or exotic foreign coins may have occasion to use a 10–power jeweler's eyepiece. The magnifying glass is the best and the one indispensable tool for detecting forgeries. Always carry your glass when you are shopping for gold coins. Always use your glass to examine carefully coins you receive through mail order as soon as you receive them. Return any that seems at all suspicious or with which you are not satisfied because it did not live up to its advertised description as to grade and condition. You will need to use your glass constantly, not only to protect yourself from forgeries, but to help you determine grading. Sometimes a coin offered as BU may, under the magnifying glass, reveal telltale signs of wear that would reduce it to AU. Don't hesitate to use your glass when buying a coin—I guarantee that the dealer will feel no inhibitions about using his if you are the one trying to sell the coin to him.

There are some older reference works on the subject of counterfeit gold coins, principally Dieffenbacher's *Counterfeit Gold Coins of the World*, but the immediacy of the problem requires constant alertness and a continual review of the numismatic journals by the collector and investor. The numismatic press does a very good job of reporting forgeries and counterfeits whenever they are discovered; by all means clip and file these articles or add them to your reference scrapbook.

Fortunately, if you are going to specialize in U.S. gold coins, or if you follow my advice and have the balance of your collection in U.S. gold, the possibility of encountering forgeries is minimal. U.S. gold coins are difficult to forge and, except for the more scarce dates and types, hardly worth the effort. Also, U.S. dealers, collectors, and investors are generally very knowledgeable about U.S. gold coins; the forgers are aware of how difficult it would be to dupe them. That is why most forgers concentrate on European and Middle Eastern coins.[2]

Although I have taken potshots at the Treasury, I must acknowledge that the Secret Service has done a good job in successfully eliminating nearly all attempts at counterfeiting or forging U.S. gold coins.[3] Local police, too, play their part in helping to prevent this kind of fraud; reports of successful arrests and prosecutions by local authorities for this crime are occasionally recorded in the press.

However, the April 1969 revisions of the Gold Regulations, which now permit the unrestricted importation of pre-1934 gold coins, add a new uncertainty to the problem of gold-coin forgeries. The former policy, which completely banned the entry of most pre-1934 gold, probably had at least one beneficial side effect, in that it made the importing of fakes and forgeries somewhat more difficult. Although there is no question that forged gold coins were smuggled into the United States prior to the lifting of the pre-1934 ban, it will obviously be a little less difficult now. U.S. laws and Treasury regulations still forbid the import and possession of counterfeit or forged gold coins, but one cannot expect every customs inspector to be a numismatic expert.

Small lots of fraudulent and fake gold coins will no doubt continue to arrive in the U.S. in much the same manner as they did before, in the pockets of returning U.S. servicemen, diplomats, business men, and tourists who are prime targets for the forgers abroad. The incidence of this kind of entry will be greater now than before the relaxation of the ban on pre-1934 imports, but to the American collector the advantages of having a far greater number of genuine pre-1934 gold coins available at perhaps a more equitable cost are well worth the slight extra risk that may now prevail regarding fakes and forgeries.

It is well to remember that the major source of forgeries will still be those smuggled in by professional criminals, who prefer to deal in large lots in order to make their efforts sufficiently profitable. Changes in the Gold Regulations probably do not affect this type of criminal activity one way or another. The Bureau of Customs, the Secret Service, and the F.B.I. will, I sincerely hope, continue to work diligently to suppress any illegal traffic in numismatic counterfeits and forgeries. Nevertheless, counterfeits, fakes, and forgeries will undoubtedly continue to turn up now and then in the numismatic market, so we should keep alert, through the numismatic and financial press, for any further developments in this area. We should also be aware of the most prominent forgeries that have already been uncovered, because of the possibility (even though it is unlikely) of being exposed to their companions. Here are some of these items, culled from my scrapbook:

ARGENTINA.   Five Pesos coins dated 1888 have been forged. The gold is too yellow, the beading about the exergue is irregular, and the design and lettering in general are quite soft, with essential details lacking or fuzzy.

AUSTRALIA.   Some common late-date sovereigns are reported to have been forged extremely well. Inspect all common-date sovereigns with a jeweler's glass.

AUSTRIA.   I don't know of any forgeries, but there are plenty of official restrikes (see chapter 11).

BELGIUM. Some very rare issues, like the 100 Francs 1911 and 1912, exist in forgeries or private restrikes, but they are said to be easy to recognize.

BRAZIL. Forging and faking of Brazilian coins is endemic. No doubt the extreme inflationary climate in Brazil has been a factor in this situation. Some of these forgeries are said to be very well done and difficult to recognize. The following gold coins are known to be forged: heavy 20,000 *Reis* pieces with four M's, 1724, 1725, 1726, 1727; 10,000 *Reis* with four M's, 1725, 1726, and 1727; 12,000 *Reis* with one large M, 1730, 1731, and 1732. Also: 6,400 *Reis*, 1832 Rio mint; 10,000 *Reis* of 1895 and 1909; 20,000 *Reis* of 1895; 6,400 *Reis* of 1822, Rio mint; 20,000 *Reis*, 1850, high collar; 20,000 *Reis* of 1851 and all dates between 1823 and 1828; 6,400 *Reis* of Peter I, 1828; 4,000 *Reis*, Peter I, all dates between 1823 and 1827.

BYZANTINE AND ANCIENT COINS. The possibility of forgeries and counterfeits here is great. This type of coin should only be bought from knowledgeable dealers in this field, who will guarantee (in writing) that the coin is genuine.

CANADA. The $10 gold pieces dated 1912 and 1914 have been forged. Two things stand out: the color is more reddish than normal, indicating modern gold, and the planchets are not of uniform thickness. Also, the beading is irregular and various other details seem weak or worn, including the fine work on the collar of George V and the faces of the lions on the shield on the reverse.

CZECHOSLOVAKIA. The 1928 gold Ducat is reported forged and is said to have easily recognized irregularities in lettering and other details.

EGYPT. Faud five-pound pieces and quite a few other Egyptian and Middle Eastern coins have been forged. Generally, they are said to be of low quality and easy to recognize.

FRANCE. A few late-date 20-franc pieces have been counterfeited very well. They are very difficult to recognize at first, and require a thorough and careful examination to identify them—but they can be detected. A 100 Francs Napoleon III dated 1856 has also been forged.

GERMANY. Rare 10- and 20-mark coins have been imitated quite well. This type of coin should be purchased only from well-known dealers who will guarantee it to be genuine.

GREAT BRITAIN. Some late-date sovereigns have been forged, including those dated 1899 and 1917. They do not have clearly defined reeding, and they feature irregular lettering.

ITALY. Italian gold coins have been extensively forged, and these fakes are designed principally for taking the tourists. A careful examination should be sufficient to detect them, but it would be wise to compare any Italian gold coin with a good enlarged photo of the original—or get a guarantee in writing. The following gold coins are known to have been imitated: 50 Lire, 1836, Carlo Alberto, Turin mint; 100 Lire, 1835, Carlo Alberto, Turin mint; 50 Lire, 1864; 100 Lire, 1872; 100 Lire, 1878, Vittorio Emanuel II, Turin mint; 50 Lire, 1884; 100 Lire, 1880; 100 Lire, 1883, Umberto I; 50 Lire, 1911, 1912; 100 Lire, 1903, 1905, 1912, 1925, Vittorio Emanuel III.

JAPAN. The large *obans* have been counterfeited and forged. A dishonest coin of this type (it is little more than stamped ingot— see Friedberg: Japan) will be hard to recognize.

MEXICO. Some rarities and some late-date common gold have been forged, but all are said to be easy to recognize.

MONTENEGRO. The gold 20 Perpera, dated 1910, is forged.

NETHERLANDS. Recent forgeries include a 10 Guilders, 1877; 10 Guilders, 1933; and 5 Guilders, 1912. An 1809 gold Ducat counterfeit has noticeably weak details and a blackish, dirty appearance An 1843 Five Guilders forgery has reddish gold and weak details.

PAPAL STATES. A forged 10 Scudi, Gregory XVI, 1835, and 100 Lire, Pius IX, 1866, are reported.

PERU. Imitations of the 50 Soles, 1930 and 1931, are reported to be easy to recognize.

SPAIN. No forgeries reported, but plenty of restrikes (see chapter 11).

TRANSYLVANIA. (Hungary) Many rarities were forged in the early part of this century. All are defective and easy to recognize.

UNITED STATES. A U.S. $5 gold of 1880 has been reported recently; reeding on the edges is not clearly defined and there are irregularities in the lettering and details. Cast forgeries of a $3 gold and $1 gold have also been seen, but should be easy to detect with a good glass.

VENEZUELA. The 100 Bolivares gold coin dated 1887 has been forged. These frauds are purposely worn to VF or EF grade to aid in the deception, but the reeding is much too shallow. The coin is heavier than the genuine piece and the inside beading on the obverse is quite uneven.

The previous list is by no means complete, but it is intended to give the reader some idea of the extent and nature of the problem, as well as to alert collectors and investors to the dangers of these specific coins. However, there should be no cause for alarm. But circumspection is in order when you are purchasing gold coins, particularly European, Eastern, and South American coins and expensive rarities. There are a few simple rules to follow when buying gold coins, and these rules plus a good glass and a little patience will keep the collector and investor out of trouble:

1. Examine coins carefully before purchasing. There is no substitute for knowledge. Know as much as you can about your business. Look for the characteristics previously described in this chapter.

2. Beware of coins offered too cheaply. If the price is well below the prevailing market, or too far below recent catalogue or auction prices, be sure you have a convincing explanation for this apparent charity.

3. Buy only from reputable dealers. Get to know your local dealers. Become acquainted with the larger dealers in the big cities nearest you. Be discreet, but find out as much as you can what other collectors' experiences have been with various dealers. It is also safe to buy from mail-order dealers of good reputation. If you have any doubts, contact the newspaper or magazine that carries their advertising; it usually will be able to inform you about the reputation and references of the dealer in question.

4. Get a written guarantee of authenticity. When purchasing any rare and expensive coin, any ancient, Byzantine or medieval gold, or any coin that is known to have been forged or counter-

feited in the past, obtain both a written guarantee of authenticity and a promise of refund in case of forgery or misrepresentation.
5. When in doubt—don't buy. If you have any reason to feel that a coin is in any way questionable, don't buy it; there are too many quality items around to take risks.

There is one type of fake that is more difficult to guard against than the outright forgery, and that is the genuine coin that has been altered in some way, such as by changing a letter or a number in the date, by removing a mint mark, etc., to make it imitate a more valuable coin in the same series. Sometimes these alterations can be discovered by careful scrutiny with a good glass, but if the coin has been altered by a skillful operator, it may take an expert with a microscope to detect it. The best defense here is to apply rule number four: if the item is scarce and expensive, and its rarity depends upon a mint mark or a date or some other small detail that can easily be altered (remember, 8s can become 3s, and 7s and 4s can become 1s), get a written guarantee of authenticity. Actually, a written authentication from a well–known dealer or numismatist will make any expensive coin easier to sell.

As for the obvious potential fakes—coins that are not catalogued anywhere, or are so "rare" that nobody seems able positively to identify them—well, they may be a new discovery, but my advice is to leave them to the numismatic experts. One cardinal rule of successful investment—any kind of investment—is to invest only in items of proven value.

Related to unidentified coins are the so-called fantasy pieces. These are coins (more accurately, items purporting to be coins) that are privately struck in order to be sold as souvenirs, propaganda, or satiric pieces. They are not really coins, even though they may have the reverse of a known coin, or bear inscriptions and denominations taken from genuine coins. They are actually private medals rather than coins. Distinguishing a fantasy from an outright fake is the fact that the producers of fantasies usually have a more or less legitimate motive and are not specifically trying to defraud the purchaser.

One recent and curiously interesting example of a fantasy is a gold "Mussolini" piece that has turned up in Italy. It bears a helmeted portrait of the late Italian dictator on the obverse, along with the date, 1943, in Roman numerals. The reverse is identical to the gold 100 Lire commemorative of 1923.[4] Other Mussolini fantasies have been reported in Italy, struck in both gold and silver, with planchets and a reverse identical to the 20 Lire silver commemorative of 1928. Apparently there are still enough die-hard Fascists around to provide a market for these items, or else they just want to see their leader's portrait on the coins of his era—an honor the sawdust caesar did not get in his lifetime.[5]

Strangely enough, I believe that fantasies like these (they probably are not produced in any great quantity) may very well have some numismatic potential—but I would not bet on it. If one really intrigues you, pay no more than 30 percent over intrinsic value for it—well, 50 percent at the most, that is, if you can actually determine intrinsic value.

Notes

CHAPTER XII

1. *Counterfeit, forgery,* and *fake* can be and are used interchangeably to describe any dishonest numismatic item. Semantically, I believe each word has a predominant meaning (see glossary).
2. Rather incredibly it has been reported that some forgeries of European and other foreign coins were actually made in the U.S. and exported to be sold to U.S. tourists and servicemen.
3. Nevertheless, we must never get careless or overconfident; look over U.S. coins just as thoroughly as any other.
4. Commemorating the first anniversary of the Fascist "March on Rome."
5. How he missed it I don't know. As an old Italian-campaign soldier I can testify that he managed to get his profile on almost everything else.

XIII

The Model Collections

"On the whole, it is patience which makes the final difference between those who succeed and those who fail in all things."
—JOHN RUSKIN

THE MODEL GOLD COLLECTIONS, OR PORTFOLIOS AS I THINK IT appropriate to call them, are based on the rather simple premise that for maximum safety, at least half the total amount invested should be in coins costing less than double their intrinsic value. The reader will note that this ideal is becoming harder and harder to realize, as the world's monetary structure shudders and creaks from crisis to crisis and ultimately to catastrophe. Nevertheless, a minimum of 50 percent of the collection should be in coins of high bullion value, hopefully costing no more than twice their net gold content at $35 per ounce.

Most of the remainder of the portfolio should consist of coins that are primarily of numismatic interest, but coins that still retain enough intrinsic value to cover perhaps 25 percent of their cost (at $35 per ounce). I also recommend that 10 percent to 15 percent of the average portfolio be represented by coins of high or very high numismatic interest, having as a result only negligible gold content value. In the more expensive collections ($5,000 or more), the proportion of high-cost numismatic-value coins can be increased to 20 or 25 percent of total market value, if desired.

As for the matter of pricing, the reader will appreciate the difficulty in trying to establish with any degree of finality something so ephemeral as retail prices for a very volatile commodity in a very shaky and inflationary economic environment. The prices shown in the portfolios are simply those the author considered to be reasonable at the time of writing. All of these prices *could* have been obtained by a *careful shopper* at some time during 1969. They are not necessarily the lowest prices recorded during this period, and definitely not the highest. There is, after all, only one certainty about prices in a free market: they will vary—from time to time, from place to place, and from dealer to dealer. There is nothing sacred about the prices given in the portfolios, or in any other part of this book; the investor will have to do the best he can with the situation that prevails at the time he is investing.

The author has, for example, BU double Eagles that were bought for $40 apiece, but I would be quite willing to continue adding to this series at $65 or $70 apiece, and perhaps someday, not too far distant, even at $80 or $85 apiece. I recall that the 50 Pesos Centenario, a beautiful coin rich in intrinsic value, sold for just $50 only a few years ago. It now brings $75, when you can find one, and I have every intention of finishing my series at this price, for I fully expect the Centenario to be in demand at $100 each before long.

The general level of prices for gold coins may very well be higher by the time this work reaches its readers; but possibly it may be somewhat lower. This situation is due to two powerful basic forces at work in the general economy, and consequently in the numismatic market as well. First, there is a *short-term deflationary trend*, caused by an increasingly overtaxed and exhausted world credit structure, and by our own government's temporary restrictive monetary and fiscal policies (which, the government hopes, will save the dollar from collapse until the SDRs can be established as a fresh source of fiat credit).

The second major force, and certainly the dominant one, is the *long–term inflationary trend*, which stems from the continuing general acceptance of, and faith in, the delusions of the fiat money, fiat credit, neo-Keynesian New Economics, and from the general world conditions outlined at the end of chapter four. With two opposite and massive economic forces contending for domination, it becomes impossible to predict near–term price movements; I assume they will be somewhat erratic. Therefore, base your general strategy on the long term, but plan your tactics to take advantage of periodic unexpected price reactions.

The recommendations and suggestions given earlier in this book are intended to be the basic guidelines for building a gold-coin collection specifically suited to the investment climate of our age; permit me to suggest that they be reread from time to time. Very briefly, the basic tactics of gold-coin collecting and investing are few in number and simple in conception: do not chase prices during periodic gold-buying panics; keep a long-term outlook; shop carefully; buy on significant reactions; take advantage of any unexpected opportunity that develops.

As I write this, BU common-date $20 gold pieces are selling for around $75; a few months ago they were somewhat higher. During the previous winter, however, profit taking and a temporary lessening of international monetary tensions had brought about a decline in the price of this coin to the $60–$65 level, down considerably from the gold-panic highs recorded in March of 1968. In recent years, the pattern of prices realized for nearly all types of gold coins has been directly affected, as one might well expect, by the ebb and flow of international monetary crises, and by the free and black market prices of gold. The following table (Fig. 33) illustrates this point.

It must be assumed that international and domestic monetary trends, the progress of inflation in various Western countries, currency devaluations or the threat of them, and fluctuations in the free market price of gold will continue strongly to influence the retail price of numismatic gold coins. In 1969, U.S. gold coins were the most active series in numismatics, with prices changing rapidly and noticeably, sometimes from week to week. At the moment, gold-coin prices again appear to be receding a bit. Perhaps the official IMF adoption of the SDR scheme will be sufficient to

Fig. 33

RECENT DEALER PRICES FOR COMMON-DATE
U.S. GOLD COINS*

Date:		Dec. 1966	July 1967	Dec. 1967	Mar. 1968	Dec. 1968	Feb. 1969	Apr. 1969	July 1969
Coin									
Lib.	$20	$48	$52	$65	$85	$64	$75	$85	$75
St. G.	$20	47	50	63	85	62	73	85	72
Lib.	$10	30	33	35	55	38	42	55	50
Ind.	$10	45	55	60	75	65	72	80	70
Lib.	$ 5	25	28	30	45	32	37	45	45
Ind.	$ 5	32	35	38	65	40	48	65	70

* Compiled from various dealers' advertised retail prices.

cause a further dip. The July 1969 announcement that the SDRs would probably be finally ratified and adopted at the fall (1969) meeting of the IMF was enough to bring on a wave of panic selling of gold shares on the New York and London stock exchanges by misguided and foolish speculators. Many well-known gold stocks fell by 50 percent or more in only a few weeks. The reaction in the gold-coin market, however, was very mild. I would say that this illustrates the difference between a market under the influence of nervous and ill-informed speculators, and one dominated by calm, rational, and knowledgeable long-term investors.

But as we have seen, gold-coin prices *do* undergo periodic short-term fluctuations in retail price, even though the long-term trend has been one of substantial advance. Any further (temporary) contractions will only present additional opportunities for those interested in gold-coin investing. And one day, perhaps sooner than expected, we will have seen the final opportunity to get in at anywhere near reasonable prices; time is running out on the 1934 gold price for the American dollar; our paper dam will inevitably be washed away. The adoption of a worldwide fiat paper currency in the form of SDRs or "paper gold" will certainly not save the dollar; in fact, it will actually serve only to intensify the world's coming monetary debacle by diluting central bank reserves to an even greater extent than the present critical level. Consequently, the ultimate return to gold and sanity, when it comes (and it is sure to come eventually), will see an even higher fixed international price for gold than was probable before the SDRs.

Therefore, shop wisely, but act decisively. Whenever you buy a coin it should be looked upon as a permanent addition to your financial and investment structure. Don't second-guess yourself by thinking you might have bought a certain coin cheaper had you waited a few days or weeks more. Investment decisions should be made calmly, rationally, and logically—that is why I have included so many charts and tables in this book. Once a commitment is made, it should just as logically and unemotionally be given ample time to mature. Do not be affected by short-term developments; short-term price reactions are opportunities to buy, not invitations to sell. Acting emotionally in financial matters is almost always a cause for bitter and costly regret at some later date. So be systematic, unhesitating, and coolly analytical in your approach to building a gold-coin collection. Decide what type of collection you would like to have; have a definite program for acquisition; then know what type of coin you are looking for. In short, the golden rule for gold-coin investing is: Buy right, sit tight.

Basically, the purpose of the model portfolios (see Figs. 34–42 in this chapter) is not to establish specific "buy points" for the coins concerned, but to present concrete examples of collections that may result from following the principles and recommendations set forth in this book.

The emphasis, of course, is on the coins of the United States; they are at present the best bargains in terms of both intrinsic and numis-

Fig. 34

MODEL $100 PORTFOLIO

No.	Item	Type	Grade	Date	Cost
1	U.S. $20	Liberty or St. Gaudens	XF-BU	Any	$65.00
1	U.S. $10	Liberty	XF-BU	Any	35.00
				Total:	$100.00

Fig. 35

MODEL $500 PORTFOLIO

No.	Item	Type	Grade	Date	Cost
2	U.S. $20	Liberty	XF-BU	Mixed	$130.00
1	U.S. $20	St. Gaudens	XF-BU	Any	65.00
1	U.S. $10	Liberty	XF-BU	Any	35.00
1	U.S. $10	Indian	XF-BU	Any	55.00
1	U.S. $ 5	Liberty	XF-BU	Any	30.00
1	U.S. $ 2½	Philadelphia Sesquicentennial Commemorative	BU	1926	55.00
1	Mex. 50 Pesos	Centenario	AU-BU	Any	70.00
1	Mex. 20 Pesos	Azteca	AU-BU	1959	30.00
1	Canada	Sovereign George V	AU-BU	Any	30.00
				Total:	$500.00

matic values. The coins of Mexico are prominently featured as they too are similarly situated. The balance of the coins in each model portfolio was selected with a view to adding a little more excitement and color to each group, as well as increasing investment potential. But each investor is advised to give reign to his own personal inclinations in this area and freely substitute coins of his own choosing that are similar in cost and numismatic potential.

For those investors with exotic tastes and ambitions, I have included three world gold portfolios, designed for specific purposes and investment groups. Of course, any collector can make his own combinations, choosing from the basic model portfolios and the world groups, or he can add U.S. coins of his preference to balance any of the world groups. The primary intention of all of these portfolio examples is to give the reader a general sense of what constitutes a good gold collection for today's conditions, rather than present rigid programs—although you can certainly use them as such, if you wish.

The model portfolios can also be readily used as guides for exclusively U.S.–type collections, simply by substituting U.S. coins of equal numismatic value and intrinsic gold content for the foreign coins on the general lists. And although I have not thought it necessary to give specific examples, one can quickly recognize that the broad selection of Mexican gold readily available, plus the gold series of Cuba, can form the basic structure for an exclusively Latin American collection, or that U.S., Mexican, and Canadian coins can be combined in an all–North American collection. There are no limits to the types of combinations possible in gold-coin collecting, except as one feels the necessity to provide effective investment potential and to minimize risks.

Where grading varies with individual coins in the portfolio, one should obviously try to buy the best grade one can get for the approximate percentage of capital recommended for that particular coin. As prices do indeed vary, especially among the coins of high numismatic value, it may help to view the dollar amounts allotted for each coin, or group of coins, as approximate percentages of the whole portfolio value (that is, a $50 coin represents 5 percent of the $1,000 portfolio, etc.).

Considering the price levels at the time of writing, I advise the reader that in some cases (such as in Fig. 34) the lowest permissible

Fig. 36

MODEL $1,000 PORTFOLIO

No.	Item		Type	Grade	Date	Cost
2	U.S.	$20	Liberty	AU-BU	Mixed	$140.00
1	U.S.	$20	Liberty	AU-BU	Scarce	85.00
2	U.S.	$20	St. Gaudens	AU-BU	Mixed	140.00
1	U.S.	$20	St. Gaudens	AU-BU	Scarce	80.00
2	U.S.	$10	Liberty	XF-BU	Mixed	85.00
1	U.S.	$10	Liberty	AU-BU	Scarce	65.00
1	U.S.	$10	Indian	XF-BU	Any	55.00
1	U.S.	$ 5	Liberty	XF-BU	Any	40.00
1	U.S.	$ 5	Indian	XF-BU	Any	60.00
1	Mex.	50 Pesos	Centenario	BU	Any	70.00
1	Mex.	20 Pesos	Azteca	BU	1959	30.00
1	Mex.	10 Pesos	Hidalgo	AU-BU	Any	20.00
1	Canada	$10	George V	XF-BU	Any	130.00

Total: $1,000.00

Fig. 37

MODEL $2,000 PORTFOLIO

No.	Item			Type	Grade	Date	Cost
5	U.S.	$20		Liberty	XF-BU	Mixed	$345.00
2	U.S.	$20		Liberty	XF-BU	Scarce	170.00
3	U.S.	$20		St. Gaudens	XF-BU	Mixed	200.00
1	U.S.	$20		St. Gaudens	AU-BU	Scarce	80.00
4	U.S.	$10		Liberty	XF-BU	Mixed	155.00
1	U.S.	$10		Liberty	AU-BU	Scarce	75.00
1	U.S.	$10		Indian	XF-BU	Any	55.00
1	U.S.	$10		Indian	AU-BU	Scarce	75.00
2	U.S.	$ 5		Liberty	XF-BU	Mixed	60.00
1	U.S.	$ 5		Liberty	AU-BU	Scarce	50.00
1	U.S.	$ 5		Indian	XF-BU	Any	35.00
1	U.S.	$ 5		Indian	AU-BU	Scarce	45.00
2	U.S.	$ 2½		Liberty	AU-BU	Mixed	135.00
1	U.S.	$ 2½		Indian	AU-BU	Any	30.00
1	U.S.	$ 2½		Philadelphia Sesquicentennial Commemorative	BU	1926	55.00
1	Mex.	50	Pesos	Centenario	BU	1921	85.00
1	Mex.	50	Pesos	Centenario	BU	1931	80.00
6	Mex.	20	Pesos	Azteca Complete series: 1917–1959	AU-BU	All	175.00
2	Mex.	10	Pesos	Hidalgo	AU-BU	Any	35.00
1	Canada			Sovereign, George V	BU	Any	30.00
1	France	20	Francs	Nap. I	XF-AU	Any	30.00
						Total:	$2,000.00

grade of certain coins had to be set at XF or AU in order to include them within the limits of a portfolio budget. But if during any future price reaction the investor is offered the opportunity to acquire for about the same price a better grade of coin of any of the types included in any of the portfolios, he should of course prefer the better grade. In other cases, however, XF or AU is actually the best grade of a particular coin that is generally available.

Having gone over some details of buying gold coins, it is now time to consider the mechanics of selling them. Fortunately this presents few problems. My recommendations that a gold-coin collection should be regarded as an insurance policy or similar long-term investment do not preclude that partial liquidation of an investor's collection may sometimes be necessary, in order to obtain ready cash for an emergency, or to get funds to invest in some other venture. There are two basic ways to sell gold coins: directly to a dealer, or on consignment through one of the major auction houses (such as Stack's). There are no special rules for selling

Fig. 38

MODEL $5,000 PORTFOLIO

No.	Item		Type	Grade	Date	Cost
12	U.S.	$20	Liberty	AU-BU	Mixed	$850.00
5	U.S.	$20	Liberty	XF-BU	Scarce	425.00
8	U.S.	$20	St. Gaudens	AU-BU	Mixed	560.00
3	U.S.	$20	St. Gaudens	XF-BU	Scarce	250.00
9	U.S.	$10	Liberty	XF-BU	Mixed	365.00
3	U.S.	$10	Liberty	XF-BU	Scarce	200.00
3	U.S.	$10	Indian	XF-BU	Mixed	165.00
2	U.S.	$10	Indian	XF-BU	Scarce	150.00
3	U.S.	$ 5	Liberty	XF-BU	Mixed	100.00
2	U.S.	$ 5	Liberty	XF-BU	Scarce	100.00
2	U.S.	$ 5	Indian	AU-BU	Mixed	70.00
1	U.S.	$ 5	Indian	AU-BU	Scarce	50.00
1	U.S.	$ 3	Indian	XF-BU	Any	310.00
11	Mex.	50 Pesos	Centenario Complete series: 1921–1931	BU	All	805.00
6	Mex.	20 Pesos	Azteca Complete series: 1917–1959	AU-BU	All	180.00
1	Canada	$10	George V	AU-BU	Any	130.00
1	Canada	$ 5	George V	AU-BU	Any	75.00
1	Great Britain		Sovereign	AU-BU	Any	15.00
1	France	20 Francs	Nap. I	XF-BU	Any	30.00
1	France	40 Francs	Nap. I	XF-BU	Any	85.00
1	Turkey	500 Piastres		XF-BU	Any	85.00
					Total:	$5,000.00

Fig. 39
MODEL $10,000 PORTFOLIO

No.	Item		Type	Grade	Date	Cost
25	U.S.	$20	Liberty	AU-BU	Mixed	$1,800.00
10	U.S.	$20	Liberty	XF-BU	Scarce	850.00
15	U.S.	$20	St. Gaudens	AU-BU	Mixed	1,000.00
5	U.S.	$20	St. Gaudens	XF-BU	Scarce	500.00
20	U.S.	$10	Liberty	AU-BU	Mixed	850.00
7	U.S.	$10	Liberty	XF-BU	Scarce	400.00
6	U.S.	$10	Indian	XF-BU	Mixed	360.00
3	U.S.	$10	Indian	XF-BU	Scarce	240.00
6	U.S.	$ 5	Liberty	XF-BU	Mixed	200.00
3	U.S.	$ 5	Liberty	AU-BU	Scarce	150.00
3	U.S.	$ 5	Indian	XF-BU	Mixed	100.00
2	U.S.	$ 5	Indian	XF-BU	Scarce	80.00
2	U.S.	$ 3	Liberty	AU-BU	Any	600.00
4	U.S.	$ 2½	Liberty	AU-BU	Mixed	200.00
2	U.S.	$ 2½	Liberty	XF-BU	Scarce	140.00
3	U.S.	$ 2½	Indian	BU	Mixed	90.00
2	U.S.	$ 2½	Indian	AU-BU	Scarce	85.00
2	U.S.	$ 1	Indian	AU-BU	Mixed	150.00
11	Mex.	50 Pesos	Centenario Complete series: 1921–1931	BU	All	805.00
6	Mex.	20 Pesos	Azteca Complete series: 1917–1959	AU-BU	All	180.00
10	Mex.	10 Pesos	Hidalgo Complete series: 1905–1959	AU-BU	All	300.00
1	Mex.	20 Pesos	Bal. Scale	XF-BU	Any	215.00
1	Canada	$10	George V	AU-BU	Any	130.00
1	Canada	$ 5	George V	AU-BU	Any	75.00
Add $500 Balanced World Gold Portfolio (Fig. 40)						500.00
					Total:	$10,000.00

except, as in buying, doing business with a dealer of established reputation.

When mailing coins to a dealer or sending a consignment to an auction house, I advise sending them by registered mail and obtaining a delivery receipt from the post office. In general it is not advisable or even possible to send small lots or individual coins to a major auction house. In most cases the auction houses place minimum estimated gross-value limits on the consignments they will accept, and these limits may be set as high as $10,000. Furthermore, the auction houses generally deduct a commission of 15 to 20 percent from the gross sales price, while the difference between the buy and sell price, on common golds at any rate, is somewhat less with most retail and mail-order dealers. The services of an auction house therefore should be reserved for the disposition of those collections of substantial size or value; it can provide special services in such cases.[1]

Most retail and mail-order dealers are usually quite anxious to buy good gold coins and will invariably pay cash on the spot. However, even an auction house, if you are in a hurry, may advance 50 to 60 percent of the estimated value of your consignment. The advertisements in the numismatic press will always provide current information concerning offers to buy and prices bid for gold coins.

Fig. 40

$500 WORLD GOLD PORTFOLIO—BALANCED VALUE

No.	Item			Type	Grade	Date	Cost
1	Austria	20	Corona	Commem.	BU	1908	$40.00
1	Austria	10	Corona	Commem.	BU	1908	30.00
1	Cuba	10	Pesos	Martí	AU-BU	Any	50.00
1	France	40	Francs	Nap. I	XF-BU	Any	85.00
1	Germany	20	Marks		AU-BU	Any	20.00
1	Hungary	20	Francs/ 8 Forint		BU	Any	15.00
1	Italy	20	Lire		AU-BU	Any	16.00
1	Mexico	50	Pesos	Centenario	BU	Any	70.00
1	Mexico	20	Pesos	Azteca	BU	1959	30.00
1	Mexico	5	Pesos	Hidalgo	AU-BU	Any	8.00
1	Mexico	2½	Pesos	Hidalgo	AU-BU	Any	6.00
1	Mexico	2	Pesos		AU-BU	Any	5.00
1	South Africa	2	Rand		BU	Any	15.00
1	Spain	100	Pesetas		AU-BU	Any	65.00
1	Sweden	20	Kronor	Oscar II	AU-BU	Any	30.00
1	Turkey	100	Piastres		AU-BU	Any	15.00

Total: $500.00

Somehow, I just can't conceive of gold coins being difficult to sell at any time in the future.

One final word about selling gold coins: prepare a detailed plan for the disposition of your gold-coin investment in the event of your sudden death. Make sure your spouse, your lawyer, and your executor (or a trusted friend or relative, whomever you intend to have settle your estate) know the procedure for selling your gold coins, and whom to contact to arrange the sale. However, if your gold-coin collection is a family affair and your spouse or perhaps one of your grown children is competent to assume the management

Fig. 41

$1,000 WORLD GOLD PORTFOLIO—HIGH INTRINSIC VALUE*

No.	Item		Type	Grade	Date	Cost
3	Australia	Sovereign		AU-BU	Any	$50.00
1	Austria	100 Corona	Fr. Jos.	BU	1915	50.00
2	Austria	20 Corona	Fr. Jos.	BU	Mixed	40.00
1	Belgium	20 Francs		AU-BU	Any	18.00
1	Bulgaria	20 Leva	Ferd. I	AU-BU	Any	20.00
1	Canada	Sovereign		AU-BU	Any	25.00
1	Cuba	5 Pesos		AU-BU	1916	32.00
2	Denmark	20 Kroner		AU-BU	Mixed	60.00
6	France	20 Francs		XF-BU	Mixed	100.00
2	Germany	20 Marks		XF-BU	Mixed	40.00
6	Great Britain	Sovereign		AU-BU	Mixed	100.00
1	Mexico	50 Pesos	Centenario	BU	Any	70.00
2	Mexico	20 Pesos	Azteca	AU-BU	Mixed	60.00
2	Mexico	10 Pesos	Hidalgo	AU-BU	Mixed	30.00
1	Mexico	5 Pesos	Hidalgo	BU	Any	10.00
2	Netherlands	10 Guilders		XF-BU	Any	45.00
1	Roumania	20 Lei	Carol I	AU-BU	Any	20.00
1	Russia	10 Roubles	Nicholas II	XF-BU	Any	20.00
3	Switzerland	20 Francs		AU-BU	Any	80.00
1	Turkey	500 Piastres		XF-BU	Any	85.00
1	Turkey	250 Piastres		XF-BU	Any	45.00

Total: $1,000.00

* U.S. and Mexican gold coins are generally the best values, as far as intrinsic gold content is concerned. See model portfolios.

Fig. 42

$1,000 WORLD GOLD PORTFOLIO—
HIGH NUMISMATIC VALUE

No.	Item		Type	Grade	Date	Cost
1	Australia	Sovereign		AU-BU	Any	$75.00
	Sydney Mint					
1	Austria	100 Corona		BU	1908	170.00
	60th Anniv.	Franz Joseph				
1	Canada	$5	George V	AU-BU	Any	75.00
1	Cuba	20 Pesos	Martí	AU-BU	1915	200.00
1	Iceland	500 Kronur	Sigurdsson	PF	1961	60.00
1	Israel	20 Pounds	Herzl	PF	1960	90.00
1	Mexico	10 Pesos	Bal. Scale	XF-BU	Any	175.00
1	Newfound-	$2	Victoria	AU-BU	Any	75.00
	land					
1	Poland	20 Zloty	900th Anniv.	BU	1925	50.00
1	Poland	10 Zloty	900th Anniv.	BU	1925	30.00

Total: $1,000.00

Note:

A hypothetical $2,500 world collection can be illustrated by combining both the $1,000 world portfolios (Figs. 41, 42) with the $500 balanced world gold selection (Fig. 40).

of it and interested in doing so, then you have only to make a provision in your will that this person should receive it.

In any case, don't neglect to set up detailed instructions and make definite provisions in your will regarding your gold-coin collection, if it is valued at any significant sum of money. Many a widow and child have been deprived of part of their rightful inheritance because of the careless and hasty disposal of coin collections by relatives and others who were ignorant of their true value.

Notes

Chapter XIII

1. In view of the total services usually provided by an auction house, the commission rates do not seem excessive. In fact, I have been told that these rates may have to be raised in the next year or two. These services include:
   - Describing the collection in detail to acceptable numismatic standards, and providing photographic illustration as warranted.
   - Printing and distributing the auction catalogues.
   - Advertising and publicizing the collection and the auction.
   - Insuring the collection against fire and theft while it is in the care of the auction house.
   - Conducting the auction itself and providing the auction gallery.
   - Providing financial and credit arrangements for the purchasers.

XIV

A Look at the Future

"The ideas of economists and political philosophers, both when they are right and when they are wrong, are more powerful than is commonly understood. Indeed the world is ruled by little else."

—JOHN MAYNARD KEYNES

PERHAPS KEYNES IS MORE DESERVING OF RESPECT AS A PHILOSopher than as an economist, for his more abstract reflections often reveal penetrating insights. He showed his genius, and that he was, by his ability to grasp so frequently the single vital point of seemingly obscure and chaotic situations. The Keynesian observation that introduces this final chapter goes a long way towards explaining why the Western nations have continued on such a disastrous economic course in recent years, despite the formidable lessons of history. It also provides a rather significant guide to the future course of events. Keynes himself was familiar with the propensity of politicians, bureaucrats, and academicians to accept others' ideas and speculations more on the basis of novelty than because of any capacity for critical evaluation. Shortly before his death in 1946, Keynes wrote: "I find myself moved, not for the first time, to remind our contemporary economists that the classical teaching embodies some permanent truths of great significance."[1]

Unfortunately the reminder was largely ignored; the promoters of the New Economics were not merely rejecting the classical doctrines; most were blissfully unaware of them. Spurred by ideas borrowed willy-nilly from the works of Keynes, Henry George, Norman Thomas, Dr. Francis E. Townsend, Huey Long, the Fabian Society, and other modern thinkers (part genius, demagogue, and crackpot), the "New Economics" was launched in 1946 with the passage of the Full Employment Act in the U.S. This act, which is still the law of the land, sanctified deficit federal spending and domestic inflation as the cure for all economic and social ills. Simultaneously, the electoral triumph of the socialist Labour government ushered in a similar new era in Great Britain.

Such is the eternal optimism of man,[2] that we can still look back after twenty years and pronounce the new economic philosophy a great success, despite the ravages of an inflation that has destroyed the free economy of vast areas of the world, brought the British to their knees, and cut the value of the U.S. dollar in half. It was this peculiar myopia that prompted *Time* magazine, in its December 31, 1965, cover story on Keynes, smugly to observe: "We are all Keynesians now." I am not at all sure that Keynes would have entirely appreciated the compliment; Keynes himself was seldom a practicing Keynesian. But the lesson is obvious; the doctrines and practices of the New Economics will continue to effect the destiny of the Western world for some time to come. The so-called practical men of the world, the great uncritical majority of politicians, bankers, stockbrokers, business men, and economic journalists, are invariably prisoners of dogmas and doctrines not of their own devising or understanding. All too easily they accept the fatuous cliché that "we will have to learn to live with inflation." Such living will prove more difficult than is generally expected.

The economic climate of the next ten years is very likely to be the most dangerous since the 1930s; the economic and political delusions that have brought us to our present state of monetary and social disorganization are too well entrenched in the popular mind to be overcome short of complete disaster. The world's economic machinery is, in my opinion, on the brink of going completely out of control—or at least out of the control of Washington. Therefore, having written a book giving investment advice, I would be remiss if I did not conclude with a forecast of the possible events of the next decade. Some of these events will be quite shocking and unexpected; they will undoubtedly unnerve many investors and cause them mistakenly to alter or abandon sound investment programs.

First, the removal of all gold backing from the dollar and other currencies guarantees that the future will see an acceleration of inflation—but such forecasts are a dime a dozen. It will not be all that simple. There will be more inflation, far more than we have previously experienced, but it will follow an erratic and unpredictable course, whipsawing many an unwary investor. The money managers will push up and push down, alternately inflating and deflating the economy in a vain attempt to preserve the collapsing international monetary structure, to save the dollar, and at the same time to fulfill the mandate of the Full Employment Act of 1946 by pursuing an expansionist domestic monetary policy. The managers face an insoluble dilemma, and will do great damage without achieving their goals.

The next major event in the worldwide economic drama that is unfolding will probably be the complete collapse of the British pound. No matter what expedients the international bankers employ, they cannot alter the fact that virtually all the monetary reserves of Great Britain have been borrowed. Another pound devaluation is inescapable, and sooner or later the reality will have to be faced that the billions loaned to England to save the pound not only will not save it, but may never be paid back. Britain is nearly bankrupt.

The French franc is also in bad shape; the Paris riots have shaken the French middle class to the core and brought back all the bad old memories. It was de Gaulle who restored trust in the franc, and the unexpected knowledge that he was not infallible has weakened it beyond repair. The August 1969 devaluation of the franc signaled a return to the old monetary instability that had plagued France before the advent of de Gaulle.

Other wholesale devaluations (including the dollar) will follow the coming breakup of the world's major currencies and as a result the world will eventually turn to "floating" currencies; that is, currencies no longer will be defined and valued in terms of a fixed amount of gold, but will become exclusively fiat instruments, allowed to fluctuate freely in the open market—like some kinds of government bonds and Treasury bills. The price of gold may be entirely freed from monetary controls and it is quite possible that the restrictions on Americans regarding the ownership of gold may be removed, but the change may come too late for most of us to benefit from it.

The period of floating exchange rates will be a most difficult and dangerous time for the gold-coin investor—or any investor, for that matter. The price of gold will no doubt fluctuate considerably during this period, in terms of dollars and other currencies, and there will be much talk that gold will lose its value entirely. There is also a very real danger that in attempting to restrain the rampant inflation that is sure to follow the wave of devaluations, or the U.S. decision to abandon gold entirely, the money managers will push down too hard on the economy.[3] Do not be surprised if the American economy is sent reeling into a severe recession, or even a depression, quite soon. But remember, when this happens the money managers will frantically reverse their position and stoke the fires of inflation more vigorously than ever.

Therefore, it is most important to the gold-coin investor not to react to any short-term uncertainty by selling. The world's monetary gold reserves are not going to be dumped on the free market, although your government may try to convince you that they will be. It is fair to ask, however, what will happen to these gold reserves in an era of floating currencies. Part of them will be retained as emergency funds for purposes of national security. Another part will be pledged to back some new international reserve currency created by the Common Market countries[4] to replace the dollar. The dollar has been able to function as a reserve currency only as long as we have maintained its convertibility; a floating nonconvertible dollar will be useless for this purpose.

Neither will SDRs nor any other international fiat money be trusted by the Europeans. The days of IMF, at least in its present form, are numbered. The Europeans may appear to play along for awhile with the present IMF arrangement and the SDR scheme, in order not to offend the powerful U.S. ally, but when the real crisis comes they will abandon IMF and set up their own fully gold-backed reserve currency.[5] The dollar and other floating currencies (perhaps including initially even some of the Europeans' own domestic fiat money) will be left to float down the drain.

Other large amounts of gold will be used to back new kinds of debt instruments. Government and corporate bonds will be issued with gold clauses guaranteeing the principal and interest in terms of fixed amounts of gold by weight, in order to insure the buyer against loss through inflation and devaluations. Believe me, before long that will be the only kind of bonds salable. Other forms of international and internal financing will also be denominated in gold, as the inflationary illness rages. The U.S. itself has already started this trend by selling nonmarketable gold-guaranteed Treasury bonds to the central banks of both Canada and Germany.[6]

It will eventually become clear, even to the Harvard Economics Department and the U.S. Treasury, that gold, far from being an anachronism, is perhaps the most valued and most demanded single commodity on this earth. Many nations of the world, particularly the U.S., will then scramble to begin rebuilding their drastically depleted gold reserves. The price of gold in terms of domestic fiat currencies will soar. Perhaps in ten years or so we will have curbed our domestic inflation sufficiently, and will have built up a national gold reserve adequate to permit a return to some system of national and international fixed exchange rates. A "permanent" price for gold will then be reestablished (at a price far higher than the present). But much hardship will ensue in the meantime.

Inflationary eras are always accompanied by waves of social and political unrest. And this, in itself an additional economic burden, will not only continue but in all probability greatly increase in the next few years.

The eventual imposition of severe economic controls, regardless of who is president, is a certainty. Classical economic philosophy may not be resurrected for many years to come, perhaps not even in our lifetime. Governments will remain addicted to the philosophies of manipulation: political, social, international, and most assuredly economic. Indeed, we will have to learn to live with inflation, but we may at the same time have to live with business stagnation, massive social discontent, and government repression. The experience of France in the post–World War II years may to a considerable degree be repeated by the U.S.; a U.S. dollar at 1/200 of its 1940 value is not beyond the realm of possibility.

Barring a major war, the economic history of the U.S. in the next five to ten years will probably evolve along these lines:

1. Accelerating inflation: galloping price increases, massive labor unrest, crippling strikes, impossible wage settlements, staggering property tax increases.

2. Wholesale worldwide devaluations, with the pound, the franc, and the lira leading the way.

3. U.S. embargo on gold exports and refusal of all further redemptions of central bank dollar holdings. Result: *de facto* devaluation of U.S. dollar in world markets.

4. U.S. action leads to: gradual worldwide abandonment of convertibility; floating exchange rates; wide fluctuations in the market price of gold; removal of all restrictions on private gold dealings; gold demonetization in the U.S. and Great Britain.

5. Collapse and breakup of the IMF; beginning of a new European Common Market gold-backed reserve currency.[7]

6. Stringent economic restrictions imposed by the U.S.; "tight money" policies resumed; partial wage and price controls begun; prime interest rates reach 10 to 15 percent.

7. Severe business depression begins in the U.S.; drastic declines in employment, stock prices, real estate, etc.; massive social unrest.

8. Panic resumption of federal deficit spending and lending, resulting in huge budget deficits—perhaps as high as $40 to $50 billion in the first year.

9. Foreign gold bonds and gold-guaranteed private debt issues appear; regular bonds and notes selling at deep discounts or virtually unsalable.

10. Only partial recovery from depression, but inflation resumes in earnest; paradoxically, purchasing power of paper dollar

declines rapidly in the midst of general economic stagnation. Crime and disorder in major cities at times almost unbearable.

11. U.S. government adopts new authoritarian economic and social policies: severe wage and price controls enforced; national police force established to assist local authorities in maintaining order and combating crime; permissive social attitudes strongly rejected by public.

12. U.S. government announces new gold policy: building of national gold reserve given first priority; all privately owned gold bullion ordered to be surrendered to Treasury at fixed price under pain of severe penalty for evasion; all gold in U.S. nationalized again (except for gold coins of recognized numismatic value); mining activity greatly stimulated by an increasing Treasury gold price, and by special grants for exploration, recovery, etc. Exports to gold-rich countries, such as Canada, South Africa, encouraged by special subsidies and government assistance.

13. National gold reserve greatly expanded; currency stabilized by a return to fixed parity with gold. "New dollar" established —old dollars exchanged at 10 to 1, 100 to 1, or who knows what, with new dollars.

14. Great international monetary meeting to establish a new system of fixed exchange rates among major trading nations. Common Market gold-certificate reserve currency adopted as new international reserve currency, resulting in a new fixed world gold price.

15. New era of international monetary cooperation begins; domestic economic restrictions eased; general prosperity resumes. But balance of power in the world substantially altered; U.S. no longer number-one trading nation—eclipsed by greatly expanded and united European economic community.

This chapter is not being written as a demonstration of psychic powers; the author claims none. I cannot and do not guarantee that all of the events I have outlined will take place, or that they will follow in the exact sequence described. But these projections are based on a long and intensive study of both economic history and human nature, and I believe they represent as accurate a view of the future as is possible to construct from that basis. There are other possibilities, of course, and they have already been mentioned in this book. The U.S. may succeed in turning the IMF into an international "engine of inflation," although I believe the odds are very much against our being allowed to manage such an "engine" for long. We may be drawn into a major war. In either of these cases the effects in terms of inflation and the price of gold are obvious. The important thing, as I see it, is not whether these events occur exactly as forecast, but whether the investor is psychologically and financially prepared for them, or for events of a similar nature.

Nowhere in this book have I suggested or intended to suggest that gold coins should be your only investment, or even your major one. Real estate, in the form of your own home or place of business, provided that it is soundly financed and not overbought, has a place in most investment programs. Certain other business investments and some common stocks, particularly gold shares, may prove rewarding in the years to come—although I think that on the whole the stock market is greatly overbought and will be a very dangerous place for all but the most nimble speculators in the next few years. But what I do say is that a gold-coin collection, if properly accumulated, will prove to be one of the safest and most rewarding areas of investment in the foreseeable future. Admittedly, gold coins are a *defensive* type of investment, but defending and protecting capital against the ravages of both inflation and business stagnation will be the major problem of the years between now and 1978 or so.

In any significant business downturn as a result of restrictive monetary policies, the high intrinsic-value coins will undoubtedly remain strong, but numismatic rarities will probably suffer important declines. The thing to do in this case is not to sell any of your coins, those of high intrinsic value or others, but to take advantage, to the best of your financial ability, of the opportunity to acquire rare items, particularly among U.S. gold coins. During any period of severely depressed prices, such opportunities may be of very short duration.

Another development that may cause concern to those who are

not prepared for it is the possibility of wide swings in the price of gold during the period of floating exchange rates. There may be one or more sharp downward reactions, and understandably these dips may cause some anxiety among gold-oriented investors. Remember, any such occurrences should be temporary; the pressures of inflation that are a built-in part of our economic and political system should inexorably reassert themselves shortly thereafter. Look upon any gold-price reactions as opportunities to complete series such as the Mexican 50, 20, and 10 Pesos, to purchase interesting common European gold coins, or to acquire missing Eagles and double Eagles at bargain prices.

Although I think one should not in any way depend on it, it is possible that with a floating dollar and demonetized gold, the U.S. may once again permit the private ownership of gold bullion. In that event, it is possible that the availability of bar gold at or near actual intrinsic value will have a depressing effect on gold coins, which usually sell at a premium (although that has definitely not been true in Europe). However, if such an effect should occur here, I believe it would be very temporary; for this reason: the inflation-scarred American public (including some of our great corporations) would quickly absorb all domestic supplies and production as a hedge against further inflation and debasement of our currency. As you know, we don't produce much gold in the U.S. We already are substantial net importers. Trying to buy foreign gold with in-convertible paper dollars will be an interesting experience; the net effect will be to drive the price of gold sky-high in terms of those dollars—and a rising price for bullion will certainly be reflected in a similar increase for intrinsic-value gold coins.

If I were offered the opportunity to buy bullion, I would not do it—except perhaps a small stamped ingot or two, just as a collector's item. I feel that the danger of government confiscation is just too great. It has been done before and it could be done again, without hesitation, whenever it is decided that such an action is "in the national interest." A major war or a worsening of the world economic situation will certainly qualify as a sufficient emergency. In short, the precedent has been established in the U.S. that the federal government can confiscate private gold (or silver) bullion pretty much at will. So speculate in gold options or futures if you must (assuming such opportunities are available), but I advise you to confine cash purchases of the metal itself to coins. Besides, bullion has no possible numismatic value or potential; and as I've reminded you, the numismatic factor in gold investments in the form of coins is too important to ignore.

If the reader is inclined to view my 15-part scenario of future events as being somewhat on the pessimistic side, I should warn you that I feel it is the most *optimistic* position I can take under the circumstances. I left out the really bad parts: the very real threat of a big war in the Middle East involving the U.S., the possibility of large-scale resumption of the Vietnam conflict, or the danger of full-scale civil insurrection in some of our major cities.

It is a dangerous world we live in. We long for security and repose, but absolute security is an impossible dream and repose does not appear to be our destiny. However, as far as our financial survival is concerned, there are certain verities that seem to survive the most catastrophic adversity. The gold coin is one of them. In the last two centuries alone, several great empires have fallen into ashes; their paper currencies, their bonds, their glory, all their pledges and promises have been consumed in the flames. Little remains of those empires but the words in the history books. But their gold coins, those that have been preserved, are now worth from five to five-thousand times their original value when issued. Surely this is a development worthy of serious investment consideration.

Notes

CHAPTER XIV

1. *Economic Journal* (June 1946).
2. "Optimism," as Voltaire once observed, "is a mania for declaring that all is well, when everything is going badly."

3. It has been done before; it is generally conceded that the sudden collapse of 1937 (and probably the recessions of 1946–49 and 1957–58), was due at least in part to such "overcorrection."

4. Under the leadership of Germany. For years de Gaulle tried desperately to prepare France for that particular role, but the French people were obviously not willing to accept the discipline it required.

5. The benefit of using a reserve currency instead of actual gold is the flexibility and convenience it affords. Nevertheless, if it is to be successful, it must be "fully backed" in the sense of sound banking practice, that is, perhaps up to 40 percent of the note circulation should be covered by actual gold deposits at some central depository, and the rest should be guaranteed by gold pledges from the member countries.

6. These interest-bearing bonds were given in lieu of gold to relieve the U.S. of balance-of-payments embarrassment, but neither country would accept them without a gold-guarantee provision.

7. The West German mark has already been accorded the status of a preferred reserve currency; the world's wealth continues to flee from nonredeemable fiat dollars and pounds, and from unstable French francs, into the security of the heavily gold-backed *deutschmark*.

Appendix I

U.S. TREASURY DEPARTMENT
Gold Regulations and Statements

GOLD COINS

TREASURY DEPARTMENT
Washington, D.C.   20220
OFFICE OF DOMESTIC GOLD AND SILVER OPERATIONS

GOLD COIN STATEMENT

1. *Regulations governing gold coins situated within the United States and places subject to its jurisdiction.*

Section 54.20 of the Gold Regulations provides that gold coins of recognized special value to collectors of rare and unusual coins may be acquired, held and disposed of within the United States or any place subject to its jurisdiction without a license. Any gold coins made before April 5, 1933 and presently situated within the United States are considered to be rare and may be held under this provision provided they were not imported without a license in contravention of the Regulations governing imports described in Item 2 below. However, regardless of the date, mutilated gold coins, restrikes (i.e., coins which have been struck recently from old dies), and counterfeits are not considered rare.

The Gold Regulations provide that gold coins made after 1933 are presumed not to be rare—they may not be held in the United States in the absence of a special determination that the particular coin has a recognized special value to collectors.

No licenses are required to export gold coins made before 1933. An export license is required for coins made after that date. Application for an export license should be made on Form TG-11 which is available upon request from the Office of Domestic Gold and Silver Operations, Treasury Department, Washington, D. C. 20220.

2. *Regulations governing imports of gold coins.*

In July of 1962, Executive Order 11037 and amendments to the Gold Regulations were issued which prohibited the unlicensed acquisition abroad by persons subject to United States jurisdiction and the unlicensed importation of any gold coins. Pursuant to these provisions licenses may be issued for the acquisition abroad and importation of rare gold coins in exceptional cases. Import licenses are granted only when this would not be inconsistent with United States gold policies. In order to be eligible for importation under this criterion the coin must have been issued for circulation within the country of issue and not for sale to the public as a means of providing gold to the private markets or of earning foreign exchange *and* it must have exceptional numismatic value. Determinations as to the numismatic value depend upon the attributes of the coin itself and not upon the nature of the individual or organization seeking to import it or the purpose for which it is to be imported. Among the factors considered are the relationship between bullion value and market value of the coin and the number of such coins struck. The Office consults with the Curator of Numismatics at the Smithsonian Institution for technical advice with regard to these matters.

Applications for licenses to acquire abroad and import gold coins should be made on Form TG-31 which may be obtained upon request from the Office of Domestic Gold and Silver Operations. This form requires a complete listing of the coins sought to be imported together with a description of each coin including the country of issue, date, mint mark, denomination, design and condition. No licenses are issued for the holding abroad by Americans of gold coins except that special authorizations may be issued for rare gold coins held by Americans temporarily abroad who wish to take their collections with them.

3. *Background information.*

The restrictions in the Gold Regulations on gold coins implement the Gold Reserve Act of 1934, the purpose of which was to improve the United States monetary system by centralizing and conserving the nation's gold stock and by prohibiting the private holding of gold as a store of value. Under this Act and the Regulations, private citizens are permitted to have gold only as needed for legitimate and customary use in industry, profession or art. Also, there have always been exemptions for gold coins of recognized special value to collectors.

Originally, the Gold Regulations were applicable only to gold and gold coins situated within the United States. However, in 1961, restrictions were placed on the acquisition, holding, etc., by United States nationals of gold situated overseas. In 1962 the special restrictions described in Item 2 above were imposed on the acquisition abroad and importation of rare gold coins for the reason that it had been brought to our attention that there appeared to be a certain amount of interest on the part of Americans in taking advantage of the exceptions in the Gold Regulations for rare gold coins to speculate in and hoard gold. Moreover, many countries began producing restrikes of their pre-1933 gold coins and there was an appreciable amount of counterfeiting of gold coins made before this date.

TREASURY DEPARTMENT
Washington, D.C. 20220

FOR RELEASE A.M. NEWSPAPERS
Saturday, April 26, 1969

Treasury Relaxes Licensing Regulations on Gold Coin Imports

The Treasury Department announced today a revision of gold coin import regulations to permit imports of gold coins minted prior to 1934 without license.

Relaxation of the licensing requirement is effective today and was made to remove an inconsistency in regulations on imported pre-1934 gold coins, which generally had to have licenses, and those regularly traded within the United States.

Gold coins minted during or after 1934, however, may be imported only with a license from the Director, Office of Domestic Gold and Silver Operations, Treasury Department, Washington, D. C. Such licenses are issued only for rare and unusual coins of recognized special value to collectors. Importation of gold coins minted in 1960 or afterwards still will not be licensed.

Before this change in the regulations, all coins made prior to April 5, 1933 could be freely bought, sold, and held within the United States. However, only rare and unusual gold coins could be imported and then only pursuant to a specific license. Under this standard, certain coins minted before 1934 did not qualify for import even though they were freely traded in the domestic market. With the change in the Regulations any gold coin may be imported which can now be legally traded within the United States.

The amendments will simplify existing restrictions on numismatists while continuing to serve the basic purpose of the Gold Regulations. The current licensing policy will be retained for coins minted after January 1, 1934.

Gold coins may still be detained at Customs stations for examination as to their authenticity. Counterfeit coins may not be imported and are subject to seizure. Restrikes, that is modern reproductions of gold coins bearing a much earlier date, will also not qualify for importation. Therefore, travelers and coin collectors should be especially careful that the coins they purchase abroad are genuine.

RULES AND REGULATIONS
TITLE 31—MONEY AND FINANCE: TREASURY
Chapter I—Monetary Offices, Department of the Treasury
PART 54—GOLD REGULATIONS
Imports of Gold Coin

Section 54.20 of the Gold Regulations is being amended to permit the importation without a license of gold coins made before 1934. Licenses will be required to import any gold coins made during 1934 or later. Licenses for importation may be issued for coins minted before 1960 which can be established to the satisfaction of the Director, Office of Domestic Gold and Silver Operations, to be of recognized special value to collectors of rare and unusual coin and to have been originally issued to circulate as coinage within the country of issue. Licenses for importation may be issued for gold coins made during or subsequent to 1960 only in cases where the particular coin was licensed for importation prior to April 30, 1969. Because the amendments relieve an existing restriction and in the case of coins made after 1933 make no change in present Regulations and licensing policies, it is found that notice and public procedure thereon are unnecessary.

Section 54.20 is amended to read:

§ 54.20   Rare coin.

(a) Gold coin of recognized special value to collectors of rare and unusual coin may be acquired, held, and transported within the United States without the necessity of holding a license therefor. Such coin may be imported, however, only as permitted by this section or §§ 54.28 to 54.30, 54.34 or licenses issued thereunder, and may be exported only in accordance with the provisions of § 54.25.

(b) Gold coin made prior to 1934 is considered to be of recognized special value to collectors of rare and unusual coin.

(c) Gold coin made during or subsequent to 1934 is presumed not to be of recognized special value to collectors of rare and unusual coin.

(d) Gold coin made prior to 1934, may be imported without the necessity of obtaining a license therefor.

(e) Gold coin made during or subsequent to 1934 may be imported only pursuant to a specific or general license issued by the Director, Office of Domestic Gold and Silver Operations. Licenses under this paragraph may be issued only for gold coin made prior to 1960, which can be established to the satisfaction of the Director to be of recognized special value to collectors of rare and unusual coin and to have been originally issued for circulation within the country of issue. Licenses may be issued for gold coin made during or subsequent to 1960 in cases where the particular coin was licensed for importation prior to April 30, 1969. Application for a specific license under this paragraph shall be executed on Form TG-31 and filed in duplicate with the Director.

(Sec. 5(b), 40 Stat. 415, as amended, secs. 3, 8, 9, 11, 48 Stat. 340, 341, 342; 12 U.S.C. 95a, 31 U.S.C. 442, 733, 734, 822b, E.O. 6260, Aug. 28, 1933, as amended by E.O. 10896, 25 F.R. 12281, E.O. 10905, 26 F.R. 321, E.O. 11037, 27 F.R. 6967; 3 CFR, 1959–63 Comp. and E.O. 6359, Oct. 25, 1933, E. O. 9193, as amended, 7 F.R. 5205; 3 CFR 1943, Cum. Supp., E.O. 10289, 16 F.R. 9499, 3 CFR, 1949–53 Comp.)

Effective date: These amendments shall become effective on publication in the FEDERAL REGISTER.

Dated: April 22, 1969.

[SEAL]   PAUL A. VOLCKER,
Under Secretary for Monetary Affairs.

[F.R. Doc. 69–4994; Filed, Apr. 25, 1969; 8:46 a.m.]

Appendix II

U.S. TREASURY DEPARTMENT
Gold Regulations and Statements

GOLD MEDALS

TREASURY DEPARTMENT
Washington, D.C. 20220
OFFICE OF DOMESTIC GOLD AND SILVER OPERATIONS

GOLD MEDAL STATEMENT

The basic principles governing the administration of the Gold Acts and Orders are that gold, as a store of value, can be held only by the Government and that private citizens and entities in the United States can acquire gold only for legitimate and customary industrial, professional and artistic use.

Historically, large medals produced in gold have not been made for sale in the United States or imported for sale to the public. Therefore, we consider them not to be a customary use of gold.

The customary use interpretation has been very strict since 1958, because at about that time we found that efforts were being made to produce, both in this country and outside of the United States, large gold medals for sale here. While such medals may command the attention of collectors, a substantial part of their sales appeal is in the knowledge of their gold content.

For many years, therefore, we have refused to consider the authorization of the acquisition abroad and the importation of gold medals manufactured for sale because in our opinion they do not comprise a customary use of gold and thus are not fabricated gold. This is formalized in section 54.4-(14)(ii) of the Gold Regulations.

TITLE 31—MONEY AND FINANCE: TREASURY
Chapter I—Monetary Offices, Department of the Treasury
PART 54—GOLD REGULATIONS
Gold Medals for Public Display and Antique Gold Medals

Section 54.4(a)(14)(iii) of the Gold Regulations is being amended to authorize the Director of the Office of Domestic Gold and Silver Operations to license the acquisition, holding, transportation and exportation of gold-plated coins or gold medals which are either antique or are for public display by an institution serving the public. Prior to this amendment, licenses could only be issued for special award medals, designed and struck in small numbers for a specific presentation. Other uses of medals have not heretofore been considered as "customary industrial, professional or artistic use" and the holding of such medals was not licensed. However, the acquisition of old medals, especially those struck over 100 years ago, will now be considered for licensing. In addition, limited numbers of commemorative medals for public display will be considered for licensing upon application by museums, libraries, and other public service institutions. Because the amendments relieve an existing restriction, it is found that notice and public procedure thereon are unnecessary.

Section 54.4(a)(14)(iii) is amended to read:

§ 54.4   Definitions.

(a) * * *

(14) * * *

(iii) The acquisition, holding, transportation, importation, or exportation of any gold-plated coins or gold medals other than: Special award medals; antique medals; and commemorative medals for regular public display by a museum or other institution serving the public.

*   *   *   *   *   *

(Sec. 5(b), 40 Stat. 415, as amended, secs. 3, 8, 9, 11, 48 Stat. 340, 341, 342; 12 U.S.C. 95a, 31 U.S.C. 442, 733, 734, 822b, E.O. 6260, Aug. 28, 1933, as amended by E.O. 10896, 25 F.R. 12281, E.O. 10905, 26 F.R. 321, E.O. 11037, 27 F.R. 6967; 3 CFR, 1959–63 Comp. and E.O. 6359, Oct. 25, 1933, E.O. 9193, as amended, 7 F.R. 5205; 3 CFR 1943, Cum. Supp., E.O. 10289, 16 F.R. 9499, 3 CFR, 1949–53 Comp.)

Effective date. These amendments shall become effective on publication in the FEDERAL REGISTER.

Dated: June 5, 1969.

[SEAL]   PAUL W. EGGERS,
General Counsel.

[F.R. Doc. 69–6860; Filed, June 10, 1969; 8:48 a.m.]

FEDERAL REGISTER, VOL. 34, NO. 111—
WEDNESDAY, JUNE 11, 1969

Appendix III

U.S. TREASURY DEPARTMENT
Gold Regulations

OFFICE OF DOMESTIC GOLD AND SILVER OPERATIONS

List of Foreign Gold Coins Minted 1934–1959
Which are Eligible for Import Under License

AFGHANISTAN	1939	½ amani (4 grams)
	1937	2 tilla (8 grams)
	1936	2 tilla (8 grams)
ALBANIA	1938	100 francs (Ahmed Zog, Wedding)
	1938	100 francs (10th Year of Rule)
	1938	50 francs (10th Year of Rule)
	1938	20 francs (Ahmed Zog, Wedding)
	1938	20 francs (10th Year of Rule)
	1937	100 francs
	1937	20 francs
AUSTRIA	1938	25 schillings
	1938	100 schillings (PROOF only)
	1937	25 schillings
	1937	100 schillings
	1936	25 schillings
	1935	25 schillings
	1935	100 schillings
CROATIA	1941	500 kuna
CZECHOSLOVAKIA	1934	5 ducats (St. Eliz. Praying & Mining Scenes)
	1934	1 ducat (St. Eliz. Praying & Mining Scenes)

	1934	2 ducats (St. Eliz. Praying & Mining Scenes)
	1934	5 ducats (St. Wenceslas on Horse & Shield)
	1934	10 ducats (St. Eliz. Praying & Mining Scenes)
EGYPT	1939	500 piastres
	1938	500 piastres
	1938	100 piastres
	1938	50 piastres
	1938	20 piastres
FRANCE	1935	100 francs
GREAT BRITAIN	1937	5 pounds PROOF
	1937	2 pounds PROOF
	1937	1 pound PROOF
	1937	½ pound PROOF
INDIA	1946	1 mohur (Hyderabad)
	1945	1 mohur (Rajkot)
	1937	½ mohur (Bikanir) (1994 Samvat)
	1937	1 mohur (Bikanir) (1994 Samvat)
ITALY	1937	100 lire
	1936	100 lire
	1936	50 lire
LIECHTENSTEIN	1956	25 franken
	1956	50 franken
	1952	100 franken
	1946	10 franken
	1946	20 franken
MEXICO	1959	20 pesos "Veinte Pesos," Aztec Calendar
	1944	2½ pesos
	1944	2 pesos
MONACO	1950	100 francs
	1950	20 francs
	1950	10 francs
	1947	20 francs
NEPAL	1938	2 mohar
	1938	1 mohar
	1937	2 mohar
	1937	1 mohar
	1936	2 mohar
	1936	1 mohar
	1935	2 mohar
	1935	1 mohar
	1934	2 mohar
	1934	1 mohar

ROUMANIA	1940	20 lei	Head, Legend—Large crown over small monogram—Carol I
	1940	20 lei	Head, Legend—Small crown over large monogram—Carol II
	1940	100 lei	Head, Legend—Small crown over large monogram
	1940	100 lei	Head, Legend—Large crown over small monogram
	1939	20 lei	Head, Large Arms
SOUTH AFRICA	1959	1 pound & ½ pound	PROOF
	1958	1 pound & ½ pound	PROOF
	1957	1 pound & ½ pound	PROOF
	1956	1 pound & ½ pound	PROOF
	1955	1 pound & ½ pound	PROOF
	1954	1 pound & ½ pound	PROOF
	1953	1 pound & ½ pound	PROOF
	1952	1 pound & ½ pound	PROOF
SWITZERLAND	1939	100 francs	
	1934	100 francs	
SYRIA	1950	1 pound & ½ pound	
TUNISIA	1956	100 francs	
	1944	100 francs	
	1943	100 francs	
	1942	100 francs	
	1939	100 francs	
	1935	100 francs	
	1934	100 francs	
TURKEY	1955	250 piastres	
	1955	500 piastres	
	1947	25 piastres (Inonu)	
	1946	100 piastres (Inonu)	
	1943	500 piastres	
	1943	250 piastres (Inonu)	
VATICAN	1959	100 lire	
	1958	100 lire	
	1957	100 lire	
	1956	100 lire	
	1955	100 lire	
	1954	100 lire	
	1953	100 lire	
	1952	100 lire	
	1951	100 lire	
	1950	100 lire	
	1948	100 lire	

1942	100 lire
1941	100 lire
1940	100 lire
1939	100 lire
1937	100 lire
1936	100 lire
1934	100 lire

May 1969

Appendix IV

U.S. TREASURY DEPARTMENT
Gold Regulations

OFFICE OF DOMESTIC GOLD AND SILVER OPERATIONS

Foreign Gold Coins Minted After January 1, 1960
Which are Eligible for Importation Under License

AFGHANISTAN	1960	2 tilla (8 grams)
ICELAND	1961	500 kronur
ISRAEL	1960	20 pounds (Herzl/Menorah)
SOUTH AFRICA	1960	1 pound & ½ pound PROOF
	1961	1 rand & 2 rands PROOF
	1962	1 rand & 2 rands PROOF
	1963	1 rand & 2 rands PROOF
	1964	1 rand & 2 rands PROOF
	1965	1 rand & 2 rands PROOF
TURKEY	1961	500 piastres
	1962	250 piastres

May 1969

Glossary

Nearly every field of study requires the use of specialized terms. Learning is partly a semantic process, and the vocabulary of economics and numismatics is particularly rich in descriptive words and phrases peculiar to those fields. The interests of the coin investor require a familiarity with the principal terms of each area, as well as a knowledge of the specialized words common to both. When these words have been used in the course of this book, I have tried, as far as possible, to use them in a definitive context. But in addition, a more formal table of definitions may prove useful. Therefore, here is a brief list of some of the specialized words that occur most frequently, not only in this book, but in the general literature of economics and numismatics.

accumulator   a collector who follows no particular direction or pattern, but who simply buys or keeps any piece of numismatic material that strikes his fancy.

bag marks   minor abrasions on uncirculated coins caused by the handling of the sealed mint bags.

billon   a very low-grade alloy of silver with copper, usually containing only 10 or 15 percent silver.

bimetallism   a monetary standard in which the monetary unit is defined and redeemed in terms of both gold and silver.

bullion   monetary metal (gold or silver) in an uncoined state; the pure metal, usually stored in bars or ingots; .999 fine.

coin (historic)   a piece of precious metal, intended for use as money, stamped with marks or inscriptions showing that it was issued by an authority or government that guarantees its weight and purity.

coin (modern)   a piece of metal marked and issued by a governmental authority to be used as money. A metal token representing the fractional parts of the monetary unit.

collector   one who collects coins or paper money in an orderly and systematic manner, according to dates, types, patterns, nationality, and similar characteristics.

counterfeit   dishonest coin or bank notes manufactured illegally, in imitation of legal tender money, with the intent to commit fraud by placing in circulation. Any false coin or note.

credit money   money that derives its value from the credit of the issuing agency. (Literally, from trust in its solvency.)

crown   a general term embracing all large silver coins, principally the most popular silver coin of any nation weighing between 20 and 35 grams.

currency   tangible money, both paper and coin.

debase   to reduce the intrinsic value (bullion content) of a coin while maintaining its face value.

debt money   same as credit money.

demonetize   when referring to a coin or note: to withdraw legal tender status. When said of metal: to cease using it to define the monetary unit.

devaluation   a redefinition of the monetary unit, which makes it worth less in terms of bullion or foreign exchange.

essai   a pattern or trial piece, prepared by a mint or under official authority, that did not get to the point of official acceptance or production.

exergue   the lower segment of a coin, sometimes set off by a horizontal bar and often displaying the date or value. The area near the bottom edge of a coin.

face value   the numerical sum stamped on a coin or paper note, as determined by the issuing authority.

fake   1. a coin or note supposedly of numismatic value, but which in reality has never had any true monetary or numismatic identity (example: a three-dollar bill). 2. a genuine coin or note that has been altered in some way to make it resemble another of greater numismatic value.

fantasy   an item resembling a coin, privately struck for souvenir, propaganda, advertising, or satiric purposes. A fake coin produced for reasons other than deceiving numismatists.

fiat credit   credit created or extended in excess of any tangible relationship to the actual value of wealth in existence; credit based on an abstract idea or theory rather than on recognizable physical assets or collateral.

fiat money   money that derives its value only from the arbitrary power of the state to compel its acceptance; not defined or redeemed in any metal or commodity; without intrinsic value. Money that is money because the government says it is. See *legal tender*.

fineness the ratio of pure metal (gold or silver) to total weight, in bars, ingots, or coins, usually expressed as a decimal percentage. U.S. standard gold coins are .900 fine, or 90 percent gold and 10 percent alloy.

forgery a false coin or note manufactured to imitate an item of numismatic value in order to defraud collectors.

fractional notes paper money with a face value less than the monetary unit.

free coinage a policy providing that anyone who deposits (gold or silver) bullion in the mint is entitled to receive in exchange coins of equal weight in grains pure of the metal deposited (less whatever small fixed seigniorage charge or ratio is established).

gold standard a metallic standard based on gold.

Gresham's Law a principle formulated by Sir Thomas Gresham (1519–1579) who noted that when coins of equal face value but different intrinsic value are put into circulation side by side, the coin with the higher intrinsic value will be hoarded and only the coin of lower intrinsic value will be permitted to remain in circulation. (It is sometimes put in the form of an aphorism: "Bad money drives out good money.") Despite the incantations of the New Economics, the events of recent years have shown rather conclusively that Gresham's Law has not been repealed.

hoarder a person who saves large quantities of common coin in the belief that the intrinsic value is greater than the face value; one who acts in accordance with Gresham's Law.

incuse a type of coin design in which the images are recessed rather than raised.

intrinsic value the actual commodity value of the metallic content of a coin.

invest to buy and hold with the expectation of obtaining a profit or increasing wealth through subsequent advances in value; to convert money into some form of wealth other than money.

legal tender whatever is declared by law to be, and therefore must be accepted as legal satisfaction for the repayment of debts and the fulfillment of money contracts. (Not all money is legal tender for all debts. Minor coins are legal tender only in small amounts. You cannot, for example, force anyone to accept a sack of pennies in payment for a $100 debt.)

matte proof a proof coin with a finely granulated or uniformly frosty surface. A crisp but nonreflecting appearance.

metallic standard refers to a money system that defines and redeems the monetary unit in terms of a fixed amount of metal, either as standard coin or bullion.

minor coin small–denomination coin not having bullion value. (As a result of the coinage act of 1965, all U.S. coins except the debased [40 percent silver] Kennedy halves will eventually be minor coin.)

mint condition refers to a regular-issue coin in a near-perfect state; never circulated.

mint set a related group of select, uncirculated, regular-issue coins, sold directly by a mint to accommodate collectors.

mirror proof a proof coin with brilliant, hard, mirrorlike background surfaces.

monetary standard the measuring value of the monetary unit, be it an actual commodity (gold or silver), credit (debt), or the legislative fiat of the state.

monetary unit the standard money, in terms of which all other types of money are defined. (In the U.S., the dollar; France, the franc; Italy, the lira; etc.)

money almost anything that is generally accepted as a medium of exchange or means of deferred payment. In modern times it includes currency, checking accounts, bank deposits, gold reserves, and certain short–term government debt instruments, such as Treasury bills and notes.

nominal value same as face value.

numismatics the study of coins, medals, and all forms of money, on a scientific basis.

numismatist a collector of numismatic items who is a serious student of their origin, history, and identification; one who engages in numismatics.

obverse the side of a coin that bears the head or principal sculpture.

offstrike a coin struck in gold from the same die used to strike a nongold coin (generally omitting the mark of value). Numismatic opinion is

very divided on whether or not offstrikes can be regarded as legitimate coins. The question seems academic; the practice is rare in modern times, and as for the early gold coins, most of them were also struck without a mark of value, as their face value depended solely on weight and purity. Modern offstrikes are intended primarily for numismatic souvenirs.

planchet   the plain metal disk ready to be stamped into a coin.

proof   a coin struck with great care and with the use of special equipment, so as to assure an unusually sharp and vivid impression. Proof coins are specifically intended for numismatic purposes.

prooflike   an uncirculated regular-issue coin in such perfect condition and so sharply struck that it compares favorably with a proof coin; refers to a mirrorlike background surface on an uncirculated coin. (Probably the result of the first run from a new die.)

proof set   a related group of proof coins, usually including all the denominations of one date or all the varieties of one type, sold by a mint to accommodate collectors.

redeemable   said of paper money when it can be readily exchanged for bullion or intrinsic-value coin at a fixed rate.

restrike   a coin struck from an original die, usually by the issuing government, but at a date after the mintage of that coin was assumed to have been concluded. In most cases the motive is to profit from numismatic demand. Sometimes restrikes bear marks that identify them as such, more often they do not. Most collectors consider the practice detrimental, if not actually dishonest.

revaluation   a redefinition of the monetary unit, which makes it worth more in terms of bullion or foreign exchange.

reverse   the side of a coin opposite the head or principal sculpture. It usually bears the seal of the state and sometimes the marks or inscriptions of value.

seigniorage   1. a small minting fee, which is obtained from the difference between the intrinsic value and the face value of standard and subsidiary coin. 2. the profit accruing to a government when the face value of its coins greatly exceeds the cost of production.

silver standard   a metallic standard based on silver.

Special Drawing Rights (SDRs)   a scheme whereby the members of the International Monetary Fund (IMF) are granted special credits or "rights" that can be utilized to settle balance-of-payments deficits. The amount of special credit granted will be related to each member nation's "pledge" or deposit with the IMF. Under this plan, a creditor nation will be obliged to accept these nonredeemable SDR "credits" whenever offered in lieu of gold. Only central banks, therefore, will be allowed or required to deal in SDRs—which is just as well; in a free market their value would probably drop to zero.

specie   the standard metallic money, gold, silver, as opposed to paper notes, etc.

speculate   to buy and sell with the hope of profiting from significant fluctuations in price.

standard coin   intrinsic-value coin with a face value equal to its bullion value (under a metallic standard).

subsidiary coin   intrinsic-value coin with a face value more than the bullion value (at the official rate).

Bibliography

Records indicate that more than 2,000 books have been published in the United States during the last century or so that have a text devoted principally to numismatics. New titles in this field are now being added at the rate of 250 to 300 per year. Include the published works on the general subjects of money, investing, gold, inflation, etc., and the list would probably number in the tens of thousands. *Coin World* publishes annually a general bibliography of numismatic books, which contains several thousand items. The subject is extensive, but the following brief list provides a beginning.

ANCIENT, BYZANTINE, MEDIEVAL, AND RENAISSANCE GOLD

Burckhardt, Jacob. *The Civilization of the Renaissance in Italy.* 6th printing. Garden City, N.Y., 1965.

Hall, V., Jr., and Stearns, J. B. *Byzantine Gold Coins.* Hanover, N.H., 1953.

Ives, H. E. *The Venetian Gold Ducat and Its Imitators.* Numismatic Notes and Monograms Series, No. 128. New York, 1954.

Klawans, Zander H. *An Outline of Ancient Greek Coins.* 2nd ed. Racine, Wis.: Whitman Division, 1964.

Wear, T. G. *Ancient Coins: How to Collect for Fun and Profit.* New York, 1964.

CATALOGUES AND REFERENCE BOOKS

Breen, Walter. *Major Varieties of U. S. Gold Dollars.* Chicago: Hewitt Bros., 1964.

————. *Major Varieties of U. S. Three Dollar Gold Pieces.* Chicago: Hewitt Bros., 1965.

————. *United States Eagles.* Chicago: Hewitt Bros., 1968.

————. *United States Half Eagles, 1839–1929.* Chicago: Hewitt Bros., 1968.

————. *Varieties of Early U. S. Half Eagles, 1795–1838.* Chicago: Hewitt Bros., 1966.

————. *Varieties of U. S. Quarter Eagles.* Chicago: Hewitt Bros., 1964.

Brown, Martin R., and Dunn, John W. *A Guide to the Grading of United States Coins*. Racine, Wis.: Whitman Division, 1969.

Burnie, R. H. *Small California and Territorial Gold Coins; Quarter Dollars, Half Dollars and Dollars*. Pascagoula, Miss., 1955.

Buttrey, Theodore V. *A Guide Book of Mexican Coins*. Racine, Wis.: Whitman Division, 1969.

Charlton, James E. *Standard Catalogue of Canadian Coins, Tokens and Paper Money*. Racine, Wis.: Whitman Division, annually.

Charlton, James E., and Willey, Robert C. *A Guide to the Grading of Canadian Decimal Coins*. Racine, Wis.: Whitman Division, 1965.

Clain-Stefanelli, Elvira. *Select Numismatic Bibliography*. New York, 1965. (This book is a cross-index of almost 5,000 U. S. and foreign numismatic books, listed by subject.)

Friedberg, Robert. *Gold Coins of the World, Complete from 600 A.D. to the Present*. 2nd ed. New York: The Coin and Currency Institute, 1965.

Hewitt, Lee F. *Price Catalogue of Modern European Gold Coins*. Chicago: Hewitt Bros., 1969.

Schlumberger, Hans. *Gold Coins of Europe Since 1800*. New York: Sterling Pub. Co., 1968.

Yeoman, R. S. *A Guide Book of United States Coins*. Racine, Wis.: Whitman Division, annually since 1947.

————. *A Handbook of United States Coins*. Racine, Wis.: Whitman Division, 1969–1970.

————. *Catalogue of Modern World Coins*. Racine, Wis.: Whitman Division, 1968.

————. *Current Coins of the World*. Racine, Wis.: Whitman Division, 1969.

COIN COLLECTING AND INVESTING

Bowers, Q. David. *Coins and Collectors*. Johnson City, N. Y.: Windsor Publications, 1964.

Clain-Stefanelli, Elvira. *Numismatics—an Ancient Science*. Paper 32, The Museum of History and Technology. Washington, D. C.: U. S. Govt. Printing Office, 1968.

Clain-Stefanelli, Vladimir. *History of the National Numismatic Collection.* Paper 31, The Museum of History and Technology. Washington, D. C.: U. S. Govt. Printing Office, 1968.

Kopkin, S., and Roberts, E. W. *Paths to Wealth Through Coin Investments.* Lynbrook, N. Y., 1965.

Reinfeld, Fred. *Coin Collector's Handbook.* Rev. ed. New York: Sterling Pub. Co., 1963.

————. *How to Build a Coin Collection.* 10th printing, rev. ed. New York: Sterling Pub. Co., 1965.

GENERAL HISTORY OF GOLD

Allen, G. *Gold, History from Ancient Times to the Present Day.* New York, 1965.

Green, Timothy. *The World of Gold.* New York: Walker & Co., 1968.

Paul, R. W. *California Gold, The Beginning of Mining in the Far West.* Lincoln, Neb., 1967.

Rist, Charles. *The Triumph of Gold.* Translated by Philip Cortney. New York: Philosophical Library, 1961.

MONEY, INFLATION, AND FINANCIAL DELUSIONS

Groseclose, Elgin. *Money and Man.* New York: Frederick Ungar, 1961.

Mackay, Charles. *Extraordinary Popular Delusions and the Madness of Crowds.* London, 1841. Reprint ed., with a Foreword by Bernard M. Baruch. New York: L. C. Page Co., 1932; 11th printing, 1960.

Rickenbacker, William F. *Death of the Dollar.* New Rochelle, N. Y.: Arlington House, 1968.

————. *Wooden Nickels, or, the Decline and Fall of Silver Coins.* New Rochelle, N. Y.: Arlington House, 1966.

Rueff, Jacques. *The Age of Inflation.* Chicago: Henry Regnery, Gateway Ed., 1964.

White, Andrew Dickson. *Fiat Money Inflation in France.* Reprint ed. Irvington, N. Y.: Foundation for Economic Education, 1959.

PERIODICALS

The following newspapers and magazines devoted to numismatics are available by subscription, or at the larger newsstands:

The Coin Collector and Shopper (Monthly)
Iola, Wisconsin 54945
(Single copy 35¢)

Coin Prices (Every other month)
"A current guide to U.S., Canadian and Mexican coin prices, continually revised to obtain realistic and up-to-date values."
Iola, Wisconsin 54945
(Yearly subscription $2.00)

Coin World (Weekly)
P.O. Box 150
Sidney, Ohio 45365
(Single copy 35¢)

COINage Magazine (Monthly)
16250 Ventura Blvd.,
Encino, California 91316
(Single copy 60¢)

Coins Magazine (Monthly)
Iola, Wisconsin 54945
(Single copy 50¢)

Hobbies Magazine (Monthly)
1006 S. Michigan Ave.
Chicago, Illinois 60605
(Has a large coin section; single copy 35¢)

Journal of Israel Numismatics (Monthly)
Cliffside Park, New Jersey
(Yearly subscription $5.00)

Numismatic News (Weekly)
Iola, Wisconsin 54945
(Single copy 25¢)

Numismatic Scrapbook Magazine (Monthly)
P.O. Box 150

Sidney, Ohio   45365
(Single copy 60¢)

The Numismatist (Monthly)
Official publication of the American Numismatic
Association, P.O. Box 2366
Colorado Springs, Colorado   80901
(Single copy 75¢)

World Coins (Monthly)
P.O. Box 150
Sidney, Ohio   45365
(Single copy 60¢)

The following publications, though not specifically concerned with numismatics, do contain articles on international monetary developments affecting gold, domestic and foreign gold mining and production, legislation concerning gold, gold-coin and other treasure finds, and treasure-hunting techniques, all of which may be of interest to the gold-oriented investor:

American Gold News (Monthly)
P.O. Box 427
San Andreas, California   95249
(Single copy 35¢)

California Mining Journal (Monthly)
P.O. Box 628
Santa Cruz, California   95060
(Single copy 40¢)

Index